Christ the Lord

Christ the Lord

The Reformation and Lordship Salvation

Edited by Michael Horton

A CURE Book

BAKER BOOK HOUSE
Grand Rapids, Michigan 49516

Library of Congress Cataloging-in-Publication Data

Christ the Lord : the Reformation and lordship salvation / edited by Michael
    Scott Horton.
        p.   cm.
    Includes bibliographical references.
    ISBN 0-8010-4374-3
    1. Salvation. 2. Grace (Theology). 3. Jesus Christ—Lordship. 4. Reformation.
    I. Horton, Michael Scott.
    BT752.C49 1992
    234—dc20   92-26910

Unless stated otherwise, Scripture references are from the HOLY BIBLE, NEW INTERNATIONAL VERSION. Copyright © 1973, 1978, 1984 International Bible Society. Used by permission of Zondervan Bible Publishers.

"Repentance in Romans," "The Law According to Jesus," "What Is Faith?" "Calvin and the Council of Trent," and "Christ Crucified between Two Thieves" were originally published in *Modern Reformation* and were revised for publication in this volume.

CURE is the logo for
Christians United for Reformation
2034 East Lincoln Avenue #209
Anaheim, CA 92806

Christians United for Reformation is a nonprofit educational foundation committed to communicating the insights of the sixteenth-century Reformation to the twentieth-century church. For more information, call during business hours at 714-956-CURE.

Contents

Foreword

I remember once attending a crowded committee meeting in a small room. As the evening wore on, the room became hot and airless. Tempers rose. The discussion became increasingly heated. It was obvious that we were going to get nowhere. Then someone threw open a window. The cool air of the night wafted in. The change in the atmosphere was immediate. People cooled down. They began to talk sense. The issues were addressed with new enthusiasm and responsibility. Good decisions were made, and everyone was happy with them. And all because of a breath of fresh air.

This book breathes fresh air into the increasingly heated debate initiated by books like John F. MacArthur, Jr.'s *Gospel According to Jesus* (1988) or Zane C. Hodges's *Absolutely Free!* (1989). Mike Horton has brought together a team of talented writers, who inject sanity and theological responsibility into the discussion of "lordship salvationism," as it has come to be popularly called. Their work brings out the inadequacies, theological and pastoral, of the extremes represented by MacArthur and Hodges, and provides a judicious and biblical alternative that remains faithful to the evangelical tradition and the Christian experience of sin and grace. This balanced and informed book will delight readers who have become alarmed at the weaknesses of both extremes in this highly polarized debate. It is a "must read" for pastors wrestling with the resulting misery and confusion within their congregations.

But the book does more than that. It reminds modern American evangelicals of their need to regain the evangelical realism of the Reformation. MacArthur's *Gospel According to Jesus* and Hodges's *Absolutely Free!* leave us longing to rediscover the balanced and realistic approach of men like Luther and Calvin. How, many Christians wonder, can we steer a middle road between some form of legalism (which simply emphasizes that we must prove we are Christians by an empirical test of discipleship, and then leaves us high and dry when we discover that we can't, on account of sin) and some disastrous form of antinomianism (which extols the virtues of "free grace," yet fails to recognize the *transformative* character of that same grace)? What can we say to the simple, honest believer who passionately wants to obey Christ, yet discovers that sin runs so deep in his nature that, despite all his prayers and tears, he still fails his Lord?

The Reformation gives us a framework to answer these questions, and many others like them. The sixteenth-century Reformers avoided the simplistic rhetoric often evident on both sides of the debate, by stressing that Christ's demands for obedience are set in the context of radical human sinfulness. As Luther put it, believers are "at one and the same time righteous and sinners [*simul iustus et peccator*]." Yet Reformation theology also stressed that the free gift of grace *changes* us. God doesn't leave us high and dry, but begins to effect what he has promised. The free gift of grace gives birth to a new obedience on our part—without reducing the gospel to hollow demands for an impossible obedience on the one hand, or crude evasions of Christian responsibility on the other.

The MacArthur-Hodges debate is for real. It deals with issues and problems that are live for many Christians today and are being hotly discussed in our churches. And it's just one example of a current debate to which the Reformation can make a powerful and helpful contribution by giving classic answers to modern questions. These answers have been tried and tested—and they work. But people don't seem to *know* about them. That's why Christians United for Reformation (CURE) has such a vital role to play. It aims to get these ideas back on the agenda, to allow the church to be challenged and refreshed by its past. In the religious fast-food world of today, CURE offers serious food, that will nourish and sustain today's church for the tasks of tomorrow.

Alister E. McGrath
Oxford University

Preface

The purpose of this volume is not to provide an exhaustive defense of what we would regard as the biblical position on the "lordship salvation" debate. Indeed, both leading spokesmen on either side, Zane Hodges and John MacArthur, Jr., have offered some reason for discomfort over the terms *lordship/no-lordship salvation*. As James Boice, J. I. Packer, and others have argued in their works, no respected, mainstream Christian thinker, writer, or preacher has ever held such extreme and unusual views concerning the nature of the gospel and saving grace as Zane Hodges. In this book, there is no doubt that we are taking a firm stand against what I would rather label the "no-effective-grace" position. While Hodges insists that he is only following the Bible, apart from any theological system, it is clear that he is missing the point of the gospel itself—to make enemies friends, to reconcile sinners to God, to break the power of sin's dominion, and to bring new and lasting life to those who before were "dead in trespasses and sins" (Eph. 2:1).

It is, in part, because of that tendency, sometimes evidenced on both sides in this debate, to pretend that one is reading the Bible without any theological influences or biases, that motivated us to get involved in this sensitive and emotional issue. Both Hodges and MacArthur claim the Reformers for support. In our estimation, there is not the slightest support for Hodges and Ryrie to claim the Reformers' favor for their novel views. The antinomi-

11

ans (that is, those who denied the necessity of Christian obedience) of the Puritan era so pressed the Reformers' defense of justification to the point where there was no place left for sanctification. However, the modern antinomianism, represented by Ryrie and Hodges chiefly, appears not to be motivated by an unbalanced fear that any talk of human responsibility will take away from God's glory, but by a fear that any talk of the effectiveness of grace will erode confidence in human responsibility and choice. In other words, the antinomians since the Reformation have erred by *denying* any human cooperation, not only in conversion and justification (which the orthodox would deny as well), but in sanctification and perseverance as well. But today's antinomians have erred by *defending* human cooperation to the point where every divine operation is wholly dependent on human willing and running, contrary to the words of the apostle Paul (Rom. 9:16).

Nevertheless, this book is not merely an endorsement of John MacArthur's position, either. We will argue that MacArthur at certain points risks confusion on some fundamental evangelical convictions, particularly between justification and sanctification. It must be said, however, that MacArthur has been most gracious in considering our concerns and we have been in dialogue with him for some time now. Significant changes have been made, as he has fine-tuned his definitions and applied a more specific theological framework to his exegesis. Revisions will appear in forthcoming editions of *The Gospel According to Jesus* and we are grateful for MacArthur's eagerness to discuss these issues. While other differences remain, there is a great deal of discussion taking place and there is every reason to believe that the chief differences lie in the realm of definitions and pastoral practice rather than substance. MacArthur's humility has been a lesson to us and we hope that we will be able to show our critics the openness he has shown us.

Nevertheless, since we are reviewing a *position,* and not a *person*, and most readers of this volume will have read the earlier edition of *The Gospel According to Jesus*, we have retained our criticisms on these points for the reader's benefit, noting MacArthur's revisions at the appropriate places. Let me also say that John has graciously allowed me to read the draft of his book, *The Gospel According to the Apostles*, which should be released about the same time as this volume. This sequel is clear, precise, and cautious, and it ought to correct the misunderstandings not only of those, like Hodges, who have misrepresented MacArthur's position through caricature and hyperbole, but even perhaps the misguided zeal of some "lordship salvation" disciples as well.

It is because both positions claim to be echoes of the Reformation that we thought the debate was in need of a more historical treatment. For that reason, one will not find in *Christ the Lord* a comprehensive exegetical treatment. While there are chapters devoted to covering the biblical material (which is, after all, our "only rule for faith and practice"), the book has a decidedly historical tone to it. It is offered unabashedly as a "Reformation response" to the positions thus far presented, not because the Reformers and their successors were infallible, but because evangelical Protestantism owes a debt of gratitude to them for digging the gold out of the rich scriptural veins through the centuries so that we could learn from those who have gone before us. Theology, preaching, teaching, counseling, and pastoral care are not done in a vacuum; we are all influenced and shaped by our own traditions, upbringing, seminary education, and church curricula, and these are all shaped by certain theological systems. It is the goal of this book to help rub the sleep from our eyes, to drive away the naive assumption that we can just be "Bible teachers" without careful theological reflection from a particular systematic point of view.

The Reformers were certainly not infallible—they would be the last to say they were—but they were wise, wiser than any of us around these days. And we would be poor stewards of the inheritance God has given us through them if we did not at least attempt to gain their counsel on these important debates.

Michael Horton
Anaheim, California

Introduction
Don't Judge a Book by Its Cover

Michael Horton

Zane Hodges is a man with a mission, not unlike his rival in the present dispute, John MacArthur, Jr. According to Hodges, Ryrie, and a number of lesser-known, but quite influential Bible teachers, men like MacArthur, whom they call "lordship teachers," are purveyors of another gospel. "Lordship teachers" are those who believe that Jesus is both Savior from sin and sovereign Lord of life for all Christians. "Let it be said clearly," Hodges warns, "*lordship salvation holds a doctrine of saving faith that is in conflict with that of Luther and Calvin and, most importantly, in conflict with God's Word*" (p. 209 n. 9).[1]

However, this introduction will attempt to demonstrate that Zane Hodges himself does not seem to appreciate that his own views are entirely inconsistent with the very biblical and Reformational position he purports to be defending. (In classic Reformed theology, this is the debate about the roles of faith and works in an individual's salvation and about the nature of justification and sanctification.) His book may be titled, *Absolutely Free!* but never judge a book by its cover.

15

Is Faith a Gift?

At the bottom of any debate about justification and assurance surely lies the doctrine of saving faith. In his appendix to *Absolutely Free!* Hodges quotes approvingly from Dr. Robert Preus, perhaps the leading conservative Lutheran scholar in our generation. In the passage cited, after criticizing the Roman Catholic insistence "that justifying faith was an act of man which could be considered a good work," Preus moves to the next great threat to that Reformation doctrine, Arminianism: "The Arminians too opposed the Lutheran doctrine by making faith (which they granted was trust) a work (*actus*) of man. Like the Romanists they had a synergistic notion of how a man came to faith. . . . These deviations from the evangelical model of justification are in force today, although in somewhat less gross form. And we have all encountered them."[2]

Indeed, we have all encountered them, not least in Zane Hodges's *Absolutely Free!* That Hodges can approvingly cite these remarks while laboring through the greater part of the book to establish that very Roman Catholic and Arminian view of saving faith as a human act and the product of a synergistic (i.e., cooperative) response of free will to divine grace demonstrates the author's confusion either as to what the Reformers taught or as to his own position.

First, Hodges notes, "MacArthur argues (pp. 172–73) that Ephesians 2:8–9 teach that 'the entire process of grace, faith, and salvation' is 'the gift of God.' This assertion is unfounded. . . . The Bible never affirms that saving faith per se is a gift." According to Hodges, MacArthur apparently gives God too much credit, since "God does everything, including the impartation of faith." Hodges appears shocked that MacArthur would go so far as to say, "Spiritual sight is a gift from God that makes one willing and able to believe." He comments, "The theology MacArthur evidently embraces is a formula for despair," since it leaves nothing for humans to do in the matter of their new birth and justification (p. 219 n. 1).

How then does one obtain this acceptance with God that is ostensibly "absolutely free"? Hodges employs terminology more

Jesus Keeps us!

characteristic of the Higher Life movement, which taught, in effect, that a higher plane of sanctification was possible for Christians who had sufficient faith, than of Holy Scripture. This despite the fact that the author insists repeatedly that he is simply letting the Bible speak for itself, without any appeal to theological systems. Chief among these terms is *appropriation*. Whereas the Reformation tradition prefers to speak of redemption "accomplished and applied" by God, Hodges chooses to refer to redemption accomplished by God and appropriated by man. Martha of Bethany "*appropriated* the gift of eternal life. . . . No wonder, then, that in one of the most fundamental passages in his entire gospel, John presents saving faith as an act of appropriation. . . . 'What you need to do,' our Lord is saying, 'is to appropriate something which I want to give you'" (p. 40).

Denying the doctrine of unconditional election ("this tragic error," Hodges calls it) and the effectiveness of God's grace in granting faith, the author adds, "Where there is a real search for God, He rewards it" (Heb. 11:6). So it was really an act of goodness and love for Jesus to allow unsaved disciples to travel with Him. He thereby enhanced their opportunity to come to saving faith in Himself (p. 86). Our Lord, however, told the disciples, "You did not choose Me, but I chose you and appointed you that you should go and bear fruit, and that your fruit should remain" (John 15:16). And shortly thereafter he said in his high-priestly prayer, "I kept them in Your name. Those whom You gave Me I have kept; and none of them is lost except the son of perdition, that the Scripture might be fulfilled" (17:12).

Chapter 10 of *Absolutely Free!*, titled "The Choice Is Yours," pursues the classical Arminian line of thinking. "Lordship thought does not understand the real nature of grace," Hodges writes. "It does not understand that God is capable of generously loving men and women who are ultimate disappointments to Him (p. 119). Here again, one is forced to wonder at the sort of grace that would leave it up to sinful individuals as to whether they would be pleasing to God. The Savior is entirely dependent on the good will of sinners in his redemptive program, according to this scheme.

Hodges also returns to the faulty, if popular, exegesis of Revelation 3:20: "Behold, I stand at the door and knock. If anyone hears My voice and opens the door, I will come in to him and dine with him, and he with Me." It is clear from the context that Jesus is addressing "the church of the Laodiceans," not the unbelieving world, as Hodges and others interpret it. A church that had become indifferent and lukewarm, self-assured as though it had everything it needed without devotion to Christ himself, required both a stern rebuke and a warm invitation to recover that intimate communion this church once enjoyed.

Unlike unbelievers, those who are regenerated are not "dead in trespasses and sins" (Eph. 2:1) and are, therefore, capable of responding to God's voice. However, if God were simply waiting for unbelievers to exercise their free will and "appropriate" the gift, he would be in for a long wait. "But natural man does not receive the things of the Spirit of God, for they are foolishness to him; nor can he know them" (1 Cor. 2:14). It was our Lord himself who declared, "No one can come to Me unless the Father who sent Me draws him" (John 6:44). If we are looking for a verse that does speak of Jesus at the door of an unbeliever's heart, we must turn to Acts 16:14, where Paul shared the gospel with Lydia: "The Lord opened her heart to heed the things spoken by Paul." After all, Jesus also identifies himself in Revelation 3 as the one "who has the key of David, He who opens and no one shuts, and shuts and no one opens" (3:7). So much for Jesus the gentleman who "would not break down their door." "It was up to them to respond. It was for them to open the door to Him," Hodges writes. "Lordship teachers" insist on God's omnipotence in salvation. But for Hodges, "The scriptural revelation knows nothing of a doctrine in which Christian love for God is guaranteed by the mere fact that one is a Christian" (pp. 130–31). At this point, Hodges moves beyond Arminianism and certainly beyond official Roman Catholic teaching, adopting a view bordering on Pelagianism.

"Somewhere on the road of our search, God meets the repentant sinner," the author writes (p. 156). What then are we to make of texts such as Romans 3:11: "There is none who understands; There is none who seeks after God"? Or Isaiah 65:1: "I was sought by those who did not ask for Me; I was found by those who did not seek Me"? It is amazing that one who so dogmatically (and, if the reader will bear the harshness, arrogantly) asserts that he

Are Hodges is an "Arminianist"?

is following the Bible alone, while anyone who disagrees with him is following a manmade system, could overlook some of the most obvious texts of Holy Scripture. One wonders who is imposing a system on the simple reading of the Bible. Furthermore, it is odd, to say the least, that Hodges is so eager to cite "Martin Luther and John Calvin, the great Reformers" (p. 143) as key witnesses for his defense while simultaneously referring to Reformed theology as "a harsh system" and "a tragic error" (pp. 85–86). This may be accounted for by his overdependence on a widely disputed thesis in historical theology that attempts to divorce Calvin from his successors. (For a detailed summary of this point, see Paul Schaefer's notes 16–19 on pp. 236–37 in this volume.)

Is Repentance the Gift of God?

Next, as faith itself is not a gift, neither is repentance, according to Hodges. Although Paul criticized the Romans for despising "the riches of [God's] goodness, forbearance, and longsuffering, not knowing that the goodness of God leads you to repentance" (Rom. 2:4), Hodges carries his Arminian view of faith to its logical conclusion. If faith is the work of humans and if God is dependent on the exercise of our free will in "appropriating" his resources, surely each aspect of God's plan of salvation is dependent on a separate and distinct decision. It is up to us whether we will justify ourselves by making a salvation decision, and it is up to us whether we will sanctify ourselves by making a lordship decision. At least the logic is consistent.

ROMANS 2:4

Hodges appeals to the Reformers once again here. First, it is true that Luther and Calvin equated repentance with regeneration (although Hodges should have pointed out that *regeneration*, for both Reformers, was a synonym for *sanctification* rather than for the gift of new life). Therefore, repentance (used in this sense of sanctification) could not possibly be a condition for justification. The author is correct to affirm that "Both [Reformers] stood firmly for the great Reformation insight expressed in the words *sola fide*—'faith alone'" and that "No other position is biblical or truly evangelical. Faith alone (not repentance *and* faith) is the sole condition for justification and eternal life" (p. 144).

[handwritten at top: We are saved from the: 1) Penalty 2) power of our sins!]

Furthermore, Hodges is, I believe, correct in his insistence that Dr. MacArthur is confusing on this point. Hodges properly cites Calvin's comments in his favor concerning this issue (an exception to the rule): "For to include faith in repentance, is repugnant to what Paul says in Acts [20:21]—that he testified 'both to the Jews, and also to the Greeks, repentance toward God, and faith toward our Lord Jesus Christ'; where he mentions faith and repentance, as two things totally distinct."[3]

Nevertheless, both MacArthur and Hodges contribute to the confusion by referring to "salvation" generally when it is not clear whether they are referring to justification or sanctification. After all, classical Protestantism has always affirmed that both the judicial declaration and the spiritual transformation are part of the same package of "salvation": having been saved from the penalty and the power of our sins. Therefore, when Hodges argues, ". . . neither Calvin nor Luther treated repentance as a *condition* for eternal salvation" (p. 144), he is far from the mark. God will always follow the gift of faith (the instrument of our justification) with the gift of persevering faith and repentance (the fruit of our justification). This, as we shall demonstrate, was the clear, consistent teaching of the Reformers.

But, once more, Hodges denies this inevitability because he denies that either faith or repentance is a gift from God. Furthermore, while he exploits Calvin's support for a distinction between faith and repentance, Hodges makes both of them separate and unrelated human contributions, dependent on human free will rather than on divine grace. The decision of faith is necessary for justification, but the decision to repent is necessary, according to Hodges, only if one wants to become a disciple.

After attributing the total "package" of salvation (including faith) to grace alone, Paul adds to the list of the gifts of grace, "For we are His workmanship, created in Christ Jesus for good works, which God prepared beforehand that we should walk in them" (Eph. 2:10). While the plain, literal reading of the text (to which dispensationalists often claim exceptional allegiance) would seem to be that God had "predestined [us] to be conformed to the image of His Son," as he says elsewhere (Rom. 8:29), Hodges discovers a different intention:

[handwritten at bottom: We were saved for His: 1) Workmanship 2) Good works]

Sometimes this text [Eph. 2:10] is misunderstood. Sometimes it is read as though it meant that the believer will most certainly walk in the good works God has prepared for him. *But Paul does not say that at all.*

Instead, Paul declares God's *purpose* for us. God *wants* us to walk in good works. . . . In neither text [John 3:17 and Eph. 2:10] do we find that there is any kind of guarantee that the stated purpose will be fulfilled [p. 73].

So, once again, the author follows his logic to its sad conclusion: God is not sovereign; he does not achieve his gracious purposes; the effectiveness of the grace he offers depends entirely on what we decide by an act of the will. Although God predestines us to good works, faith is not a free gift of God, but the work of man.[4] Why then, indeed, should the grace of God lead us to repentance?

Is Perseverance the Gift of God?

Next, we come to Hodges's denial of God's grace even in preserving his people in faith. The Reformed side of the Protestant divide has insisted that the Bible clearly teaches that Jesus Christ "will also confirm you to the end," since "God is faithful, by whom you were called" (1 Cor. 1:8–9). After all, "God is faithful, who will not allow you to be tempted beyond what you are able, but with the temptation will also make the way of escape, that you may be able to bear it" (1 Cor. 10:13). And we "are kept by the power of God through faith for salvation ready to be revealed in the last time" (1 Pet. 1:5). Paul declared his confidence "that He who has begun a good work in you will complete it until the day of Jesus Christ" (Phil. 1:6). Jude characterized genuine believers as those who "are called, sanctified by God the Father, and preserved in Jesus Christ" (1:1). And what of those who do not seem to persevere? Did they ever really possess saving, justifying faith, or were they like the seeds that fell on rocky ground or were choked by the weeds before they took root (Luke 8:14–15)? Apparently the latter; as John writes, "They went out from us, but they were not of us; for if they had been of us, they would have continued with us; but they went out that they might be made manifest, that none of them were of us" (1 John 2:19).

As faith, according to Hodges, is the work of man, and repentance is also credited to human decision, so too it is up to the believer as to whether he or she wishes to persevere in faith. Grace does not guarantee this, in Hodges's scheme. In fact, Hodges follows his own logic by calling his particular version of eternal security "the forever appropriation," which he distinguishes from "the forever gift" of eternal life. In other words, the believer is "safe and secure from all alarm," not because he is resting on Christ, but because he is resting on the fact that he made a decision, walked an aisle, or signed a piece of paper with the date of this evangelical ritual recorded for his future assurance. "The Bible predicates salvation on an *act* of faith, not on the *continuity* of faith," Hodges writes (p. 63), whereas we maintain that the Bible predicates salvation on neither the act nor the continuity of faith, but on the object of faith—namely, Jesus Christ the Righteous.

Now Hodges's "believer" is free to put his or her Bible on the shelf, ignore Christ, and never attend the preaching of the Word or the administration of the sacraments. In fact, according to Hodges, this newly converted Christian is free to become an atheist. But, no reason to worry, the contract has been signed; God is stuck with him or her. I realize this is strong language, but I assure you that it is no caricature:

> Of course, our faith in Christ *should* continue. But the claim that it absolutely must, or necessarily does, has no support at all in the Bible. . . . According to those who hold this [lordship] view, effective Christian living is virtually an inevitable result of new birth. But this view is as remote from the Bible as east is remote from west. . . .
>
> What they [Paul's words in Rom. 7] do describe is the astounding enigma of Christian experience. The believer in Jesus is alive in spirit, while still inhabiting a physical house which is as dead to God's life as it can possibly be. . . . The simple fact is that the New Testament never takes for granted that believers will see discipleship through to the end. And it never makes this kind of perseverance either a condition or a proof of final salvation from hell. . . .
>
> But if anyone supposes that no true Christian could quit, or would quit, they have not been paying attention to the Bible. They need to reread their New Testament. This time, with their eyes

open. . . . Indeed, discipleship is neither a condition nor a proof of actual regeneration. . . . But, on the other hand, we certainly must not assume that a person who has "dropped out" of the process is necessarily *un*saved. They may in fact have found their spiritual education more taxing than expected; they may have failed to count the cost correctly. . . . Salvation is absolutely free; discipleship most certainly is not. . . .

It is impossible, so lordship teachers tell us, for the faith of a believer to collapse entirely. The shield of faith can never really be stripped from a Christian's hand, for if the shield is lost, so the logic of this position runs, it was not really a shield at all since the person in question was not a true believer to begin with! . . . God, they [lordship teachers] say, guarantees the believer's perseverance in the faith. Unfortunately, this dogmatic claim does not have the support of the Bible.

On the contrary, the New Testament is altogether clear that maintaining our faith in God involves a struggle whose outcome is not guaranteed simply by the fact that we are saved. . . . Nowhere does the Word of God guarantee that the believer's faith inevitably will endure. [pp. 63, 69, 71, 80, 83, 88, 104, 111]

So, at last, we come to the conclusion of Hodges's logic: Faith is not a gift; repentance is not a gift; perseverance in sanctification or even in continued trust in Christ—none of this is a gift. It is all the work of humans, should they decide to "appropriate" the items they choose.

Are Rewards a Gift?

Whenever the church becomes unclear on the doctrine of justification, strange notions appear. For instance, when the sacramental system of the medieval church commanded penance and satisfaction for sins in this life, the question arose, "Then what happens to people who do not properly deal with their sins in this life?" The answer the medieval church proposed (with the support of some obscure references from a few later church fathers) was purgatory. In purgatory, one could atone for the obedience he or she had lacked in this life, with the assistance of grace. Of course, this struck at the heart of the assertion that the merit of Christ completely satisfied God's judgment. The Reformers maintained that those who do not stand in perfect righteousness before God will not be given a chance to "purge" themselves of the remaining sin. They will be condemned for all eternity, the Scriptures teach clearly. That is why Protestants insist that God requires a perfect righteousness, and the only way this may be obtained is through faith in the finished work of Christ.

Today we see the confusion over justification leading again to strange notions, which, although different in key respects, are motivated by the same concern to have human merit play at least some role in the process. This is evident in Hodges's teaching, made popular partly by television preacher Charles Stanley, pastor of Atlanta's First Baptist Church. The following citations are taken from Stanley's book, *Eternal Security*, a popular defense of Hodges's position.[5]

Stanley argues, "Each of us will be judged on the basis of individual opportunities and abilities." The parable of the talents (Matt. 25:14–30) makes Christ's meaning clear, he says, "Those who demonstrate in this life an ability and willingness to properly use and invest what God has entrusted to them will be given more to use and invest in his future kingdom." Remember that for dispensationalists, the kingdom is only future. It is not the present reign of Christ through the gospel, but the future reign of Christ through the law. Next, Stanley offers what he considers the obvious explanation for the place described in Matthew 25:30 as "outer darkness":

> The final verse of this parable is so severe that many commentators assume it is a description of hell. It is not. . . . The point of this parable is that in God's future kingdom, those who were faithful in this life will be rewarded and those who were not will lose any potential reward . . . . Before we can understand the full impact of the parable, we must first determine what the "outer darkness" refers to in the context of the parable. It certainly does not mean hell in the parable. How could a master throw a slave into hell? . . . But what actual place was Jesus referring to in the parable? He gave us only one hint: "In that place there shall be weeping and gnashing of teeth." . . . To be in the "outer darkness" is to be in the kingdom of God but outside the circle of men and women whose

What?
→ you got
To Be Kidding!

faithfulness on this earth earned them a special rank or position of authority.

In other words, this place of "weeping and gnashing of teeth" is inside the kingdom of God itself, inside the realm where we are told, "And God will wipe away every tear from their eyes; there shall be no more death, nor sorrow, nor crying; and there shall be no more pain, for the former things have passed away" (Rev. 21:4). But Stanley goes on:

> The kingdom of God will not be the same for all believers. Let me put it another way. Some believers will have rewards for their earthly faithfulness; others will not. . . . Some will reign with Christ; others will not (2 Tim. 2:12). Some will be rich in the kingdom of God; others will be poor (see Luke. 12:21, 33). Some will be given true riches; others will not (see Luke 16:11). Some will be given heavenly treasures of their own; others will not (see Luke 16:12). Some will reign and rule with Christ; others will not (see Rev. 3:21). A careful study of these passages reveals one common denominator. Privilege in the kingdom of God is determined by one's faithfulness in this life.

What?

Evidently, in spite of the consummation, in spite of the eradication of evil, sin, and suffering, there will nevertheless remain a Third World in the kingdom of God for "carnal Christians."

> This truth may come as a shock. Maybe you have always thought that everyone would be equal in the kingdom of God. . . . The clearest proof comes from Jesus' reply to Peter when he asked the Master about what he and the other apostles would receive for their sacrifices: "Then Peter answered and said to Him, 'Behold, we have left everything and followed You; what then will there be for us?'" Jesus did not reprimand him for being selfish and self-centered. Neither did He attempt to correct Peter's theology. Peter's question was justified.

Stanley then leads his readers in an exercise that the Reformers would have known quite well from their childhood homilies:

Now, imagine standing before God and seeing all you have lived for reduced to ashes. How do you think you would feel? How do you think you would respond? Picture yourself watching saint after saint rewarded for faithfulness and service to the King—and all the time knowing that you had just as many opportunities but did nothing about them. We cannot conceive of the agony and frustration we would feel if we were to undergo such an ordeal; the realization that our unfaithfulness had cost us eternally would be devastating. And so it will be for many believers. Just as those who are found faithful will rejoice, so those who suffer loss will weep. As some are celebrated for their faithfulness, others will gnash their teeth in frustration over their own shortsightedness and greed. We do not know how long this time of rejoicing and sorrow will last. Those whose works are burned will not weep and gnash their teeth for eternity. At some point we know God will comfort those who have suffered loss (see Rev. 21:4). . . . . Anyone who takes Jesus' kingdom teaching seriously knows that believers do not get away with sin. Every sinful deed will be examined. On the other side of the coin, we can rest assured that none of our good deeds will go unnoticed, either.

Notice how Stanley, who footnotes Hodges frequently throughout this discussion, brings merit into the process of salvation. "Anyone who takes Jesus' kingdom teaching seriously knows that believers do not get away with sin," he argues. Hence, "To be in the 'outer darkness' is to be in the kingdom of God but outside the circle of men and women whose faithfulness on this earth earned them a special rank or position of authority." Stanley and Hodges have merely managed to move purgatory geographically. No longer is it a place outside of heaven and hell, but it is within the kingdom of God itself. The amazing claim here is that there would even be such a thing as a "circle of men and women whose faithfulness on this earth earned them a special rank." This has much more in common with medieval dogma than with evangelical Christianity. Evangelical Christianity, from its inception, has always been quick to proclaim with the psalmist, "Blessed is he whose transgressions are forgiven, whose sins are covered. Blessed is the man *whose sin the* LORD *does not count against him*" (Ps. 32:1–2 NIV, emphasis mine).

what?

Finally, Stanley closes this discussion with a pastoral illustration:

> Several years ago I did a series in our church on the topic of rewards. As the series progressed, I began to notice a change taking place in the life of one of our high school students. Ken had never been much of a spiritual leader in our Youth Department. In fact, I learned that up until that time, he had for the most part gone the way of the world. But something about the series caught his attention. Every week he moved closer and closer to the front of the sanctuary. By the end of the series, he was on the front row. . . . [At the end of the series] he said, "I was always under the assumption that as long as a person had trusted Christ, and knew he was going to heaven, that was pretty much it. I figured that in heaven we would all be equal. That being the case, I really didn't see any point in giving up anything down here. What difference would it make? When you began talking about rewards I was shocked. I had never heard anything like that before. All of a sudden I started thinking about every thing I did. I began to realize that every moment counted. I quit drinking, I quit going to parties, I started inviting my friends to church. Everything changed. I guess before that, I really wasn't motivated. Once I realized that what I do now determines what eternity will be like, I got busy."

I do hope that Ken's newfound theology did not lead him into either the arrogance or the despair that consumes many of its adherents. The motivation he expresses is the same works-righteousness that fueled the pre-evangelical fears of the Reformers. One could be saved without becoming "spiritual," but the truly committed were not content with an extended time in purgatory. They wanted to earn their rank. Just as Stanley thinks Peter's selfishness was justified, so, he thinks, is Ken's. Without the fear of punishment or the hope of rewards, there is no motivation; this is what Ken expresses and Stanley approves. In fact, Stanley adds,

> . . . believers who have been lulled into thinking that, once they have a ticket to heaven, they can "relax" do not realize that "Every moment counts." No deed goes unnoticed. All of us must give an account. No one gets by with anything. If you are a believer living

for Christ, this news should be encouraging. If, however, you are
one of those believers who has been content just to know you are
on your way to heaven, this information should be disturbing. It
is my prayer that you will renew your commitment to Christ and
begin living for Him.

This is nothing new. Many of us were raised with such allu-
sions to "being saved, but singed." Of course, if justification by the
imputed righteousness of Christ is real, there is not one sin for
which a believer can be judged. This wonderful truth is clearly
denied in the sort of teaching one often hears in dispensational
churches on the subject of rewards.

Once again, if there is anyone who supposes that the Chafer-
Ryrie-Hodges-Stanley (dispensational Arminian) position promotes a gospel that is "absolutely free," he or she has not had to
endure sermons, Sunday school materials, camps, and evangelistic services that send the confusing signals we have been discussing. The irony is that Stanley quotes approvingly not only
from Hodges's *Absolutely Free!* but also from a book titled *Grace in
Eclipse: A Study on Eternal Rewards.* This is ironic because, far from
defending grace against the incursion of some medieval form of
works-righteousness, Hodges and his supporters are assisting in
that very eclipse.

Are we not on safer ground, once more, to take the view of
these "rewards" texts in the Bible exemplified in the following
commentary from Calvin?

> First, let us be heartily convinced that the Kingdom of Heaven is
> not servants' wages, but sons' inheritance [Eph. 1:18]. . . .
>
> Therefore, let us not consider that the Holy Spirit approves the
> worthiness of our works by this sort of promise, as if they merited
> such a reward. For Scripture leaves us no reason to be exalted in
> God's sight. . . . In short, [Christ] usually so deals with [the godly]
> that wherever they turn their eyes, as far as this world extends,
> they are confronted solely with despair. Thus Paul says, "We are
> of all men most to be pitied if we hope only in this world." [1 Cor.
> 15:19p.]. Lest they fail amidst these great tribulations, the Lord is
> with them, warning them to hold their heads higher, to direct their
> eyes farther so as to find in him that blessedness which they do

not see in the world. He calls this blessedness "prize," "reward," "recompense" [cf. Matt. 5:12; 6:1ff., etc.), not weighing the merit of works, but signifying that it is a compensation for their miseries, tribulations, slanders, etc. . . .

Only let us not imagine the correlation between merit and reward on which the Sophists [a pejorative for the Roman Catholic theologians—M. H.] rudely insist because they do not consider the end that we have set forth. . . . Whoever, then, deduces merit of works from this, or weighs works and reward together, wanders very far from God's own plan. . . .

If anyone wishes to jump from God's pure kindness to the value of works, by these testimonies he will not be helped to build up his error.[6]

After all, let us never forget that in the new heavens and new earth, every Christian will cast his or her crown at the feet of Jesus Christ, falling at his feet to worship. For who among us can boast about a gift? Even our best works, corrupted by sinful motives, could not earn for us a special place in heaven, as Stanley and Hodges argue. The Heidelberg Catechism puts it well: "Even the very best we do in this life is imperfect and stained with sin (Isa. 64:6). Q: How then can you say that the good we do does not earn anything when God promises to reward it in this life and the next? A: This reward is not earned; it is a gift of grace (Luke 17:10; 2 Tim. 4:7–8)." Thus, in Revelation 19:12 we read, "His eyes were like a flame of fire, and on his head were many crowns"—our crowns.

Is Anything the Gift of God?

In fact, Hodges cannot even seem to get the definition of justification right. When describing "the single act of trust" that saves (presumably, he means "justifies"), Hodges writes, "For at the precise instant when a man or woman believes in Christ, at that moment eternity itself invades human experience and transforms our [sic] inner beings into something wonderfully and permanently new" (p. 62). This is precisely the confusion of justification and sanctification (or inner renewal) that characterized the Roman Catholic position that Hodges is so eager to attribute to

MacArthur. Furthermore, faith alone is necessary "to be saved," according to Hodges, but repentance is the way to "get on harmonious terms with God" (p. 146). How one can say that "getting on harmonious terms with God" is anything other than justification is baffling, to say the least. For, as Paul wrote, "Therefore, having been justified by faith, we have peace [harmonious terms] with God" (Rom. 5:1).

Other odd statements that undermine Hodges's claim to be defending the "grace" position include his assertion that believers who have a "besetting wickedness" may experience "a premature and untimely death through sin" (p. 121). He comments that James's warnings about dead faith ("Can faith save him?" [2:14]) refer to physical, not spiritual life. Physical salvation is dependent on works: "And he [James] has already insisted that *this kind* of salvation can only be effected by obedience—by good works (1:22–25). . . . If we speak of prolonging human life by godliness, we are speaking of something faith alone cannot achieve" (p. 125). As if this were not enough, we are reminded of Hodges's remark, "Salvation is absolutely free; discipleship most certainly is not" (p. 88). Did not the apostle Paul have an ironically similar teaching in view when he asked the Galatians, "Are you so foolish? Having begun in the Spirit, are you now being made perfect by the flesh?" (Gal. 3:3). Was Jesus downplaying the cost of discipleship when he declared, "Come to Me, all you who labor and are heavy laden, and I will give you rest. Take My yoke upon you and learn from Me, for I am gentle and lowly in heart, and you will find rest for your souls. For My yoke is easy and My burden is light" (Matt. 11:28–30).

Here we must bring this critique to a pastoral reflection, and for that I will have to explain why this issue is so important to me. I was raised in Bible churches pastored by those who had been taught by Zane Hodges, Charles Ryrie, and other proponents of the "carnal Christian" teaching. I attended Christian camps and conferences, leading to a five-year stint at a Christian university whose roots were deep within the soil of Keswick, "Higher Life," dispensational teaching. Michael Coccoris (one of the proponents of the Ryrie-Hodges position) spoke frequently in chapel and during conferences, as did others with similar views, such as Bill

Bright. As a teenager I had discovered the writings of the Reformers and the later exponents of that system. The more deeply I
delved into these works, the more cynical I became toward the
schizophrenia I had experienced all along in trying to get from
the bottom of the spiritual ladder to the point where I could finally
be victorious, fully surrendered, yielded, and consecrated.

Of course, the official theology of our church declared that those
who did not wish to go first-class could refuse discipleship (that
included a legalistic lifestyle). But nobody I knew wanted to settle for lost rewards or for being looked down upon by God or, perhaps more importantly, by other Christians, so being a "carnal
Christian" was simply not an option. The bulk of the preaching,
teaching, and personal exhortation was concerned with getting
people into the category of "spiritual Christian"; this consisted of
all those who had Jesus "on the throne" of their lives. Who wanted
to be saved without being "in fellowship" with God?

The Higher Life teaching insisted that we were to "let go and
let God"—that is, to become passive channels of God's Spirit. To
become actively involved in sanctification was to allow the flesh
to do that which only the Spirit could perform. Therefore, not
only did we have to worry about obedience; we had to wonder
whether we were being obedient "in the flesh." "The great
Reformer," as Hodges calls Calvin (while rejecting that Reformer's
entire theological system) is hardly a witness in the defense of
the Chafer-Ryrie-Hodges/Keswick, dispensational position.
Notice the Genevan's stern warning to a remarkably similar sect
in his own day:

> Certain Anabaptists of our day conjure up some sort of frenzied
> excess instead of spiritual regeneration. The children of God, they
> assert, restored to the state of innocence, now need not take care
> to bridle the lust of the flesh, but should rather follow the Spirit as
> their guide, under whose impulsion they can never go astray. It
> would be incredible that a man's mind should fall into such mad-
> ness, if they did not openly and haughtily blab this dogma of theirs.
> The thing is indeed monstrous! . . . . "Take away," say the Anabap-
> tists, "vain fear—the Spirit will command no evil of you if you but

yield yourself, confidently and boldly, to his prompting." Who
would not be astonished at these monstrosities?[7]

According to the Reformation position, regeneration inevitably
results in a changed life. Anyone who is truly born again by grace
alone will be a "new creature," and therefore will be eager to love
and obey God even when he or she ends up falling short of the
mark constantly, as we all do. Looking back at those calls to "higher
life," realizing that there is no such thing as a Christian who wants
to be simply carnal, I can see how the call to enter into the "victorious Christian life" was appealing to all of us. We wanted it desperately. We would do anything for it. And, as Hodges put it, discipleship is not free in this system. It is not a gift for every believer,
no matter how small the faith or how weak the obedience. It is
for "successful runners" (p. 83).

Those who do not come from this background may assume that
because the dispensationalist side of the debate is "antinomian"
(that is, it denies the validity of the law) it is therefore oriented
toward Christian liberty at the expense of holiness, but this is not
the necessary conclusion. In most cases with which I have been
familiar (including my own), those who have been nurtured in
this environment are far from free. Many live in constant fear of
whether they are "carnal Christians" because they have not
become "successful runners." If their quiet times are irregular; if
they have too much interest in "the world"; if secular work doesn't
leave time for "ministry"; if they enjoy entertainment, dancing,
drinking, smoking, and social involvement with non-Christians—
all of these things are dead giveaways of the carnal Christian.

It might be fine for Hodges and Ryrie to tell them that they will
be saved anyway, but that is not enough for those who love God
and want to be pleasing to him. What they really need is Christ
as the sufficiency for their faith, their justification, their sanctification and growth, their obedience and perseverance in faith to
the end. They do not merely need him in order to "appropriate"
salvation; they need to be appropriated by someone outside of
themselves. This comfort they will not receive from Arminian dispensationalists who make sharp dichotomies between flesh and
spirit, the new man and the old man, carnal and spiritual. They

need to hear that there are not two classes of Christians, but that they own all of the blessings of salvation regardless of the level of their piety or devotion. We are not either carnal Christians or spiritual Christians; rather, all Christians are simultaneously sinful and spiritual—not because of their "surrender," but because of Christ's. We are all in the same category, simply at different points along the way.

The message of the Reformation has been salve in the wounds of many, including this writer. I am not a Christian with great faith or with praiseworthy character, but a Christian who is confident that I share with every regenerate Christian "every spiritual blessing in the heavenly places in Christ" (Eph. 1:3). I am simultaneously sinful and justified, as I am simultaneously at peace with God because of Christ's imputed righteousness, but at war with myself because of Christ's imparted righteousness. I am not a "successful runner," but I am "looking unto Jesus, the author and finisher of [my] faith" (Heb. 12:2). I trust and obey Christ (however feebly), and I know that I will continue trusting and obeying until the day I die—not because I have appropriated Christ, but because he has appropriated me.

The position defended by Zane Hodges is not a recovery of the evangelical message, but the back door to the medieval notions he so cheerfully consigns to the "lordship salvation" proponents. Hodges denies total depravity and unconditional election (it's up to the unbeliever to respond of his own free will). He advocates the very medieval and Arminian synergism that Dr. Preus criticizes in the quote Hodges approvingly cites! Hodges insists that the cross did not guarantee the salvation of anyone (p. 73), and that keeping faith and persevering in Christian growth are difficult and expensive exercises. He denies the perseverance of the saints (or, better, God's perseverance with his saints), but, unlike most Arminians, claims that this does not affect Christian's eternal destiny. In short, when Hodges argues that MacArthur's conviction that "'the entire process of grace, faith, and salvation' is 'the gift of God'" is "unfounded" (p. 219 n. 1), the former cannot possibly expect us to conclude that he is the defender of grace in the face of "lordship salvation." No one has ever accused an Arminian of out-preaching a Calvinist on the doctrine of grace, and there is every reason to believe that this general impression has not been affected in the least by Hodges's arguments.

To be sure, "to an alarming degree [the evangelical church] has lost touch with the unconditional love of God," and "in the process, the marvelous truth of justification by faith, apart from works, recedes into shadows not unlike those which darkened the days before the Reformation." True, "what replaces this doctrine is a kind of faith/works synthesis which differs only insignificantly from official Roman Catholic dogma" (pp. 18–20). This recovery of justification by grace is at the center of our work at Christians United for Reformation. But, as we have seen, Hodges himself is ill-suited to defend himself against the charge of departing from the Reformation's teaching on these points (synergism, faith as mere assent, the defectability of faith, dependence on human initiative throughout the process, and so on). He fails to make the proper distinctions necessary to avoid the confusion he attributes to those he is criticizing. To claim Luther and Calvin, quoting them selectively, while repudiating their theologies, reveals a serious failure to come to grips with the issues involved in the historical debate.

As we have seen, both on the theological and the pastoral level, the grace Hodges offers is not amazing. Nothing is a gift; everything depends on human initiative. The author's offer is not absolutely free. In fact, it may cost many their very lives.

The Gospel According to Jesus

After such serious criticisms of *Absolutely Free!* one might conclude that this volume will cast its lot with Hodges's most popular critic, John MacArthur, Jr. But that conclusion is not wholly accurate.

If legalism is the opposite pole of antinomianism, one might place MacArthur on the former pole, but this too would be hasty, for MacArthur affirms in very clear terms the basic definitions of confessional Protestantism relating to this subject. Although Hodges accuses MacArthur of being unaware of the relevant literature (p. 208 n. 9), it is obvious that the latter has a greater appreciation than the former, for the whole teaching of those he cites as expositors and stands much more directly in the line of Reformation (that is, evangelical) Christianity.

For instance, MacArthur writes,

> Let me say as clearly as possible right now that salvation is by God's sovereign grace and grace alone. Nothing a lost, degenerate, spiritually dead sinner can do will in any way contribute to salvation. Saving faith, repentance, commitment, and obedience are all divine works, wrought by the Holy Spirit in the heart of everyone who is saved. . . . There are no human works in the saving act, but God's work of salvation includes a change of intent, will, desire, and attitude that inevitably produces the fruit of the Spirit. [p. xiii][8]

Further, in answer to the charge that accepting Christ as Lord is a work, MacArthur replies, "We do not 'make' Christ Lord; He *is* Lord! . . . acknowledging His lordship is no more a human work than repentance (cf. 2 Tim. 2:25) or faith itself (cf. Eph. 2:8–9) (p. 28). Against earlier versions of dispensationalism, MacArthur comments, "Salvation has *always* been by grace through faith, not by the works of the law (Gal. 2:16)" (p. 26), and he insists, "We may sin (1 John 2:1)—we *will* sin—but the process of sanctification can never stall completely" (p. 33). ". . . sanctification is a *characteristic* of all those who are redeemed, not a *condition* for their receiving salvation" (p. 188). Other statements could be added, and if this were the one, single message we read throughout *The Gospel According to Jesus*, we would have no criticisms of MacArthur's treatment. However, this is not the only message one is likely to find in this otherwise commendable work.

What Is Saving Faith?

Kim Riddlebarger will discuss the essence of saving faith in chapter 4. For our purposes, it is enough to say here that MacArthur in a praiseworthy zeal to defend the lordship of Christ, sometimes presents his readers with confusing interpretations.

When MacArthur writes, "Real faith results in obedience" (p. 46), there is nothing with which we would take issue. However, when he adds repeatedly such statements as the following, we cannot help but take issue with him: "Disobedience is unbelief"

(p. 47). "True faith is humble submissive obedience" (p. 140). "We have seen already that repentance is a critical element of genuine faith . . ." (p. 172). "In other words, faith encompasses obedience. . . . faith is not complete unless it is obedient" (p. 173), and we could go on.

The fruit of genuine faith is grateful obedience; nevertheless, in order to clear the garden of the antinomian weeds, the danger is that we may pull up some precious flowers along the way. Martin Luther coined the phrase, "justified by faith alone, but not by a faith that is alone." This simple formula was calculated, on the one hand, to protect the doctrine of justification against the additions of human works as merit or even as unmeritorious conditions to the forensic declaration; and on the other hand, to guard against the antinomian menace, that both Luther and Calvin faced, that denied the inseparable union of faith and repentance; justification and sanctification.

Faith produces obedience, but to suggest that faith is obedience is to confuse justification with sanctification. Thus, when MacArthur writes, "repentance is a critical element of genuine faith" (p. 172), he is inconsistent with the Reformation position. Defending the evangelical doctrine of saving faith against the Roman Catholic position, Calvin wrote the following:

> For their inclusion of faith under repentance disagrees with what Paul says in Acts: "Testifying both to Jews and Gentiles of repentance to God, and of faith . . . in Jesus Christ" [Acts 20:21]. There he reckons repentance and faith as two different things. What then? Can true repentance stand, apart from faith? Not at all. But even though they cannot be separated, they ought to be distinguished. As faith is not without hope, yet faith and hope are different things, so repentance and faith, although they are held together by a permanent bond, require to be joined rather than confused.[9]

Not only did Calvin guard against confusing faith and repentance; he argued that the former produced the latter:

> However, our immediate transition [in the discussion—M. H.] will be from faith to repentance. For when this topic is rightly under-

stood it will better appear how man is justified by faith alone, and simple pardon; nevertheless actual holiness of life, so to speak, is not separated from free imputation of righteousness. Now it ought to be a fact beyond controversy that repentance not only constantly follows faith, but is also born of faith. . . . There are some, however, who suppose that repentance precedes faith, rather than flows from it, or is produced by it as fruit from a tree. Such persons have never known the power of repentance, and are moved to feel this way by an unduly slight argument.[10]

Furthermore, the classical evangelical definition of saving faith encompasses three elements: knowledge (an intellectual grasp of the facts), assent (the conclusion that these facts are true), and trust (the conviction that these true facts are true in my case and for my salvation). MacArthur argues that the elements of saving faith are knowledge, assent, and "the determination of the will to obey truth." After all, "faith is not complete unless it is obedient" (p. 173). He quotes Louis Berkhof, whose *Systematic Theology* is the standard contemporary summary of Reformed theology, in his favor:

> Berkhof sees three elements to genuine faith: An intellectual element (*notitia*), which is the understanding of truth; an emotional element (*assensus*), that is the conviction and affirmation of truth; and a volitional element (*fiducia*), which is the determination of the will to obey truth. [p. 173]

Nevertheless, this is not actually what Berkhof says. The section where Berkhof lists these three classical Protestant elements states nothing at all about "the determination of the will to obey truth." Berkhof has much to say about *fiducia*, but it is all along the lines of trust, which is how this third element has been understood by evangelicals since the Reformation. As Berkhof summarizes, "This third element consists in a personal trust in Christ as Saviour and Lord, including a surrender of the soul as guilty and defiled to Christ." It also includes the reception of Christ "as the source of pardon and spiritual life."[11] While it is clear that Berkhof would never sever the relationship between saving faith and the determination of the will to obey the truth, he certainly does not confuse the two either, as MacArthur implies of Berkhof and certainly accomplished himself.

In fact, Berkhof shares the Continental Reformed view that assurance of salvation does not require earnest introspection, but that it is part of the very essence of faith itself. Berkhof's warning against what he called "pietistic nomism" (from *nomos*, law) could be easily directed at the fundamentalism out of which MacArthur comes, although that is, happily, not where MacArthur seems entirely to stand these days:

> Pietistic nomism asserted that assurance does not belong to the very being, but only to the well-being of faith; and that it can only be secured, except by special revelation, only by continuous and conscientious introspection. All kinds of 'marks of the spiritual life,' derived not from Scripture, but from the lives of approved Christians, became the standard of self-examination. The outcome proved, however, that this method was not calculated to produce assurance, but rather tended to lead to ever-increasing doubt, confusion, and uncertainty. [Louis Berkhof, *Systematic Theology* (Grand Rapids: Eerdmans, 1941), 508]

While I am certainly not accusing MacArthur of "pietistic nomism," it is interesting to note Berkhof's disdain for "continuous and conscientious introspection," searching for "marks of the spiritual life" (often nonbiblical taboos) as means of attaining assurance. It must be said that this is not an enterprise that interests those who are more oriented toward the Reformation. There is certainly an important place for introspection—taking spiritual inventory, for the purpose of sending us back to Christ and his cross, confessing our sins, praying for the strength to change, and accepting his forgiveness. Nevertheless, inward-looking piety has more in common with the errors of modern evangelicalism than with the ethos of Reformational evangelicalism.

Since many of the supporters of the "lordship salvation" position do not come from the Reformation perspective, but from a legalistic background, it is essential that MacArthur's position (and ours generally) be clearly distinguished from the "pietistic nomism" which continues to grip large segments of the evangelical community.

Faith, according to Reformation theology, is not conversion, obeying God's commands, repentance, or commitment to live a new life. It produces inevitably all of these effects (contra Hodges), but it is not itself to be confused with its effects (contra MacArthur). This is an essential issue, of course, because what is at stake is the biblical and evangelical doctrine of *sola fide* (faith alone).

If, for instance, anyone would have said at any time throughout our Protestant history, "I am justified before God by faith and works," any informed layperson would have been convinced that such a person was a Roman Catholic or at least an extreme Arminian. After all, faith is not enough, according to Thomas Aquinas, because his definition of faith is knowledge of and assent to the teachings of the church, not a trusting reliance on the person and work of Christ himself. Therefore, to faith was added love, and this faith formed by love was to produce the obedience necessary for justification.

I know that this is not what John MacArthur means, but his language certainly does cause some confusion in this important area. For instance, is there really any substantial difference between saying one is justified by faith and works (that is, obedience) and saying one is justified by faith alone, but faith includes works (obedience) in its definition, and until one's faith is obedient, it is not justifying? Surely not. If obedience is a work (and who would deny this?), and "faith is humble, submissive obedience," then MacArthur is telling us that faith is works. He seems to be saying that we are justified, not by faith and works (the Roman Catholic view) or by a faith that works (the Protestant view), but indeed by a faith that is works, for "faith is not complete unless it is obedient" (p. 173).

Rome was convinced that mere knowledge and assent (the elements of faith in its definition) could not justify, and the Reformers concurred. Of course, this would be "devil's faith," as James referred to it. Nevertheless, what the Reformers insisted was missing in the Roman Catholic formula was the element of trust. In other words, faith did not need works in order to become justifying; rather, knowledge and assent needed trust in order to become saving faith!

MacArthur, it seems, is so disturbed by the antinomianism of his opponents that, in order to make what he calls easy-believism more untenable, he insists that the believer is justified by knowledge, assent, and *obedience* (or, at least, "the determination of the will to obey truth"), rather than by knowledge, assent, and trust. Granted, the formulation is different from official Roman Catholic teaching, but it merely moves the element of works into the definition of faith itself. This leaves the impression that, if a believer is repeating the same sin, he or she must not be justified yet, since "repentance is a critical element of genuine faith" (p. 172) and "faith is not complete unless it is obedient" (p. 173).

Further, MacArthur (like Hodges) rarely refers to "justification," but primarily to "salvation." In fact, in the index to *The Gospel According to Jesus* the entry *sanctification* includes a number of references, while for *justification* we read, "See Salvation." While MacArthur is not responsible for creating the index, surely this is an imbalance in any presentation that claims to represent "the gospel according to Jesus" (see n.16). Thus, are we to conclude that MacArthur intends *justification* by his use of the word *salvation* in the following quote? "Those who think of salvation as merely a legal transaction, a reckoning apart from practical righteousness, will have a difficult time with this warning of Jesus [in Matt. 7:21–23]. It puts salvation in very practical terms. It reiterates the key statement of the Sermon on the Mount: 'For I say to you, that unless your righteousness surpasses that of the scribes and Pharisees, you shall not enter the kingdom of heaven' (Matt. 5:20)" (p. 188). Most often, *justification* is what contemporary evangelicals mean by *salvation*, but if this is MacArthur's meaning, he is in serious conflict with the biblical teaching on justification at this point. If this is not his interpretation and *salvation* refers to something other than the event in which one is set right with God, these distinctions should be clarified for the reader.

First, we must insist that justification *is* "merely a legal transaction, a reckoning apart from practical righteousness." We dare not defend against the separation of justification from practical righteousness by denying the distinction between them. Second, the real purpose of the text in Matthew 5:20 is to drive the hearers to recognize that the external righteousness imposed by the Pharisees was hypocritical. What we require is a righteousness that not only covers obvious, scandalous sins, but that covers the internal corruption of our hearts and attitudes. And this righteousness, we learn elsewhere in the Gospels and Epistles, is outside of us, imputed to us legally apart from our own practical righteousness. If MacArthur by *salvation* here refers to sanctification, then the issue of practical righteousness is quite appropriate. But failing to make key distinctions along the way, the author often, as he does here, leaves the reader with the impression that justification itself includes both a legal and a practical aspect. This is quite foreign to the evangelical position.

MacArthur appeared to make this confusion more directly obvious in a message on Romans 4:9–12, which has appeared in his Bible study booklets and on his radio broadcast:

> And we've been learning that justification, then, or God imputing to us his righteousness, God putting his righteousness to our account, must be seen in two ways. First of all, it is a forensic declaration, that is, it is a statement of God relative to judicial reality. . . . I heard recently that a preacher said, "When we are saved, it is only a legal pronouncement; there's no change at all. It is simply that God declares us righteous, contrary to the real fact, but based on the death of Jesus Christ." That is not true. There is a declaration, there is a legal statement, but there is a second aspect, and theologians would call this the ontology of justification, or the reality of it. And it is this: that God not only declares us to be righteous, based on the satisfying work of Christ, but in Christ he *makes us righteous*. We are *made* righteous. . . . And so you must see, then, in justification by faith, both of those elements. *That which is declared about us, that we are from now on right with God, can only be declared because in fact it is true that we have been recreated in his image.* . . .

MacArthur then illustrates his point with the story of the prodigal son. Justification has, ever since the Reformation, drawn on the illustration of a robe of righteousness because in this legal declaration God covers our nakedness and shame with the verdict of

Christ's righteousness. But MacArthur here sees this covering with the robe of righteousness in a different sense:

> But robing him in the robe to prepare him to sit at the father's table is equivalent to that ontological [sic] or that reality of a changed life. And so there must be both. . . . *And it's as if the son cannot receive all the blessedness of the father's table until he is robed in the right robe.* . . . And so we are reminded by this marvelous parable that there must be a stated fact about our [being] made righteous with God, but there also must be a reality behind that, because God doesn't say things about us that aren't in fact true. [GC 45–27 on Romans 4:9–12, "Grace to You," radio broadcast, Grace Community Church, Panorama City, California; also in MacArthur's booklet on Romans 1–8, 239, 307]

The importance of this departure from historic evangelical definitions cannot be overestimated. First, these statements embrace, unintentionally, a classic Roman Catholic understanding of justification. According to the Counter-Reformation Council of Trent (1563), "Justification . . . is not only a remission of sins but also the sanctification and renewal of the inward man through the voluntary reception of the grace and gifts whereby an unjust man becomes just. . . ." After condemning the notion that one can be "justified before God by his own works" (Canon 1) and that grace does nothing more than assist free will to merit eternal life (Canon 2), Trent nevertheless insists that justification involves a double aspect: a declaration and an actual inner renewal. The Reformers objected to this teaching more strongly than to any other; in fact, one can safely say that this *was* the Reformation debate. Again and again one finds the Reformers attacking the confusion of justification and sanctification.

Not only does MacArthur seem here to repeat the Roman Catholic confusion of justification and sanctification; he actually makes the forensic declaration depend on a real moral change in the person's behavior. First, the robe is "the reality of a changed life" not the declaration of a changed status, as the Reformers would have understood it. Second, "the son cannot receive all the blessedness of the father's table until he is robed in the right robe. And so there must be more than a declaration involved." In other words, God cannot declare one righteous before there is moral change. The legal declaration depends on moral transformation in MacArthur's statements here, just as surely as in Trent's. To his credit, however, MacArthur seems to flatly contradict these very comments elsewhere, namely, in *The Gospel According to Jesus* (cf. 187).

These concerns have been brought to MacArthur's attention and although there has not yet been any public retraction, these comments have been removed from the future copies of the tapes and editions of the booklet by MacArthur's staff. I have also been informed that MacArthur has corrected his position on this issue. After carefully assessing these comments, it does bring at least this writer to the conclusion that the parties involved in this controversy would do well to go back to the sources, particularly those of the Reformation debate, in order to clarify their language. One ought to give MacArthur the benefit of the doubt that he does in fact hold an orthodox evangelical doctrine of justification, but it is surely not the view expressed in these remarks, remarks read, heard, approved by Christians around the world who think this is "lordship salvation." It is time for those who claim the Reformation heritage, on both sides of the debate, to gain greater clarity on these utterly basic definitions before they engage in sensitive theological debates. The laity are confused enough by our debates as it is.

Our "determination of the will to obey truth," our repentance, our surrender, and our commitment—none of this has anything whatsoever to do with our justification. All these things are simply necessary (that is, inevitable) fruits of justification. The tendency to condition justification on moral transformation is always a departure from the biblical message. Richard Muller, a modern scholar of Protestant orthodoxy, notes concerning the Roman Catholic idea of justification conditioned upon moral renewal, "This conception of faith is denied by the Reformers and the Protestant orthodox insofar as it implies the necessity of works for justification and insofar as it rests on a concept of created grace (*gratia creata*) implanted or infused into man."[12]

The Reformers also spoke of faith as passive reception. It was not something for a person to do, but something for a person to believe and trust as having been done for him or her. MacArthur wants to maintain the classic doctrine of "faith alone," but when "faith" is obedience, active effort, surrender, and commitment, one wonders how that position can be maintained. Even if MacArthur argues, as he does, contrary to Hodges, that obedience and repentance are gifts of a sovereign God, he is still saying nothing that Thomas Aquinas or many Tridentine fathers would have denied. They believed that faith and obedience were God's works within a person, but the Reformers countered that these were not part of justification. We are not justified by God's work within us, but by his work for us, and this is received through faith (knowledge, assent, and trust) alone.

MacArthur adds W. E. Vine's definition of faith as including even "conduct inspired by such surrender" (173–74). If we are justified by faith and if faith is surrender, obedience, and conduct inspired by such surrender, then we are justified by works. The logic seems unavoidable:

> We are justified by faith alone.
> Faith is surrender, obedience, and conduct inspired by such surrender.
> Therefore, we are justified by surrender, obedience, and conduct inspired by such obedience.

Again, we would be on better ground if we were to take the Reformers' view, expressed by Calvin when he wrote, ". . . not even spiritual works come into account when the power of justifying is ascribed to faith."[13]

What Is the Gospel?

In chapter 6 of *The Gospel According to Jesus*, "He Challenges an Eager Seeker," MacArthur takes up the story of the rich young ruler who came to Jesus to find out what he must do to be saved, since he probably saw Jesus as the new rabbi who had the latest rules for getting into heaven (Matt. 19:16–26). "'But if you want to enter into life, keep the commandments,'" Jesus told the ruler. "He said to [Jesus], 'Which ones?'" After Jesus rehearsed the Ten Commandments, the ruler answered amazingly, "'All these things I have kept from my youth. What do I still lack?'" In other words, give me a law I haven't already fulfilled. "Jesus said to him, 'If you want to be perfect, go, sell what you have and give it to the poor, and you will have treasure in heaven; and come, follow Me.'" The rich young ruler was not willing to do this, that demonstrated that he had not kept the law, as he had not loved his neighbor as himself. He "went away sorrowful."

The exegesis of this passage that one will find in most evangelical churches committed to the Reformation faith and message centers on our Lord's use here of what is called the "theological" use of the law. The moral law is useful to frame civil society (first use) and to inform believers of God's will for their lives (third use). But according to its second use it comes to judge and sentence us as we are in our own righteousness. Whenever we pretend to offer God anything of our own, he brings the law to us as a mirror, and we see our shame. This is the only interpretation of what our Lord is doing in this passage that is consistent with the whole teaching of the New Testament concerning the use of the law.

Nevertheless, MacArthur disagrees with this exegesis, upon which so much in this debate depends: "Many readers of this Matthew 19 passage have taken the young man to task for his question. They say his mistake was in asking, 'What good thing shall I *do*?' In other words, he had a works-oriented mindset" (p. 82).

This interpretation, however, is not the purpose of the passage, MacArthur insists, even though he acknowledges that the ruler was self-righteous and was seeking to be justified by his own efforts. "Our Lord gave this young man a test. He had to choose between his possessions and Jesus Christ. He failed the test. No matter what he believed, since he was unwilling to forsake all, he could not be a disciple of Christ. Salvation is for those who are willing to forsake everything" (p. 78).

This leads us to ask, what if the ruler *had* sold everything? If the point of the Epistle here is that "salvation is for those who are willing to forsake everything," then this command is not according to the second use of the law (to drive us to Christ), but is part of the gospel. In other words, Jesus offered a promise that could be fulfilled upon rendering sufficient obedience. MacArthur seems to be saying that instead of functioning as the law telling us that we have not fulfilled its requirements to love our neighbor as we love ourselves, this passage is the gospel offering us salvation if we are at least *willing* to fulfill this duty. It is not an antinomian like Hodges, but the biblical theologian Calvin who writes the following concerning the Roman Catholic exegesis of this passage:

> I do not want to pursue the individual testimonies that the stupid Sorbonnists [Roman Catholic theologians at the University of Paris—M.H.] of today have groundlessly torn from Scripture—whatever first came to hand—to fling at us. . . . The lawyer, accustomed to the persuasion of law righteousness, blinded himself with confidence in works. . . . Therefore he is rightly sent back to the law wherein there is a perfect mirror of righteousness.
>
> With a clear voice we too proclaim that these commandments are to be kept if one seeks life in works. And Christians must know this doctrine, for how could they flee to Christ unless they recognized that they had plunged from the way of life over the brink of death? . . . Therefore, since we are barred from law righteousness, we must betake ourselves to another help, that is, to faith in Christ. For this reason, as the Lord in this passage recalls to the law a teacher of the law whom he knew to be puffed up with empty confidence in works, in order that he may learn he is a sinner, subject to the dreadful judgment of eternal death, so elsewhere he comforts with the promise of grace without any mention of the law others who have already been humbled by this sort of knowledge: "Come to me all who labor and are heavy-laden, and I will refresh you . . . and you will find rest for your souls" [Matt. 11:28–29].[14]

In other words, Jesus' comment was not a test to see whether the young man was willing to surrender all, but a challenge to his pretensions of law-keeping. In Calvin's exegesis, the problem was that the young man did not keep the law at all, and therefore, should have fled to Christ; in MacArthur's, the problem was that he did not keep the law enough, and therefore, should have sold his possessions.

MacArthur adds to this something that is, to say the least, an unguarded statement: "What kind of evangelism is this? Jesus would have failed personal evangelism class in almost every Bible college or seminary I know! He gave a message of works, and at this point did not even mention faith or the facts of redemption" (p. 79). How can MacArthur consider "a message of works" without "faith or the facts of redemption" evangelism? Elsewhere, MacArthur does provide sound definitions of the gospel, but in instances such as this, confusion arises as to whether the gospel according to MacArthur is, "Do this and you shall live" or "Live and you shall do this," especially when he concludes of this episode, "Here is the ultimate test: will this man obey the Lord?" (p. 86). This does not mean, MacArthur hastens to add, that we must all give everything we have to the poor, "but we *do* have to be willing" to do this. Therefore, this encounter becomes, in MacArthur's scenario, a call to greater holiness, not a revelation of the desperation of pretenses to holiness.

Let us, then, apply this exegesis in a pastoral situation. Bob was driving along his city's main street, well within the speed limit, and a man ran into the middle of the street, pretending to have been hit by Bob's car. It was obvious to Bob that this was a scam, but the scam included "witnesses" who were willing to testify that Bob was speeding. Without a second thought, Bob planned on hiring a lawyer and fighting the suit, but later he recalled having read in *The Gospel According to Jesus*, "We must be eager to do whatever [Jesus] asks," or we have every reason to doubt our salvation (p. 87). Further, it is clear that Jesus demands in Matthew 5:39–40, "But I tell you not to resist an evil person. . . . If anyone wants to sue you and take away your tunic, let him have your cloak also." MacArthur says of the rich young ruler, "Here is the ultimate test: will this man obey the Lord?" (p. 86). So, would he not also call this Bob's "ultimate test"? Will Bob obey? If not, should he not doubt his salvation?

However, is it not more consistent with the whole teaching of Scripture to argue that the purpose of the Sermon on the Mount, as well as the story of the rich young ruler, was to use the law as the mirror that showed just how unrighteous those were who thought they were obeying it by conforming outwardly? Adultery is not merely the act, but the lust in the heart; murder and theft fit the same picture. The point is to take from "law-keepers" any illusion that they are actually pulling it off.

MacArthur appears to make room for this point when considering the rich young ruler (p. 84), but obscures the issue by making this primary focus a secondary focus through his question, "Will this man obey the Lord?" He causes even greater confusion when he argues, "This passage crushes the claim of those who say the Sermon on the Mount is not gospel, but law." In fact, he emphasizes, the Sermon on the Mount (which is a restatement of the moral law) "is pure gospel" (p. 179). MacArthur even titles this chapter, "The Way of Salvation." Does this mean that one cannot expect to attain adoption until he or she has overcome hatred of enemies (cf. Matt. 5:44–45)? Calvin's commentary is to be preferred over MacArthur's on this issue. He writes, "No one wins this distinction [of sonship] for himself, no one begins to be a son of God from the time he loves his enemies. . . ."[15] Since Rick Ritchie covers this subject in chapter 3 in this volume, we will set aside a fuller treatment for now.

What Is Repentance?

MacArthur correctly defines repentance as a vigorous, lifelong process, in contrast to Hodges's assertion that it is merely turning to Christ. Yet, while Hodges confuses repentance with faith MacArthur confuses faith with repentance in *The Gospel According to Jesus*, although after fruitful dialogues we understand that this will be changed in future editions.[16]

Again, the reader must not get the impression that the classical Reformation position tolerates the separation of saving faith and genuine repentance, as though one could be justified through faith alone and not make a commitment to leave sin and follow Jesus Christ at all costs. But MacArthur's definition of faith here is actually an effective definition of repentance, not faith. Nevertheless, if "disobedience is unbelief" (p. 47), according to MacArthur, then would he not also say that the converse could be equally true:

obedience is belief? This is the confusion of the cause (faith) and its effect (repentance), as Calvin argues from a number of texts that repentance follows faith logically, if not psychologically or chronologically.[17]

This distinction is especially important in that the proper nature of faith is rest and trust in the finished work of Christ. As Calvin writes,

> For a conditional promise that sends us back to our own works does not promise life unless we discern its presence in ourselves. Therefore, if we would not have our faith tremble and waver, we must buttress it with the promise of salvation, that is willingly and freely offered to us by the Lord in consideration of our misery rather than our deserts. . . . He [the apostle Paul—M.H.] distinguishes the gospel both from the precepts of the law and from the promises, since there is nothing that can establish faith except that generous embassy by that God reconciles the world to himself [cf. II Cor. 5:19–20].[18]

And yet, this does not mean that one may have a savior without a lord: "Therefore, when we say that faith must rest upon a freely given promise, we do not deny that believers embrace and grasp the Word of God in every respect: but we point out the promise of mercy as the proper goal of faith,"[19] not the call to discipleship itself.

Discipleship is given to and required of all the justified, but it is not itself the good news in which we place our confidence, trust, and hope. Repentance ought indeed to be preached along with the call to faith, as the flip side of the coin of conversion, but these two must be distinguished if we are to maintain "faith alone."

Confidence ✓
Trust ✓
&
Hope ✓

What Is Assurance?

"If disobedience and rebellion continue unabated there is reason to doubt the reality of a person's faith," according to MacArthur (p. 113). And yet the apostle Paul writes, "For what I am doing, I do not understand. For what I will to do, that I do not practice; but what I hate, that I do. . . . For the good that I will to do, I do not do; but the evil I will not to do, that I prac-

Discipleship is given to & Required of All The Justified – true Born-Again Believers, But it is not the good news in which we place our Confidence, Trust & Hope!

Not Conforming to God's Law "is" what causes; the, strains, struggles & tensions Misunderst And the Definite Need For the Cross of Jesus Christ!

tice" (Rom. 7:5, 19). Would we have to doubt the reality of Paul's faith because "disobedience and rebellion continue unabated"? MacArthur himself recognizes that this passage from Romans 7 is referring to the apostle after his conversion and is therefore a realistic picture of the Christian life (p. 174 n. 14). Nevertheless, MacArthur may have been on safer ground to have said, "If there is no struggle against the disobedience and rebellion, there is reason to doubt the reality of a person's faith." In other words, evidence of the new birth is not whether we are, on the whole, achieving victory at any given point, but whether we are at war! While Paul struggles in this way, he adds, "For I delight in the law of God according to the inward man. But I see another law in my members, warring against the law of my mind, and bringing me into captivity to the law of sin that is in my members" (Rom. 7:22–23). While the regenerate do not cease sinning, they also do not cease hating their sin and struggling to eradicate it. The believer loves God's law because it is written on his or her heart (Jer. 31:33–34), but it is his or her inability to conform perfectly to it that creates this tension in the Christian life, this war within.

① Do not cease sinning!
② Hate it!
③ Struggle Against it!

While MacArthur may not intend for readers to come away from his remarks prepared to conclude that they are not Christians because they find themselves committing the same sins repeatedly, I do not think this is an unwarranted conclusion based on his comments. This general impression is only furthered by MacArthur's discussion of the "narrow gate":

> One cannot get through a turnstile with armloads of suitcases. The narrow gate Jesus describes is not wide enough for superstars who want to enter with all their valuables. . . . Whoever we are, whatever it is we treasure, when we reach the narrow gate we can expect to drop everything. The baggage of self-righteousness, selfishness, sin, or materialism must be left outside, or we'll never make it through. The good news is that although the gate is narrow, it is wide enough to accommodate the chief of sinners (cf. 1 Tim. 1:15). [p. 183]

Simultaneously Just & a Sinner!

What are we to conclude from this remarkable statement? What happens when the unbeliever of Romans 7 discovers the baggage in his trunk again? The Bible teaches what Luther and Calvin reproduced in the formula *simul iustus et peccator*. In other words, the believer is "simultaneously justified and sinful." While MacArthur acknowledges this truth, comments such as this one risk confusing the average layperson, unless proper distinctions are drawn.

This question of assurance is at the root of the present controversy. After all, it is not enough to be saved by grace. We must also have assurance that we are saved by grace. This question has been debated not only outside the Reformation churches, but within them as well. Chief among the issues involved is what the Protestant orthodox have called the "practical syllogism." Simply stated, those who are struggling with their assurance ought to comfort themselves with the following syllogism:

A) The elect bear fruit.
B) I bear fruit.
Conclusion: I am one of the elect.

Whenever Luther, Calvin, or the other Reformers declared Christ's promise that a good tree bears good fruit, they were employing the practical syllogism. Nevertheless, the Reformers were quite anxious to hold together faith and assurance as responses that demand Christ alone as their object. In other words, one is not justified through faith alone and then assured some time later by examining his or her works. Rather, justifying faith carries with it (in its very definition: trust) a certain confidence and assurance that the promise is true for me, even though my faith and assurance may be weak.

MacArthur, as we have seen, not only takes the focus for our assurance off of the finished work of Christ, but even raises questions about the focus for faith itself. Is faith resting in Christ's life and death or in ours? We must be careful not to react to the antinomian threat by driving the sheep back to themselves, away from Christ. The Sermon on the Mount and other calls to discipleship and the bearing of fruit are addressed to all Christians in this age,

but these words belong to the category of *law* (that is, divine commands that we are to obey) not *gospel* (that is, "good news" for
those who meet the legal conditions by their own obedience). As
Calvin warned, "If consciences wish to attain any certainty in this
matter, they ought to give no place to the law." And yet, no Christian can "rightly infer from this that the law is superfluous for
believers, since it does not stop teaching and exhorting and urg-
ing them to good, even though before God's judgment seat it has
no place in their consciences,"[20] either for justification or assurance. At certain points, it must be said, both Hodges and
MacArthur make it sound as though discipleship is a matter of
great strain, as though Christ's yoke were not easy and his burden light. The Radical Anabaptists during the Reformation also
challenged the Reformers for preaching "a sinful sweet Christ,"
while they preferred to follow "a bitter Christ." The comparison
does not end here, for as the historian Timothy George notes, "For
the Radicals, repentance always preceded faith, in contrast to the
teachings of Calvin, who reversed this order and interpreted
repentance as a fruit of faith."[21]

We would all do well to heed Calvin's advice in this matter:

PROV. 20:9
I CHRO. 8:36

Now if we ask in what way the conscience can be made quiet before
God, we shall find the only way to be that unmerited righteousness be conferred upon us as a gift of God. Let us ever bear in mind
Solomon's question: "Who will say, 'I have made my heart clean;
I am pure from my sin'?" [Prov. 20:9]. Surely there is no one who
is not sunken in infinite filth! Let even the most perfect man
descend into his conscience and call his deeds to account, what
then will be the outcome for him? Will he sweetly rest as if all
things were well composed between him and God and not, rather,
be torn by dire torments, since if he be judged by works, he will
feel grounds for condemnation within himself? The conscience, if
it looks to God, must either have sure peace with his judgment or
be besieged by the terrors of hell. Therefore we profit nothing in
discussing righteousness unless we establish a righteousness so
steadfast that it can support our soul in the judgment of God. . . .
For no one can ever confidently trust in it [one's obedience—M.H.]
because no one will ever come to be really convinced in his own
mind that he has satisfied the law, as surely no one ever fully sat-

isfies it through works. . . . First, then, doubt would enter the minds of all men, and at length despair, while each one reckoned for himself how great a weight of debt still pressed upon him, and how far away he was from the condition laid down for him. See faith already oppressed and extinguished! . . . Therefore, on this point [assurance—M.H.] we must establish, and as it were, deeply fix all our hope, paying no regard to our works, to seek any help from them. . . . For, as regards justification, faith is something merely passive, bringing nothing of ours [not even repentance and a determination of the will to obey—M.H.] to the recovering of God's favor but receiving from Christ that which we lack.[22]

While our obedience can support and lend the aid of a character witness to our profession, we are not to ground our assurance in such obedience:

They [acts of obedience—M.H.] have no place in laying a foundation to strengthen the conscience, but are of value only when taken *a posteriori*. For there is nowhere that fear that is able to furnish full assurance. And the saints are conscious of possessing only such an integrity as intermingled with many vestiges of the flesh. . . . For if they begin to judge their salvation by good works, nothing will be more uncertain or more feeble. . . . From this it comes about that the believer's conscience feels more fear and consternation than assurance. . . . If righteousness is supported by works, in God's sight it must entirely collapse; and it is confined solely to God's mercy, solely to communion with Christ, and therefore solely to faith.[23]

How then do we distinguish true believers from hypocrites? Did Jesus not teach that the church or kingdom of Christ is like a field, with wheat and tares? The servants asked the master if he wanted them to pull up the tares, and the master replied, "No, lest while you gather up the tares you also uproot the wheat with them. Let both grow together until the harvest . . ." (Matt. 13:28–30). Calvin comments, ". . . to know who are His is a prerogative belonging solely to God [II Tim. 2:19]. . . . For those who seemed utterly lost and quite behind hope are by his goodness called back to the way; while those who more than others seemed to stand firm often fall."[24]

Conclusion

The issues raised during the Protestant Reformation are being debated hotly again, as even the evangelical world appears to be as confused as the medieval church was on these points. Both Zane Hodges and John MacArthur are self-described dispensationalists, and yet both claim the Reformers for their support. But neither appears to be saying what Luther and Calvin insisted was the biblical message, although MacArthur at least affirms the basic Reformation tenets.

With MacArthur, I am convinced that there are many in our churches who are not regenerated by the power of the Holy Spirit. The United States claims fifty million "born again" Christians, and yet the culture sinks deeper and deeper into decadence, frequently with Christian spokespersons themselves leading the way. Our lives are, taken statistically, wasteful, proud, unproductive, and self-indulgent, and we feel more at home in shopping malls than in the house of God. Why are we—so many of us—living this way even though we claim to be born again?

Here, I must diverge a bit from MacArthur. He would argue that the problem is that unregenerate believers are not obedient enough. Like the rich young ruler, they have not passed the test; they have not surrendered all at the turnstile. However, I would argue instead that the reason why so many Christians are anemic is that they do not understand the gospel. In the gospel message, in the facts of redemption and reconciliation, we discover "the power of God to salvation" (Rom. 1:16). If faith is the root of all the believer's obedience and faith comes only by hearing the good news of God's saving work in Christ, apart from our own works, then justifying faith is the answer to this great problem, not mere moral pleas or threats.

In fact, I would argue that the reason so many unbelievers can sit comfortably in our churches and even call themselves born-again Christians is that we give them very little to deny. The offensive message of the cross has been replaced with "God loves you

To Confess Sin & Sinfulness is Two Different things! —we must confess the things we do — the sin —But Also our state — our Sinfulness!

Don't Judge a Book by Its Cover 55

and has a wonderful plan for your life," with the cross tucked somewhere underneath it. I would like to offer the following two reasons why we might not be seeing the health and spiritual maturity God expects of us in our personal holiness:

(1) *Hypocrisy.* Many think they are living holy lives because they *think there good with No Fault!* do not have the slightest comprehension of biblical holiness. They have never stood, like Isaiah in his vision, before the Holy Creator, and felt their "righteousness" crawl into the corner for shelter from the divine glory. They think that because they avoid certain movies, rock music, nightclubs, and non-Christians in general, they are not, at least, great sinners. But they *are* great sinners. Not only because they are proud and obnoxious to both God and man in their self-righteousness—like the Pharisee who thanked God for his piety, while the sinner cried out for mercy— but because they are hypocrites who cannot confess their sinfulness (1 John 1:9). They have never known the terror of God's law; their consciences have felt rather like that of the rich young ruler who responded to Jesus' recitation, "All these things I have kept from my youth" (Matt. 19:20). Because they have never had premarital sex or been drunk, they are certain that they do not require self-examination and a swift flight back to the cross. They may not be "spiritual giants," they concede, but they're "good Christian folks"—mediocre, external, and superficial in their devotion. They have never been condemned in their righteousness by the law, so they shall never be justified by Christ's righteousness.

(2) *Despair.* The rest, better off by far and ready for the gospel's peace, despair. They have heard the calls to holiness—by surrendering or laying all on the altar or by rededicating their lives, hoping this time it will work. They are not told that they are dead to sin's dominion because of the once-and-for-all work of Christ. Rather, they are expected to enter into or attain that higher life, being harassed regularly into attempting something that they should be told has already been done for them. Instead of living against sin with the recognition that Christ has already won victory, they are certain that they must themselves become "victorious Christians." After successive frustrated attempts, they give up.

[Handwritten margin notes: In 1 Cor. 1:30: 1) Holy 2) Righteous 3) Sanctified 4) Reconciled — who we ARE spiritually! Called to live who's we ARE "In Christ" Not to Become what we Are not yet.]

The solution is simple. As Christ is the answer to our guilt and condemnation (through justification), so he is the answer to our bondage and corruption (sanctification). He takes away not only the verdict, but also the slavery. To justify us in the heavenly court without giving us the gifts that, by virtue of that heavenly verdict, belong to us would be cruel and unjust on God's part. No, he does not simply put money into our bank account and then leave us stranded along the side of the road, beaten and bruised. Holiness is not an option for the Christian. But hold on—I can hear the hearts racing: "Holiness, the impossible dream?" To be sure, "but with God all things are possible" (Matt. 19:26). Holiness is not an option, it is a requirement. But this is not a threat; it's a promise. What God began he will finish (Phil. 1:6). In Christ we already are holy, righteous, sanctified, reconciled (1 Cor. 1:30). Now we are called to live what we are, not to become what we are not yet.

Understanding these words takes the load off of the despairing, because they realize for the first time that God wants to give them the righteous status they could not attain by "yielding" and "surrendering." And it converts the hypocrites by showing them the offensiveness of their own "holiness" and "righteousness," driving them to Christ for shelter from God's wrath. For hypocrisy, we need the law; for despair, the gospel. The answer is never to confuse or separate the two, but to clearly proclaim Christ, our Prophet, Priest, and King.

Zane Hodges's gospel as we have seen, is far from "absolutely free." Very little is attributed to God, and much is attributed to human decision and activity. While Hodges is an antinomian, MacArthur is surely no legalist. And yet, even though MacArthur's conclusions are a vast improvement, we still must dig deeper into the Scriptures and into our Reformation heritage (from which both authors quote generously, but often selectively) to discover a better explanation; toward that end this volume hopes to contribute in some slight measure.

Let me conclude this introduction with two statements the great Calvinist John Newton, author of "Amazing Grace," made as he faced the threats of antinomianism and legalism in his day. Notice that legalism is always the root of antinomianism:

[Handwritten margin note (vertical, left): Surrendering & Yielding came effortless & naturally when we accept God's Righteous Status!]

Of the antinomians,

Satan labours to drive unstable souls from one extreme to another, and has too often succeeded. Wearied with vain endeavours to keep the law, that they might obtain life by it [legalism], and afterwards taking up with a notion of the Gospel devoid of power [antinomianism], they have at length despised that obedience that is the honour of the Christian, and essentially belongs to his character, and have abused the grace of God to licentiousness. But we have not so learned Christ.[25]

Of the legalists,

Their experience seems to lead them to talk of themselves, of the change that is wrought in them, and the much that depends upon their own watchfulness and striving. We likewise would be thankful if we could perceive a change wrought in us by the power of grace; we desire to be found watching. But whenever our hopes are most alive, it is less from a view of imperfect beginnings of grace in our hearts than from an apprehension of him who is our all in all. His person, his love, his sufferings, his intercession, compassion, fulness and faithfulness—these are our delightful themes, which leave us little leisure, when in our best frames, to speak of ourselves.[26]

Part 1

Light from Scripture

Repentance in Romans

Robert B. Strimple

I want to turn your attention now to the sixth chapter of Paul's letter to the Romans, not only because of the intrinsic importance of its teaching for Christians in all ages, but also because of the way it speaks to a most significant theological controversy that is raging in American evangelicalism today. The church of Christ needs to be alerted to the false teaching at issue because it does not concern some minor matter or some peripheral doctrine. It focuses directly on the central message of Christianity. It focuses directly on the very nature of the Christian gospel.

It is helpful, in discussing a controversy or a false teaching, to give it some convenient label. The false teachers I have in mind here call the view they *oppose* the doctrine of "lordship salvation." So those who are being attacked by this false teaching often label it, in return, the doctrine of "no-lordship salvation." I don't know how happy that teaching is to wear that label, but since it is in fairly widespread use, I shall use it here.

"No-lordship salvation" has been described by James Boice as a doctrine that reveals "the greatest weakness of contemporary evangelical Christianity in America. . . . It is a tragic error. It is the idea—where did it ever come from?—that one can be a Christian without being a follower of the Lord Jesus Christ."[1] As that teaching is often expressed: To be saved one must receive Christ as Savior. Receiving Christ as lord of one's life is another matter. However commendable and desirable we might think it is to have Christ as the lord of one's life, they maintain, that bears absolutely no relationship to the matter of one's eternal salvation.

It has become very common in evangelical churches in recent years to hear preachers attacking the doctrine of lordship salvation. And that new phrase makes it sound as if the preacher who opposes it opposes some novel theological position. The fact is, however, that what is now being called lordship salvation is simply historic Protestant theology! What *is* novel is this present-day opposition to that theology and that gospel.

To understand Zane Hodges, the "no-lordship" position's chief advocate, however, and to understand the great appeal of his theology for many evangelicals, you must understand that his motive in all that he says can appear to be solidly biblical. Indeed, it can appear to be most commendable and vitally important. To understand Hodges's theology you must recognize that all that he says is geared to preserving in its purity the gospel of justification by grace through faith in Jesus Christ. Justification is by faith, as Paul explains in the first five chapters of his letter to the Romans. And, as Martin Luther wrote in the margin of his copy of that letter, it is by faith ALONE! Just remember that, Hodges says, and then everything else that the New Testament talks about will fall into place and you will see that none of it has any relationship to the believer's justification—that is to say, to his or her eternal salvation, the possession of eternal life.

If you understand what Hodges has said there, you already know what he will say about every Christian virtue spoken of in the New Testament. You already know what he is going to say in every chapter on every subject in his books. Repenting of my sin, becoming Christ's disciple, obeying Christ, manifesting the fruit of the Spirit, doing good works, loving God and my neighbor, even the matter of whether I go on believing in Christ, of continuing in my faith—no matter what good things you might want to say in favor of any of those responses, or even of all of them, none of that can have any bearing whatsoever on whether I have eternal life. To say that it does, Hodges insists, is to fall into the Roman Catholic error, which is the same at root as the Judaizing error that Paul faced—that is, the error of believing that salvation is by works, or perhaps by faith and works.

Hodges speaks of "the idea" that "has gained ground that true saving faith is somehow distinguishable from false kinds of faith, primarily by means of its results or 'fruits.'"[2] But that, Hodges insists, is a totally unbiblical idea. Now, it might surprise the reader greatly, that "by their fruits shall you know them" is a totally unbiblical idea. That a person's possession of eternal life in Christ is necessarily evidenced by that person's life of faith, hope, love, joy, peace, kindness, self-control—is thought to be a totally unbiblical idea. And I suspect, I certainly hope, that you would immediately think of many New Testament passages to which you could turn to refute Hodges here, passages like 1 John 2–3 and James 2, passages that insist that true faith in Christ is a faith that works through love (Gal. 5:6).

Does Justification by Faith Equal Antinomianism?

Paul begins the sixth chapter of Romans with a question: "What shall we say, then? Shall we go on sinning so that grace may increase?" And with that question the apostle turns his attention in this letter to an important new area of gospel truth. For five chapters before this he has been developing one wonderful theme, the heart of the gospel, the theme of justification. He has been answering the question that is of such basic concern to every sinner: how can I be right with God? How can I be accepted by God as one who has fulfilled his holy demand for righteousness?

And Paul has emphasized that such acceptance, such standing before God, can never be attained on the basis of law-keeping or personal good works. The perfectly righteous God demands perfect righteousness, but who of us has that to present before God? Surely the very best among us is a lawbreaker. There is none righteous as God is righteous. Therefore, as Paul concludes in Romans

3:20, no human being can be received by God as right on the basis of his or her good deeds.

There would seem to be no hope for us sinners then. But into the night of human hopelessness the light of God's love and God's grace appears! God announces that in love *he* will provide that righteousness which in justice he demands. He will send his Son as our new Covenant Head, who will perfectly fulfill all the law's demands, even taking the execution of the sentence of that holy law upon himself in the sinner's place. Having taken all the sinner's guilt upon himself, he credits all his righteousness to the account of every sinner who simply responds in trust, in faith, in self-abandonment to the Savior.

This gospel is obviously a divine gospel, because no human being would ever have conceived it. It is so contrary to the thinking of sinful humans that Paul spends the better part of three chapters (3, 4, and 5) making it clear. At the end of chapter 5, Paul's presentation of the gospel of justification by grace through faith alone has left itself open to an obvious and serious objection. Will the preaching of such a gospel not simply encourage people to continue on in their sin? If Christ has already paid the penalty for my sins—past, present, and future sins—if I have already been credited with Christ's perfect righteousness, if my holiness of life has not had the least part to play in saving me, then why should I be concerned about sin in my life at all? Why try to do good? Why strive to live a righteous life?

The objection can be put even more sharply. In Romans 5:20 Paul says, "where sin increased, grace increased all the more." The magnitude of God's grace is seen all the more clearly when it is contrasted with the extent of sin. Well then, someone might say, if the worse our sin the greater God's grace is seen to be, I will really magnify God's grace by becoming the worst possible sinner!

The one who speaks this way is not being serious, of course. The question of Romans 6:1 is an attempt to ridicule Paul's gospel by reducing it to absurdity. In every age down through history, however, those who take a legalistic approach to religion raise this objection. The traditional Roman Catholic theology, liberal Protestantism, cults of various types—all insist that by preaching the gospel of salvation by God's free grace alone we take away the only effective motivation for holy living, and we open the door to lawlessness and sin. And this is a very serious objection indeed to our gospel.

Notice, however, that the legalist's objection to Paul's gospel is at the same time the antinomian's distortion of the gospel. That label, *antinomian* (*nomos* [Greek] = law), has been given to those who teach that, since we are justified by grace through faith and not by our works, we may continue to give ourselves over to sin's mastery and still be saved. The church has always had to be on the lookout for such dangerously false teaching. The teaching of "no-lordship salvation" is simply the latest form of this heresy, and the only thing new about it, perhaps, is how open, how shockingly blatant it is in its antinomianism. Note well, therefore, how in this sixth chapter of Romans the apostle Paul answers both the legalist's objection to his gospel and the antinomian's distortion of it.[3] To the legalist he says: The justified person, remember, is also the sanctified person. Paul seems to be saying that, for clarity in presentation, he has separated justification and sanctification to discuss each in turn, since one cannot say everything at once. Yet he asserts that, in reality, justification and sanctification cannot be separated. Both flow to the believer from the virtue of Christ's death and the power of his resurrection.

The believer's very real (though deeply mysterious) union with Christ produces not only justification but sanctification as well. And just as justification is not through the merit of works of law-keeping, so sanctification is not through any supposed power of the law, because the law has no power. Sanctification is through the power of Christ's risen life and the indwelling Spirit, that same Spirit who raised Christ from the dead. In Romans 3–5 Paul has spoken of justification by faith. We might well say that he now goes on to speak of sanctification by faith, because just as justification is not through the merits of law-keeping, so sanctification is not through the Christian's own power to keep the law. Rather, it is through the power of Christ's risen life and the indwelling Spirit, which becomes the Christian's possession through faith. It is the believer's union with Christ, a union with Christ in his death and in his resurrection symbolized and sealed in the act of baptism, that makes real not only his or her justification but his or her sanctification as well.

And thus Paul answers also the antinomian's distortion of the gospel. To make being under grace an excuse for carelessness about sin (see Rom. 6:15) is an indication that one is not really under grace at all. If one knows nothing of victory over sin in his or her life, there is no reason to believe that such a person has been justified. The matter, as the apostle views it, is no less serious than this.

In many evangelical circles, teaching concerning the so-called victorious Christian life has been very popular over the years, but often its message has been a distorted one. We need to see clearly that in the perspective of the inspired apostle the *victorious* life, the life of victory over sin, is the *Christian* life. Paul in this sixth chapter of Romans is not speaking of some super-normal Christian experience, but simply of the facts about any believer. If you approach Romans 6, as many Christians do, with the assumption that Paul is speaking here of what should be true of all Christians, you will never understand this chapter. Paul is not speaking here of what *should* be true of all Christians; he is speaking here of what *is* true of all Christians. Sanctification, deliverance from sin's dominion over your life, is not merely the purpose of justification. Purposes, by definition, can fail. Sanctification, being set free from sin's dominion, is God's gift to you, along with justification; it is the inevitable partner of justification.

If we understand Paul's words in this chapter aright, we shall find them full of serious warning. Many years ago, a book was published entitled *Calories Don't Count*. Many hopeful Americans snapped up that book, scrapped their diets—and soon found themselves in serious trouble with their weight. The sad fact is that calories do count. Many preachers and evangelical writers in our day encourage spiritual laziness by asserting that what one does simply doesn't matter. One can be a "carnal Christian," after all, and still be a Christian.[4]

Hodges is now telling *former* believers that even though faith in Christ is something they used to have, but don't have any longer, they still have eternal life.[5] The truth is that works do count, because they are the inevitable fruit testifying to the reality of the life of the risen Christ in our lives.

Thus, Paul's words in Romans 6, understood rightly, are full of serious warning. But notice that his words are also full of blessed assurances and wonderful promises. For example, when Paul says in verse 14, "sin shall not be your master," this is not a command. It is not as though Paul were saying, "Sin is mastering you, Christian. Don't let it!" Nor is his statement a promise of a future blessing: "There is a day coming when sin shall no longer be your master." It is simply a statement of fact: "sin shall not be your master." And Paul says "*shall* not be your master" to express the absolute certainty of this fact.

Now, do not misunderstand. There are commands in this chapter, in verses 11, 12, and 13. But these commands are based not on what should be true of all Christians, but perhaps is not true in your case. These commands are based on what *is* true of all Christians, including you. For example, in verse 11 we are not commanded to *become* dead to sin and alive to God. This has already happened by virtue of our union with Christ. And it is not by "counting" or "considering" or "reckoning" these things to be facts regarding us that they become facts regarding us. We are to "count" or "consider" them to be facts regarding us for the best possible reason—because they *are* facts!

In verse 12 when Paul informs the believer, "Therefore do not let sin reign in your mortal body," his argument is not, "sin reigns in you; don't let it," but rather, "sin does not have the dominion in your life." That's the point of the whole chapter (see vv. 14, 17, and 18): "Sin does not have dominion in your life; you have been set free from sin's mastery. Therefore, don't let sin reign in your life."

It would be cruel mockery to say to a slave who has not been set free, "Do not behave like a slave." He might well respond, "But that's what I am. I am a slave!" But to say the same thing to a former slave who has been set free is very meaningful, because he now must exercise the privileges, rights, powers, and responsibilities of his liberation. Think of the Reconstruction period in the South immediately after the Civil War, a difficult time of transition for many former slaves. We can well imagine two false ways a former slave might have been tempted to go. He might have been unwilling to take the risks of a new life of freedom and might have tried to continue to live, to all intents and purposes, like a slave still. Or he might have used his newfound freedom as an excuse for licentiousness and a life of anarchy and lawlessness. But what was needed was for each former slave to begin to live a life of responsible freedom.

Again, please do not misunderstand. "You have been set free from sin" (vv. 18 and 22) does not at all mean that you are now "sinless." The apostle Paul sees sin as a power under whose bondage the sinner lives, hopeless to ever gain the victory over that slave master by his or her own strength—until by faith that sinner is united to the Savior and, by the power of the Spirit of the risen Christ, sin is cast down from its throne. If you trust in Christ, sin is no longer master over you. You have now another master and lord, the triune God. This is not something for you to do, but something for you to believe.

But Paul knows that the battle against sin continues in the believer's life, and will continue until the end. The Christian will always find himself or herself on the front line in that battle. But, whereas outside Christ one was situated in enemy territory, where sin and death were in command, now the believer has been "rescued . . . from the dominion of darkness and brought . . . into the kingdom of the Son he loves" (Col. 1:13). Here in this life, in this age, we continue to fight the good fight. But we are called upon to use our new freedom in Christ to fight earnestly against sin in all its deadly forms.[6]

In Romans 6:6 Paul writes, "our old self was crucified with him [Christ]" in order that our new self, the man or woman we now are in union with Christ, might be a man or a woman filled with the power of Christ's risen life, a victor over sin, and a servant of God. Since, therefore, God has, in the words of the hymnwriter, broken "the power of cancelled sin," let us live as liberated men and women in gratitude for God's grace. Because Christ is the author and finisher of our faith, we can be confident that our Christian lives will be fruitful.

The Law 2
According to Jesus

Rick Ritchie

"Must one submit to the lordship of Christ in order to be saved?"
What often remains unnoticed in the current debate is that, while the two sides differ in their answer to this one question, they both come to the question with a common theological background, dispensationalism, which determines in advance the possible range of answers. We might call the proponents of the two positions "Dispensational Lordship Salvationists" and "Dispensational Decisional Salvationists." Before we offer our support on one side of the debate, we ought to take notice of the fact that both parties occupy the same theological continent and have pledged allegiance to the same doctrinal constitution. The better question for us might not be, Which side shall we support? but, How can we avoid the mine fields of both positions and find our way back to our true country?

In *The Gospel According to Jesus,* John MacArthur sets forth his position, which has been labeled "lordship salvationism." MacArthur says that he does not particularly like this label; it was invented by his opponents, and it pulls his position on Christ's lordship out of its biblical context. He sees teaching the necessity of surrendering to the lordship of Christ as one aspect, though an indispensable aspect, of the broader task of gospel preaching. When his opponents labeled his position, that gave them the opportunity to set the parameters of the discussion and give it an unbiblical focus. MacArthur would prefer to be allowed to preach the gospel biblically rather than defend one aspect of the message.

When evaluating the positions of MacArthur and his opponents, I feel the same way. MacArthur laments the fact that, by focusing our attention on one controversial aspect of the gospel, his opponents have made it difficult for him to present his position adequately because the lordship salvation question is not itself a biblical question. It is difficult to provide a balanced treatment of a subject in answer to an imbalanced question. If this is true, both MacArthur and his opponents, by determining the meaning of the terms used in the debate according to the distinctive theological system that they share, have made it even more difficult for Reformation Christians to set forth *their* answer to the lordship salvation question. It is not easy to provide a relevant treatment of the subject when many of those who have followed this debate disagree on the meanings of crucial terms.

The Dispensational Grid

To many American Christians, dispensationalism is not just a peripheral set of doctrines tacked onto a core of beliefs held in common with the rest of Christendom. Dispensationalism is the grid on which these Christians hang all of their doctrines, even the ones they claim to derive from other Protestant theologies. When dispensationalism is the interpretive grid by which theology is understood, it affects even the understanding of those doctrines which originated outside of the dispensationalist system.

When we witness MacArthur and his adversaries using Luther and other Reformation theologians to support their respective positions, we might be tempted to think that they are our cousins in the Reformation faith; however, even when they use the same vocabulary as the Reformers, their interpretive grid has already given to certain key terms a meaning that is foreign to the theology of the Reformation. This is never more evident than where they speak of "law" and "gospel."

Is the Sermon on the Mount the Gospel?

MacArthur's opponents claim that in their presentation of what they call free grace, they are simply presenting the old Reformation teaching. While Reformation theology did indeed teach free grace, what MacArthur's opponents describe ought to be called lawless grace. MacArthur is correct in criticizing the rampant antinomianism of this doctrine. Where we would question him is not in his criticism of his opponents, but in his attempt to support his criticisms by appealing to the Reformation, especially where MacArthur counters the neglect of the Sermon on the Mount by dispensationalism by suggesting that Martin Luther taught that the Sermon on the Mount was gospel and not law.

In classical dispensationalism, there is an age of law and an age of grace. One age follows another. The Old Testament saints were citizens of a distinct nation, Israel, which had been singled out for the privilege of receiving the Law. We, in contrast, are a different people, the church, living in a different age, the age of grace. While there may be valid principles that can be derived from the Mosaic law, it was not intended for the church. In dispensationalism, to label a teaching as "law" means that that teaching is not intended for today.

When MacArthur says that the Sermon on the Mount is gospel and not law, he is distancing himself from a view which relegates the Sermon on the Mount to a different age. He is placing the Sermon on the Mount before the world as a teaching with which it must come to terms.

MacArthur has done a service by insisting on the relevance of the Sermon on the Mount for the present age. He has correctly identified the Sermon's audience. What he has missed is its primary purpose. Like the Mosaic law in the Old Testament, the Sermon on the Mount was given to let us know of our need for a savior. Its primary purpose is to condemn, not to save.

MacArthur chastises his opponents for banishing the Sermon on the Mount to another age on the grounds of its legal nature.

While he is correct in applying the Sermon on the Mount to the present day, his opponents are correct in seeing that it is legal. The fact that the Sermon on the Mount is an explication of the law does not confine its relevance to a past or future age.

In Reformation theology we stress that both law and gospel are operative in both Old and New Testament times. We can see law in operation in the New Testament in the Sermon on the Mount. We can see grace operative in the Old Testament in the protoe-vangelion (Gen. 3:15) and in the faith of the Old Testament saints in the coming Messiah (Heb. 11, esp. vv. 24–26). Law and gospel are not confined to distinct ages.

Yet, while the law and the gospel are both found in the Old and New Testaments, they differ. According to Luther: "The Law and Gospel are two doctrines that are absolutely contrary. To place righteousness in the Law is, therefore, simply fighting against the Gospel. For the Law is an extractor, requiring of us that we should work and give; in a word, it wants to have (something) from us. But the Gospel exacts nothing of us; it gives freely and enjoins us to hold out our hands and take what it offers."[2]

Even though MacArthur manages to distance himself from dispensationalism in its compartmentalization of God's saving work, he brings considerable confusion to his reflections on the Sermon on the Mount by his failure to properly identify law as law.

The law demands while the gospel gives. We need to know from the law what God demands of us before we recognize our need to be saved by the gospel. On account of this, even though the gospel differs from the law in its role (as condemnation differs from forgiveness!) it depends upon the law. If we want people to know how badly they need the gospel, we need to preach the law to them in its impossibly demanding vigor, even today.

Like John MacArthur before him, Martin Luther had to contend with adversaries who said that the Sermon on the Mount did not apply to them, and his writings are especially stern:

> According to them [Luther's opponents], Christ does not intend everything that He teaches in the fifth chapter [of Matthew] to be regarded by Christians as a command for them to observe; but he gave much of it as advice to those who would try to be perfect, to

be kept by anyone who pleases. This in spite of Christ's angry threat that no one will enter the kingdom of heaven who abolishes the least of these commandments (Matt. 5:19); and he explicitly calls them commandments.[3]

Unlike MacArthur, Luther regarded this sermon as law, however, as we can see from the fact that he referred to Christ's words in the Sermon on the Mount as commandments. Because of this, when MacArthur claims that Luther regarded the Sermon on the Mount as gospel and not law, he cannot be fully correct.

Since Luther understood the law in terms of what God demands of us, and the gospel in terms of what God gives to us, he was sometimes able to find both law and gospel in the same passage, sometimes even in the same statement! The law is not the gospel; we are condemned by the law and saved by the gospel. A given passage can contain both, however.

In his Large Catechism, for example, Luther explicates the Ten Commandments in such a way that they portray God as one who can be trusted. He speaks of the "gracious offer," the "cordial invitation," and the "rich . . . promise" that God brings to us in the first commandment. Luther can find gospel in the Ten Commandments. Elsewhere, he states very clearly that we are not saved by keeping the Ten Commandments, but that they show us our sin and condemn us. He finds law in them as well. If we read a passage to learn of God's holy justice and see what God demands of us, this is law, and will condemn us. If we are reading the same passage to see what it tells us of God's mercy and promises, our trust can be awakened, and this trust is saving faith.

If Luther was able to find both law and gospel in the Ten Commandments, then surely he could have found both in the Sermon on the Mount. MacArthur is wrong, then, when he says Luther argued that the Sermon on the Mount was not law. But what about his statement that Luther said that the Sermon on the Mount was gospel? That is certainly correct, isn't it? Yes, but not in the way MacArthur understood it.

For MacArthur, to say that the Sermon on the Mount is gospel means that the Christian is called to live according to its demands, and by living this way the Christian will be saved. This conclusion is further supported by the very title of his chapter on the sermon, "The Way of Salvation." MacArthur is compelled by other texts (e.g., 1 John 1:8) to admit that Christians will still sin, but says that the Sermon on the Mount, being part of the gospel, demands wholehearted discipleship along with faith as a condition of salvation. He says that this is still all of grace, because God gives us both the faith and the obedience.

For Luther, on the other hand, to say that the Sermon on the Mount is gospel means that in the Sermon on the Mount we can find promises where God does not demand from us, but gives to us. For Luther the gospel, by definition, does not make demands of us. This does not mean that there are no demands placed on the believer, but demands are in the category of law, not gospel. MacArthur's reading of the Sermon on the Mount is, in Lutheran terms, "law" because it makes demands of us. This is absolutely legitimate, in itself. The Sermon on the Mount can be read as law. That is its primary reading. It is to be read as law to drive us to the cross. To say, however, that MacArthur's reading of the Sermon on the Mount is the gospel is to say that the law is the gospel. This is definitely not legitimate! To confuse law and gospel is the most disastrous theological error one can make. Luther said that where this distinction is lacking "one cannot tell a Christian from a heathen or a Jew."[3]

A good theologian can find gospel in some of the most unlikely places. The Gentile woman who came to Jesus was able to find grounds for trust in him even when he sent her away saying that it was not right to throw the children's food to the dogs (Matt. 15:22–28). Because the woman was looking for what God would freely give to her in his words, she found gospel. We might find gospel almost anywhere, but not when we are reading to determine what God demands of us. If we are reading a passage to find out what God demands of us, we will find law. This will even be true if we read a passage like John 3:16—which was intended as gospel—as a demand made upon us by God to produce faith in ourselves. We are not saved by fulfilling God's demands.

The Rich Young Ruler

We have seen how the dispensationalist grid alters the meaning of the terms *law* and *gospel*. When an appeal is made to the Reformers' writings in order to back up contemporary teachings, we need to read with care, for contemporary writers often do not understand the Reformers' language even when they use common theological terms. Our Lord's conversation with the rich young ruler (Matt. 19:16–22; Mark 10:17–22; Luke 18:18–25) is another passage fraught with peril for those who do not distinguish properly between law and gospel. At first this seems to be an ideal passage from which to derive MacArthur's contention that the gospel makes demands. In this passage, we witness Jesus sending a young man away from him without salvation. According to MacArthur, it is patently clear that the reason the young man walked away condemned was that he would not submit to the lordship of Christ.

Nevertheless, the young man did not walk away having rejected the gospel. Jesus had not preached the gospel to him. The young man had asked what good thing he could do to be saved. He was trying to save himself by keeping the law. Theoretically, this is possible. If any of us were born free of original sin and lived a perfect life, obeying God's commandments flawlessly, we would go to heaven because we earned it. Jesus was aware that the man standing before him was a sinner. The young man did not know this about himself. Jesus' intention was to reveal his sin to him, so he began his subversion of the man's self-righteousness by running through the commandments. The young ruler said that he had kept them all from birth. In response to this, Jesus told him that he lacked one thing. He told him to sell all his possessions and give them to the poor. The man walked away dejected.

Elsewhere Jesus told his hearers that unless their righteousness exceeded that of the scribes and Pharisees, they would never enter the kingdom of heaven. Many find in this verse the key to why the young man was not saved. He, like the Pharisees, said that he had kept the commandments, but perhaps that was not enough. Viewed from this perspective, it takes more than outward obedience to be saved.

Perhaps we come to this strange conclusion on account of the wrong starting point. We err if we believe that the young man really lacked only one thing, for elsewhere we are told that if we break the law in one point, we break it in all points (James 2:10). The man thought that he was a pretty good person who had kept the commandments and just needed a little advice to help him become perfect. Instead of countering the man's claim that he had kept the commandments, Jesus presented him with merely one of the commandments in its full rigor to destroy the man's self-confidence. The young ruler was a lawbreaker. Not only had he failed to keep the one commandment Jesus had not mentioned previously, the one against coveting, but, as James tells us, he had broken all of the commandments.

MacArthur recognizes much of what I have outlined here. He knows that the man fell short of God's demands, and he ably demonstrates how the man's covetousness demonstrated a lack of dependence on God. The problem is that, after a good reading of how Jesus applied the law to the man, MacArthur turns around and calls this the gospel, as if the man could have been saved by following Jesus' instructions. It is to be admitted that the man's lack of discipleship was the result of the absence of faith. It is to be admitted (contra MacArthur's opponents) that, had the man possessed faith, discipleship would have been an inevitable result. The question is whether faith would have resulted if the man had agreed to follow this Jewish teacher, whose identity he did not know. The answer one can expect to hear from the Reformation camp is unanimous: Certainly not!

We are rightly reminded by MacArthur that faith without works is dead. My fear is that MacArthur thinks that we can reverse this equation and add works to dead faith to create living faith. The rich young ruler had not recognized that Christ was God. He could not have had living faith apart from recognizing the identity of Christ. Had he abandoned his possessions to follow Christ, he would have merely added works to his dead faith. Most of us have probably tried to picture what the scene would have been if the man had abandoned his possessions. We are wrong if we picture Christ rejoicing over the salvation of a new convert. Instead, I picture Jesus coming up with a new way to prove to the man that he could not keep the law. Otherwise, the incident would have only strengthened the man's self-righteousness.

One place where I fear that MacArthur's teaching will produce the most damage is with those who wonder if they have followed Christ at a great enough cost to be saved. The conversation with the rich young ruler is a "law" passage and is therefore rigorous, as the law demands perfection. MacArthur realizes from other passages that Christians continue to sin. He tries to combine his understanding of Jesus' law-preaching as gospel with the Bible's teaching on the imperfection of the Christian. The result is his teaching that the Christian must *be willing* to follow Jesus regardless of cost and *willing to* obey him in all he commands, although he or she occasionally will fail. The problem is that in our Christian experience, occasional failure is proof that we were not truly willing to obey in these particular cases.

In addition, this requirement of "inner willingness" to do anything that the Lord has commanded for salvation will itself become a tyrannical principle in the life of anyone who seriously desires to be saved. In order to demonstrate this, I will follow the logical implications of this teaching through a hypothetical situation, one in which many Christians could find themselves, to demonstrate what MacArthur's position seems to mean.[4]

The Case of Linda Leadfoot

Linda Leadfoot enjoyed driving. Next to the fish on the back of her car, she used to have a bumper sticker that said, "Faster than a speeding ticket!" To the amazement of her friends, Linda peeled the sticker off last month after hearing a sermon on Romans 13 where the pastor interpreted the verse on obeying the governing authorities to mean that when we go past the speed limit, we are disobeying God.

Linda peeled the sticker off the back of her car with resolve. She would be an obedient Christian. A couple of weeks later her friends noticed that she came to church frazzled. Last night, she was in tears after the service.

"I don't know if I'm saved," she told some of her friends. "I haven't been able to submit my driving to the lordship of Christ."

Her friends were puzzled. "A few weeks ago," she explained, "the pastor gave that sermon on Romans 13. Submitting to the lordship of Christ means submitting to the speed laws, because he commands it."

"But he also said that none of us obeys the law perfectly," one of them responded. "And isn't it just the inner willingness to obey that matters? You displayed that when you peeled that sticker off your car."

Linda appreciated her friends' attempts to reassure her, but they obviously had not taken things as seriously as she. "An inner willingness? Does any of us really have it? Sure, I wanted to follow the sermon, but for how long? Only until my foot hit the gas pedal. I have even been able to hold to the speed limit a good portion of the time. You tell me that I do not need to be able to obey perfectly, but that an inner willingness will be enough. The problem is, I have found that the outward obedience is sometimes easier than the inner willingness. It is easier for me to control my foot than my heart. I have driven the speed limit and wished I could just speed freely without fearing for my salvation. It got to the point last week where I was hating those other drivers with their Christian bumper stickers who were leaving me in the dust. Then they come to church happy, and I, the obedient one, have been miserable and guilty for hating them." Linda tried to make sure that she wasn't glaring at her friends as she said this.

"But you have a general intention to obey. Isn't that enough?"

"How can I know my intention? Not from the fact that I run the words 'I want to drive slowly' through my head. No, every time I get into the car, I know that what I want to do is drive fast. I know from the pastor's sermon that I can be forgiven for past speeding, but what will happen to me when I continually wish to disobey?"

"Linda, this is silly. Who ever heard of people questioning their salvation over the speed limit? The pastor's illustration was about sexual immorality."

"There was nothing in the sermon to suggest that this didn't apply to speeding. The issue is obedience and disobedience, not cars versus sex. What makes this so terrible is that I know that speeding is not the only issue. It's just the first issue that I have begun dealing with. What will become of my life when I am compelled to submit in every area? My driving alone has been enough to make me want to get rid of my car. I'll never be able to pull it off."

"But Linda, isn't salvation all of grace?"

"Yes, I know it is. But if part of the grace is the desire to obey, I wonder if I was left out. Then I look around, especially at the ones who so happily quote the pastor's sermons, and wonder if they were left out. In fact, I wonder if anyone wasn't left out."

The Procrustean Bed

What should Linda do? What should her friends say to her? Is she bound to a life of misery? Must she remain in a state of doubt concerning her spiritual state? I know the advice that she is likely to receive. She will be told that Satan is attacking her. She will be told that the very fact that she is concerned means that she is all right. The problem is that MacArthur offers no means of measuring whether one's discipleship is good enough to allow one recourse to the cross in cases of failure. It preaches law passages presenting impossible demands that only Christ could fulfill as passages of the gospel, but then tones the demands down by admitting the existence of Christian imperfection.

MacArthur's appeal to the biblical teachings on Christian imperfection in order to make his position viable is a Procrustean bed. The law found in the Sermon on the Mount and the conversation with the rich young ruler allows for no imperfection. Since MacArthur takes these passages to be the gospel, he uses the Christian imperfection passages as a scalpel to trim down their demands to fit our sins.

MacArthur's softening of Jesus' demands in the Sermon on the Mount appears arbitrary. There is a better conclusion than MacArthur's or Linda's: reading law as law and gospel as gospel. If we do this we will not present discipleship as optional, as Hodges, Ryrie, and similar antinomians do; nor will we present it as saving, as MacArthur appears to do.

Conclusion

I have a real fear for the evangelical church in America if either of the two well-known positions of Hodges and MacArthur wins the day. If MacArthur's opponents win, we will see increasing antinomianism in our churches and even more shocked faces on the day of last judgment than we might have otherwise. If MacArthur wins, I see few "carnal Christians" (read "unbelievers") being turned from error, but I see the most sensitive and committed Christians setting out on a course that will shipwreck their confidence and assurance, embitter them against fellow Christians, and deprive them of the very gratitude that fuels discipleship. Our most serious Christians today may be our most dejected brethren tomorrow. Our only hope in avoiding either of these scenarios is to recover the old Reformation teaching of law and gospel.

What Is Faith? 3

Kim Riddlebarger

Whenever a serious doctrinal debate arises among conscientious Christians, we would do well to remember the words of Paul, "No doubt there have to be differences among you to show which of you have God's approval" (1 Cor. 11:19). Theological debate for the sake of discovering truth, if unpleasant, is a necessary aspect of church life. Theological debate to promote division among the brethren is a sin. The situation under review here is surely the former. There can be no doubt that the debate between John MacArthur and those advocating his so-called lordship salvation position, and Zane Hodges and his followers, who reject MacArthur's position as a dangerous legalism, is one of the most significant theological debates to arise in recent decades among American evangelicals.

But from my perspective, this debate, at least so far, has shown that perhaps neither side has God's approval. One would have hoped that, given the publication of major books by MacArthur and Hodges on the subject, the issues at stake would become clearly focused and that one or the other would gradually win the debate by the weight and strength of his arguments. Unfortunately, this is not yet happening because during much of the debate each side has managed to talk past the other. At many points in their arguments, both fail to establish clear definitions for very critical theological terminology. And at other points of both presentations, what an author gives with his left hand he quickly retracts with the right. This is especially true with the doctrine of faith in the debate. Instead of making the doctrine readily understandable for those in the pews struggling to comprehend better what the Bible teaches about faith, this disputation has largely been a disappointment.

Perhaps the best way to proceed with such a heated topic is to look at the doctrine of faith as presented by both Zane Hodges and John MacArthur and then to develop the necessary biblical and exegetical concerns. Not surprisingly, since many evangelicals do not look at doctrinal questions historically, we find here two very zealous and very capable combatants struggling to reinvent the wheel. Many of the issues with which these two are struggling have already been debated by great minds, and we would be foolish to overlook their contributions to the subject. I am thinking of the Reformers and of those in the Protestant scholastic tradition who developed their rediscoveries after the Reformation. For it is here that I think many of the problems arising in today's debate, such as confusing definitions and questionable exegesis by both parties involved, can be identified and corrected. As a Protestant, I am fully committed to the concept of *sola scriptura*— which means that I am convinced that this debate ultimately can be settled only by careful exegesis and exposition of the relevant biblical texts. I am also convinced that during the more than one hundred years from John Calvin (d. 1564) to François Turretin (d. 1687) some very good work on the subject of faith was completed. We may find, to our surprise, that many of our modern questions were answered from the pages of Scripture by the Protestant scholastics, as they debated some of the same subjects with their contemporaries. Thus my approach will be critical, biblical, and historical.

Zane C. Hodges's book, *Absolutely Free!*[1] contains some rather surprising doctrinal formulations. Surprising, because Hodges's position reflects so clearly the synergism and semi-Pelagianism of the medieval church, something Protestants have historically rejected. In response to John MacArthur's earlier volume, *The Gospel According to Jesus*,[2] Hodges takes pains to help his readers understand the urgency of the "lordship salvationism debate": "Lordship salvation teachers express alarm when the gospel is presented to men as a gift that is absolutely free. . . . But the cure which they propose is far worse than the disease they believe they have diagnosed" (p. 47).[3] Lordship salvation is perceived to be but an ill-informed response to the increasing moral and ethical apathy in today's church, and one which, according to Hodges, intrinsically denies the free offer of the gospel. Therefore, the consequence of lordship salvation—a denial of the biblical doctrine of faith—is truly much worse than any casual attitude toward moral and ethical issues among professing Christians, which the lordship position is supposedly intended to correct.

Zane Hodges's development of the doctrine of faith, initially at least, appears to be set out very clearly. "What faith really is, in biblical language, is receiving the testimony of God. It is the *inward conviction* that what God says to us in the gospel is true. That— and that alone—is saving faith" (p. 31). Faith is the inward conviction that the testimony of God as revealed in the Bible is true. Hodges adds, "Faith, then, is taking God at His Word. Saving faith is taking God at His Word in the gospel. It is nothing less than this. But it is also nothing more" (p. 32). It is important to notice the great stress that is placed on priority of the intellect in Hodges's system. "The facts presented to [Martha in John 11:25–26] by the Lord are more than great facts. They are *saving* facts. That is, they are *divinely revealed facts which are to be believed for salvation*" (p. 39, italics in original). Hodges argues for the simplicity of the biblical meaning of faith, which, he asserts, is readily apparent to English speaking readers:

> Let it be clearly stated here that English words like to "believe," or "faith" function as fully adequate equivalents to their Greek counterparts. There is not some hidden residue of meaning in the Greek words that is not conveyed by their normal English renderings. Although some have affirmed that there is, this claim betrays an inadequate or misguided view of biblical linguistics. [pp. 28–29]

This view appears to reflect traditional concerns, but things get confusing very quickly. Hodges is acutely aware of the charges that are leveled against him by his opponents, specifically John MacArthur, who argues that Hodges equates faith with "mere intellectual assent." In other words, the faith that saves is simply the acknowledgment of the truth of the propositions that are to be believed. In this case, this means taking God at his word. Hodges, however, takes preemptive action against his critics. "Lordship thinkers," he argues, have confused the issue of faith by adding misleading qualifying terminology to the biblical word *faith*—by using *faith* in conjunction with other pejorative and pre-scriptive adjectives such as "saving faith" and "false faith" (pp. 27–28, 207 n. 3).[4] He continues, "What was really missing in false faith, so they [the lordship group] affirmed, were the elements of true repentance and submission to God. Thus, saving faith ought not to be defined in terms of trust alone, but also in terms of com-mitment to the will of God. In the absence of this kind of sub-mission, they insisted, one could not describe his faith as biblical saving faith" (p. 27). Thus, according to Hodges, the lordship posi-tion is in error because it confuses the simplicity of the biblical meaning of faith as taking God at his word and because it adds pejorative adjectives or unbiblical conditions to faith, such as repentance or submission to Christ's lordship. Hodges continues, "the most misleading of all the lordship code-word expressions is the phrase 'intellectual (or, mental) assent'" (p. 30). Thus, a major bone of contention in this debate is the definition of the basic bib-lical word *faith*.

There is nothing wrong with faith defined in an "intellectual" sense, says Hodges. But "the Bible knows nothing about an intel-lectual faith as over against some other kind of faith (like emo-tional or volitional). What the Bible does recognize is the obvi-ous distinction between faith and unbelief!" He concludes, "It is an unproductive waste of time to employ the popular categories—intellect, emotion, or will—as a way of analyzing the mechanics of faith" (pp. 30–31). However, these are categories that Protes-tants have used since the time of the Reformation to deal with many of the same questions that are raised in this debate. Accord-ing to this historic Protestant understanding, faith is seen as a composite of three necessary elements: knowledge, assent, and trust. That is, one must have knowledge about the Christian message (*notitia*—knowledge, which involves the intellect), one must arrive at the conviction that what the Bible claims is in fact true (*assensus*—assent, wherein the intellect comes to believe that the content of *notitia* is true), and last, one must believe that what the Bible says is true *for me*. I must act upon what I know and believe to be true (*fiducia*—trust in Christ, which is an act of the will). Hodges rejects these categories out of hand. Hence, tremendous confusion results.

At last Hodges laments, "People know whether they believe something or not, and that is the real issue where God is concerned. But lordship salvation drives its adherents into a psychological shadowland. We are told that true faith has volitional and emotional elements" (p. 31). But where does Scripture make such a distinction? asks Hodges. We accept the testimony of God. We take him at his word; we believe him. Lordship thinkers import a complex faculty psychology, employing terms such as *mind, will,* and *emotions,* to explain what the Scriptures present in a very simple manner. Faith is taking God at his word, believing what God says.

But what is actually presented in Hodges's system is not the simple, though intellectual, view of faith that he proclaims. While stating that he denies the usefulness and perhaps even the validity of the classical Protestant view of faith as including knowledge, assent, and trust, he entertains the question, With what faculty does one believe and trust the word of God? Is it only the mind (thereby making faith assent to the truth of biblical propositions—even propositions regarding one's own salvation), or is faith a matter of the will (in which one must appropriate the grace of God in order to be saved), or is faith the activity of the heart (that is, the "emotions," where one feels subjectively compelled to place one's trust in Christ)? Or perhaps, is the answer to be found by arguing that the whole person, including the mind, the will, and the emotions, turns to Christ by trusting God and taking him at his word? The way Hodges handles this is very problematic.

That Hodges is aware of this problem of defining faith as assent to the truth of biblical propositions, is clear. While describing

Martha's reply to Christ in John 11:27, he makes the following assertions:

> It is one of the tragic aspects of evangelical thought today that we have lost much of our appreciation for the majesty of simple faith in Christ. . . .
> The New Testament does not share our modern point of view. . . . They were in no way inclined to depreciate the worth of "believing the facts" about the Son of God. . . . The facts presented to [Martha] by the Lord are more than great facts. They are *saving* facts. That is, they are *divinely revealed facts which are to be believed for salvation.* Thus, Jesus' words to Martha are John's way of telling us what it means to believe that Jesus is the Christ, the Son of God. [pp. 38–39]

One would assume that this indicates that Hodges is, in fact, defining faith as intellectual assent to the truth of our Lord's words. Martha "believed" that what Jesus said was true; therefore, Martha exercised faith, in the biblical sense. But, as you may suspect by now, there is more.

> Not all facts about God are saving facts. To believe, for example, in the unity of God (that God is One) saves no one. Every orthodox Jew in the Roman world believed *that.* So in fact, claims an opponent of James, do the demons (James 2:19). To be sure, the unity of God is glorious Christian truth. But it does not contain within itself the truth of the gospel.
> But to believe that Jesus is the Christ—*in John's sense of that term*—is to believe saving truth. It is, in fact, to believe the very truth that Martha of Bethany believed. . . .
> Thus, by believing the amazing facts about the person of Christ, Martha was *trusting* Him. She was placing her eternal destiny in His hands. [p. 39]

Hodges has imported an additional category, trust. So we are now left to extricate ourselves from the maze he has erected. Is faith assent to the truth of propositions of Scripture, or is it trust in the Savior found in those propositions, or is it both? Hodges does not say. And thus when MacArthur accuses Hodges of advocating a doctrine of faith as "mere intellectual assent" from passages such as those quoted, Hodges can backtrack and argue that people such as Martha "trusted" Christ, they believed his word, and that this is not some mere intellectual act of assenting to the truth of the propositions given her by our Lord. Such equivocation is hardly helpful in resolving this debate.

While Hodges's definition of faith is confusing, it is not nearly as disturbing as the role that he assigns to faith in his overall discussion of the doctrine of salvation. The supposed resolution of the dilemma of defining faith as assent, Hodges argues, is to be found in the object of faith. "Everything depended on the *truth* of what [Martha] believed. It was not at all a question of what *kind* of faith she had" (p. 39). Thus the object of faith, the one to be believed, is the issue, not the type or kind of faith that one exercises. What is disturbing to Christians from a historic Protestant and Reformation perspective is the way in which this concept of faith is worked into Hodges's synergistic *ordo salutis,* or "order of salvation." "Martha believed the facts about Jesus which it was necessary for her to believe in order to be saved. But in so doing she had actually *appropriated* the gift of eternal life. . . . She had received the testimony of God about His Son (1 John 5:9–13). And in so doing, she had appropriated eternal life itself" (p. 40, cf. pp. 106–7). This raises two very serious questions about Hodges's scheme. First, what about the object of one's faith? Can we "believe" in Jesus Christ in the biblical sense, if we do not intend to submit to his authority, his "lordship," as the debate implies? Second, is faith the *cause* or the *instrument* by which we are saved?

In answering the second question first, it must be pointed out that, yes, Protestants have historically argued something that sounds like Hodges's original assertion—the object of faith, Jesus Christ, saves the sinner by grace, *through* faith. Christ's death is the ground of salvation, and faith in Christ is the instrumental cause,[5] whereby we receive Christ's saving benefits. But notice carefully that in Hodges's scheme it is faith that "appropriates" eternal life. Faith becomes, not the instrument cause, the efficient cause of salvation, which is made available by God to those who will believe. Therefore, grace is now an "effect" received by one exercising faith, which in turn becomes the "cause" of the grace received. While grace is not mentioned in Hodges's discussion at this point at all, it may be implied, however, that when the will appropriates eternal life by "receiving" Jesus Christ, then grace is granted in the "gift" of the new birth. But how can the new birth be said to be a gift *if* we must exercise faith to receive it? The new birth becomes, as Paul says, a reward (Rom. 4:5). Faith is the one thing *we* contribute. It is *the* saving work. But this must be true, says Hodges, or we deny human responsibility, reducing men and women to mere puppets (p. 86).

The question must be raised then as to how men and women who are dead in sin can choose to "receive" eternal life, when they are hostile to God and opposed to God by their very nature. In Hodges's system, the grace of God is not at all a cause of salvation, it is a type of "effect." Faith is the efficient cause of eternal life, because through its exercise one "appropriates" eternal life: then one receives the effect of faith, the gift of eternal life. That Hodges's view of faith approaches "mere" assent is also made clear when it is placed in the context of the *ordo salutis*. "This sin-burdened woman [the Samaritan woman at the well in John 4:7–26] could not obtain eternal life unless she obtained crucial information. She needed to know something about this offer, and she needed to know something about the Person who was placing the offer before her" (pp. 40–41). The Samaritan woman did not need the regenerating grace of God to respond, she only needed true information about Jesus Christ so that she could respond correctly. Why? Because she had within herself the ability to process correct information, act upon it, and thereby be saved. This is decisional regeneration pure and simple, and despite Hodges's protests to the contrary, here he *has* defined faith as mere assent. All we need is correct information. In Hodges's system it is our "decision for Christ" that is the *causa efficiens* (the efficient cause) of regeneration, not God the Holy Spirit, whom the Scripture declares regenerated us in his grace while we were dead in sin (Eph. 2:5). Despite the usual equivocation (this time Hodges says that faith regenerates and then later says that the Word of God is the "life-giving seed"), in two places he makes the point that it is our response, not the grace of God, that saves us:

The truth that Jesus is the Christ—the truth that He is the Giver of eternal life to every believer—is saving truth. Belief in this truth *produces immediate—and permanent—new birth.*

It follows, therefore, that there is no such thing as believing the saving message without possessing eternal life at the same time. "Everyone"—not just some or many—but "Everyone who believes that Jesus is the Christ is born of God." There are no exceptions at all. [p. 42, emphasis mine]

When all is said and done, therefore, there is simply no substitute for the real miracle of new birth. . . .

It is the consistent testimony of the New Testament Scriptures that God's Word in the gospel is what produces the miracle of regeneration. It—and it alone—is the powerful, life-giving seed which takes root in the human heart when that Word is received there in faith. . . . For if the "facts" in question constitute God's saving message to men and women, then those facts are God's truth. Those facts are embodied and expressed in God's Word. And where God's Word is, there also is God's power. . . . What happens to those who believe this invitation?

A *miracle* happens to them. [pp. 48–49]

. . . there is no thought of looking and looking and looking [to Christ]. Just as the single drink of living water was an effective appropriation, so too is the single look of faith. . . . For now, however, it is sufficient to observe that the Bible predicates salvation on an *act* of faith, not on the *continuity* of faith. Just as surely as regeneration occurs at a point in time for each individual, so surely does saving faith. [pp. 62–63]

Once the gift of eternal life has been "appropriated," there is no need to ever proceed a step further in the Christian life. Discipleship, defined as "basically the experience of *spiritual education*" (p. 136), is optional. There is an "obvious difference between the gift of life and being a pupil of Jesus Christ" (p. 68). Thus one must believe in Christ as Savior, by trusting in the truth of God's Word on the matter, but one need not submit to Christ as Lord, in the sense of becoming his disciple. ". . . to suggest that some kind of personal surrender of the will is a part of the saving transaction in Acts 16:31, is to violently thrust into the text ideas which it does not contain" (p. 170). One may call upon the name of the Lord so as to be saved, and one is eternally saved once faith is exercised, but nevertheless, there is no biblical requirement to submit to Christ's authority as Lord (p. 169).

Faith and Works

The relationship, or lack thereof, between faith and works becomes another important theme for Hodges. "Nothing," in this case, salvation, "can be by grace and by works at the same time. *They are mutually exclusive.* To mix them is to alter in a radical way their character. Either grace would cease to be grace, or works would cease to be works" (p. 72, emphasis mine). This kind of formulation is not at all helpful. Since MacArthur has included submission to Christ in his own definition of faith, argues Hodges, Hodges in turn responds by defining faith and works as "mutually exclusive." If by this Hodges means that faith and works are not the same thing and must not be confused or collapsed into one another in attempting to formulate a definition of saving faith, classical Protestantism would concur. But if he means that faith and works have no necessary or intrinsic relationship to one another in the *ordo salutis*, the Protestant orthodox would surely disagree. And it is the latter relationship, that faith and works are *not* connected in any way, that is made clear in the following: "And who could forget the marvelous declaration found in the second chapter of Paul's epistle to the Ephesians? In that famous text, 'For by grace you have been saved through faith, and that not of yourselves; it is the gift of God, not of works, lest anyone should boast' (Eph. 2:8–9), Paul assures us that works play no role whatsoever in salvation" (pp. 72–73). Even though we may recall that Hodges defined salvation elsewhere in quite opposite terms than Paul does here (saying, in effect, that it is *by faith* you have been saved *through grace*), Hodges again equivocates and cites verse 8 as proof that "the saving experience is by grace through faith alone. It is God's free gift to us" (p. 73).

You may be anticipating that Ephesians 2:10 offers what Hodges would consider to be a stinging rebuke to his assertion that there is no necessary connection existing between faith and works. But, on the contrary, writes Hodges (equivocating yet again!),

> . . . works do have a role in the Christian's experience *after* spiritual birth and justification. In the passage cited above, Paul goes on to say so: "For we are His workmanship, created in Christ Jesus for good works, which God has prepared beforehand that we should walk in them" (Eph. 2:10).
>
> Sometimes this text is misunderstood. Sometimes it is read as though it meant that the believer will most certainly walk in the good works God has prepared for him. *But Paul does not say that at all.*
>
> Instead, Paul declares God's *purpose* for us. God *wants* us to walk in good works. Whether we do so or not depends on the many biblical factors which are relevant to spiritual development. [p. 73].

So Hodges writes, "there is no confusion [in Jesus' words in John 6:60–71] between discipleship and salvation, as there is today in lordship theology" (p. 87). This is the case because there is no necessary biblical connection between faith and works. One begins by faith and is saved eternally. Discipleship is optional. "'It is possible,' Jesus is saying" (in Hodges's comments on Luke 14:29–30), "'that you might start out as a "pupil" of mine, but that you might not be able to stay the course. You may not be able to finish'" (p. 80). In fact, concludes Hodges, "Nowhere does the Word of God guarantee that the believer's faith inevitably will endure" (p. 111). Since we are saved by faith ("our decision") and receive the gift of eternal life at that moment, "the believer's basic relationship to God is unaffected by the overthrow of one's faith" (p. 111). Only those who desire to progress in the faith need to work. "To make progress in the faith, the believer must do more than just listen to God's truth. The believer needs to obey it" (p. 122). But then, *why* should the believer make progress in the faith since this is not necessary? Failure to progress involves the inevitable loss of rewards.

One last issue needs to be addressed before moving on to developing MacArthur's doctrine of faith, and that is Hodges's treatment of faith in the Book of James. Since Hodges's earlier comments seem so out of line with James's comments, that "faith without deeds is dead," it is necessary to look at Hodges's interpretation of such texts. In treating James 2:26, Hodges makes the following remarks:

> In the closing verse of his famous discussion about faith and works, James writes: "For as the body without the spirit is dead, so faith without works is dead also" (James 2:26). . . . Yet, in one of the strangest distortions of Scripture that has ever occurred, many theologians and Bible interpreters have decided that a "dead faith" must necessarily have always been dead.
>
> But why draw such a deduction as this? James compares "dead faith" to a dead body. Surely this was not a loose or careless analogy on his part. If "dead faith" had never been alive, why not compare it to a stone or some other inanimate object?
>
> But clearly, James has chosen this analogy precisely because it is especially suited to make his point. What James is worried about is a Christian whose faith has lost all of its vitality and productiveness. He is worried about the man or woman whose faith has ceased to move and act, just as a dead body has ceased to move and act. [pp. 125–26]

Thus, as we would expect, Hodges places James's category of "dead faith" into his doctrine of the separation of individual salvation from discipleship, wherein a believer, who has once had faith and now does not, is still a Christian, even if his or her faith is dead or absent. He or she is still a Christian, because he or she *once* believed and was given eternal life. But even though *now* there is no evidence of present faith, faith does not ever need to be exercised again. Regeneration is not lost, nor is this taken as proof that regeneration was never really present.

Hodges's distinctive view of faith, then, includes the following elements. First, faith is defined primarily as assent to the truth of biblical propositions, that is, taking God at his word, believing that what he says is true. A corollary of this is the conviction that one does not need to submit to Christ's authority as Lord as part of belief, or in order to believe what God says about salvation in Jesus Christ. Second, faith functions as the efficient cause of regeneration. An act of faith produces eternal life, which subsequently cannot be lost. Third, since the act of faith is the cause of the believer's receiving of the gift of eternal life, it is not necessary for someone to continue to exercise faith in the truth of biblical propositions, including belief in Christ as savior, to be saved. Such a person loses rewards but maintains eternal life. Fourth, faith and works have no necessary biblical connection, either as cause (faith) and effect (works), or by seeing works as the evidence of saving faith. Good works, discipleship, and submission to Christ's authority are purely optional.

Where Hodges takes one approach, it will come as no surprise that MacArthur takes quite another. It is clear from his response to MacArthur that Hodges attempts to eliminate any aspect of obedience or repentance from faith, and it is also clear, on the other hand, that MacArthur insists that faith has a necessary relationship to obedience and repentance. And thus, the debate between the two turns largely on the nature of faith and on whether or not any biblical relationship exists between faith and repentance, and faith and works.

In MacArthur's system, definitions are again important. MacArthur insists, "Salvation is solely by grace through faith (Eph. 2:8). That truth is the biblical watershed for all we teach. But it means nothing if we begin with a misunderstanding of grace or a faulty definition of faith" (p. 31). This is agreed upon by both parties involved—the definition of faith is paramount to all else.

In remarks obviously directed at Hodges, MacArthur writes, "Faith, like grace, is not static. Saving faith is more than just understanding the facts and mentally acquiescing. It is inseparable from repentance, surrender," presumably to Christ's lordship, "and a supernatural eagerness to obey. The biblical concept of saving faith includes all those elements" (p. 31). Those who deny the lordship position by arguing that it is inherently legalistic "assume that because Scripture contrasts faith and works, faith may be devoid of works. They set up a concept of faith that eliminates submission, yieldedness, or turning from sin, and they categorize all the practical elements of salvation as human works" (p. 31).

That demonstrating a necessary link between faith and repentance is the primary thrust of MacArthur's overall argument surfaces even when MacArthur applies the classical model to his definition of faith. Citing Reformed theologian Louis Berkhof, MacArthur writes:

> Berkhof sees three elements to genuine faith: An intellectual element (*notitia*), which is the understanding of truth; an emotional element (*assensus*), which is the conviction and affirmation of truth; and a volitional element (*fiducia*), which is the determination of the will to obey truth. Modern popular theology tends to recognize *notitia* and often *assensus* but eliminate *fiducia*. Yet faith is not complete unless it is obedient. [p. 173]

While MacArthur attempts to present his position as something quite compatible with the classical Protestant model, Hodges takes him to task for misquoting Berkhof: "MacArthur seriously distorts a well-known theological definition of faith when he writes, 'Berkhof sees three elements to genuine faith. . . .' This is astoundingly inaccurate. *Assensus* is *not* an 'emotional element,' and *fiducia* means trust and *not* 'a determination to obey the truth'" (Hodges, p. 207 n. 5).

Hodges is absolutely correct here, though. Berkhof speaks of *fiducia* as a volitional element, which "consists in a personal trust in Christ as savior and Lord, including a surrender of the soul as guilty and defiled to Christ, and a reception and appropriation of Christ as the source of pardon and spiritual life."[6] The act of the will, for Berkhof, is one of receiving the benefits of Christ. Faith is an instrumental cause; therefore, there is not a word in Berkhof about obedience, or repentance in his definition of faith. MacArthur's use of the threefold model for faith, as presented here, is *outside* of the classical Protestant understanding of that model. Here again, we see the unclarity in defining basic terminology that lies at the root of the whole debate.

Certainly, MacArthur is attempting to defend his position that one cannot come to Christ (in the biblical sense of that phrase) unless one submits to Christ's lordship or authority—something to which Berkhof and classical Protestantism would agree. But instead of arguing for a necessary connection between faith and repentance in the *ordo salutis* (that is, while faith is not repentance, and repentance is not faith, one is not present in the life of a Christian without the other), MacArthur defines faith itself as *including* repentance, or *as* repentance, or *as* obedience. There is tremendous confusion here, even to the point that MacArthur misreads Berkhof, to make his own point. And thus, here lies the fundamental problem raised by MacArthur's presentation of the lordship position: What is the relationship between faith and repentance?

As we unpack MacArthur's arguments on this point, one thing becomes clear—MacArthur does not like Hodges's definition of faith, arguing the following: "Salvation *is* a gift, but it is appropriated only through a faith that goes beyond merely understanding and assenting to the truth. Demons have that kind of 'faith' (James 2:19). True believers, on the other hand, are characterized by faith that is as repulsed by the life of sin as it is attracted to the mercy of the Savior" (MacArthur, p. 32). He continues, "James describes spurious faith as pure hypocrisy, mere cognitive assent, devoid of any verifying works—no different from the demons' belief. Obviously, there is more to saving faith than merely conceding a set of facts. Faith without works is useless. Yet some in contemporary evangelicalism refuse to allow for any kind of relationship between faith and works" (p. 170). Faith defined as mere assent is nothing of which demons are not capable. Faith must be something more than Hodges's definition of simply believing the truth of the propositions of Scripture. Faith must be directly connected to repentance in some sense, and someone who exercises the kind of faith that saves must submit to Christ's authority as Lord. Thus MacArthur can write:

> Our Lord's point in relating that account [Luke 18:13] was to demonstrate that repentance is at the core of saving faith. The Greek word for repentance, *metanoia,* literally means "to think after." It implies a change of mind, and some who oppose lordship salvation have tried to limit its meaning to that. But a definition of repentance cannot be drawn solely from the etymology of the Greek word.
>
> Repentance . . . far from being a human work . . . is the inevitable result of *God's* work in a human heart. [p. 32][7]

What does MacArthur mean when he says that "repentance is at the core of saving faith"? I take him to mean that repentance is a constituent element of saving faith—a necessary, but not a sufficient, condition. "The Bible does not recognize faith that lacks this element of active repentance" (p. 32). But admittedly, there is a great deal of unclarity here in MacArthur's use of terminology. Does he mean that faith is linked to repentance in the sense that those who place their faith (trust) in Christ will *also* repent of their sins, or does he mean that repentance is part of the exercise of saving faith itself? MacArthur goes on to say, with a confusing use of terms, "True faith is never seen as passive—it is always obedient. In fact, Scripture often equates faith with obedience (John 3:63; Rom. 1:5; 16:26; 2 Thess. 1:8). . . . Salvation by faith does not eliminate works *per se*" (pp. 32–33). But in what sense is faith obedient? Is saving faith a "work" in any sense? How do we know if we have believed? How do we know that we are saved? And how is faith related to repentance?

I have concluded that, in MacArthur's scheme, faith is not linked to repentance in the way in which the Reformed have historically argued. For MacArthur, the faith that saves includes repentance and obedience as elements that compose the saving faith itself. That we may take this to be the case is strengthened by statements indicating that we may be sure that saving faith *has not* been exercised if obedience, repentance, and other such vague terms as *yieldedness* are absent from faith:

> No aspect of salvation is merited by human works (Titus 3:5–7). Thus salvation cannot be defective in any dimension. As a part of His saving work, God will produce repentance, faith, sanctification, yieldedness, obedience, and ultimately glorification. Since He is not dependent on human effort in producing those elements, an experience that lacks any of them cannot be the saving work of God. [p. 33]

Unlike Hodges, however, MacArthur does side with historic Protestantism in asserting that salvation is the work of God, not the work of God and man cooperating. In his treatment of Ephesians 2:8–10, for example, he stands in marked opposition to Hodges:

> Salvation by faith does not eliminate works *per se*. It does away with works that are the result of human effort alone (Eph. 2:8). It abolishes any attempt to merit God's favor by our works (v. 9). But it does not deter God's foreordained purpose that our walk of faith should be characterized by good works (v. 10). We must remember above all that salvation is a sovereign work of God. [MacArthur, p. 33]

MacArthur concludes that faith must be maintained throughout one's life. "The modern definition of faith eliminates repentance, erases the moral elements of believing, obviates the work of God in the sinner's heart, and makes an ongoing trust in the Lord optional" (p. 171). In contrast to Hodges's assertion that saving faith is but one brief glance at Christ, MacArthur states, "Endurance is the mark of those who will reign with Christ in His kingdom. . . . As a divine gift, faith is neither transient nor impotent. It has an abiding quality that guarantees its endurance to the end" (pp. 172–73). On these essential points, MacArthur is well within the bounds of historic Protestantism.

In summarizing MacArthur's *The Gospel According to Jesus*, the primary point is that faith is necessarily linked to repentance, obedience, good works, and submission to Christ's authority—his lordship. Repentance and obedience are essential components of saving faith. A second point is that a believer's assurance is also linked to this definition of faith as including repentance and obedience, because a believer draws assurance from his or her obedience, submission, and yieldedness to Christ's authority. Therefore, those who know that they have yielded and are producing tangible fruit have the assurance of their salvation. Those who do not, have no such assurance. The confusion in all of this comes from the very simple, but fundamental failure to define what exactly is meant by the term *faith*. MacArthur never does define it clearly. When he uses the classical categories, he misquotes Berkhof and presents a definition contrary to this source that he is quoting as support for his argument. All that MacArthur has told us is that the faith that saves includes certain elements, such as obedience, submission, repentance, and so on. This serves to generate a mass of confusion, which is one of the few things the "lordship controversy" has succeeded in doing.

What Is Faith?

Since the reason the lordship controversy has been so heated and so unable to come to a clear and definitive resolution is that important terms have *not* been defined, it is my contention that a quick review of the biblical data—the terminology used in Scripture for "faith" and "believing"—will help to end some of the problems. Of course, it must be pointed out that an exhaustive lexical and exegetical study is well beyond the scope of this review, and much of this work has already been done very effectively by others.[8] But granted that caveat, a survey of the biblical data will be essential if we are to formulate a workable definition of faith.

In the Old Testament, the verb translated *to believe* comes to us from the Hebrew *heemin*,[9] from which we derive the commonly used expression *amen*. The noun form (*emuna*) "denotes faithfulness in the sense of trustworthiness."[10] There is only one text in the entirety of the Old Testament that speaks of faith as an active response to God. In Habakkuk 2:4, the prophet writes that "the righteous will live by his faith," a passage cited in the New Testament by the author of Hebrews (10:37–38) and by Paul (Rom. 1:17; Gal. 3:11). B. B. Warfield, the great Reformed theologian from Princeton at the turn of the century, states that the term *faith* is used here to draw a sharp contrast between "arrogant self-sufficiency and faithful dependence upon God,"[11] the latter exhibited by the righteous man, in contrast to the proud Chaldeans who opposed God. "This faith, which forms the distinctive feature of the righteous man, and by which he obtains life, is obviously no mere assent." In fact, "it is a profound and abiding possession, an ingrained attitude of mind and heart towards God which affects and gives character to all the activities."[12] Warfield concludes, "to believe in God, in the Old Testament sense, is thus not merely to assent to His word, but with firm and unwavering confidence to rest in security and trustfulness upon Him."[13] That is, not only is assent to the truthfulness of God's word involved, but so is an act of trust in the God who is speaking. The New Testament, on the other hand, abounds with the terminology for "faith," both in the noun (*faith*) and verb (*believe*) forms.

> The disparity in the use of the terms "faith" and "believe" in the two testaments is certainly in a formal aspect very great. In contrast with their extreme rarity in the Old Testament, they are both, though somewhat unevenly distributed and varying with relative frequency, distinctly characteristic of the whole New Testament language, and oddly enough occur equally often (about 240 times each). . . . In the Old Testament again, "faith" occurs in the active sense in but a single passage; in the New Testament it is the passive sense which is rare. In the Old Testament in only about half of its occurrences is the verb "to believe" used in a religious sense; in the New Testament it has become so clearly a technical religious term, that it occurs very rarely in any other sense.[14]

The varied use of the term can be seen when we notice that the apostle John, for example, prefers the verb form *to believe,* and Paul, the noun, *faith*. Thus, examining the "technical religious sense" of this term is necessary to formulate a biblical definition of faith and believing.

There are three major types of constructions in the New Testament where this terminology is used. The first type is where the term *to believe* (*pisteuien*) takes a noun in the dative case for its object. There are about forty-five instances of this in the New Testament, and the object can be a thing, such as the word of God ("I believe everything that agrees with the Law and that is written in the Prophets"—Acts 24:14), or a person. And "when its object is a person it is rarely another than God or Jesus."[15] This can be seen in a passage like John 5:46, "If you believed Moses you would believe me." This type of construction "expresses believing assent."[16] That is, the intellectual element is predominant.

When we look at constructions where the verb *to believe* is used with various prepositions, "we enter a region in which the deeper sense of the word—that of a firm, trustful reliance—comes into its full rights."[17] As J. I. Packer notes, when used with the two most common prepositions (*en* and *epi*), what is indicated is "restful reliance on that to which, or him to whom, credit is given."[18] In Matthew 27:42, the Jewish leaders express this by ridiculing Christ, "Let him come down now from the cross, and we will believe in him." We see the same thing in Acts 16:31, where Paul and Silas exhort their erstwhile jailer to "Believe in [*epi*] the Lord Jesus, and you will be saved." As Warfield points out, the biblical evidence is quite substantial. He cites numerous texts with this construction and concludes that even

> a glance over these passages will bring clearly out the pregnancy of the meaning conveyed. It may be more of a question wherein the pregnancy resides. It is probably sufficient to find it in the sense conveyed by the verb itself, while the proposition adjoins only to the person towards whom the strong feeling expressed by the verb is directed. In any event, what these passages express is *"an absolute transference of trust from ourselves to another," a complete self-surrender to Christ.*[19]

That the term *believe* includes *both* aspects of assent and trust is quite evident.

The absolute use of the verb is common—twenty-nine times in John, twenty-three in Paul, twenty-two in Acts, fifteen in the gospels, and one each in Hebrews, James, Jude, and 1 Peter. "Four times in a single chapter of John it is used of belief in a specific fact—the great fact central to Christianity of the resurrection of Christ." In John 20:8, we find John reporting that "the other disciple, who had reached the tomb first, also went inside. He saw and believed." This leads Warfield to surmise that "a survey of these passages will show very clearly that in the New Testament to believe is a technical term to express reliance on Christ for salvation."[20]

When the noun form is used the meaning is varied. However it, is never used in defining or describing man's faith in other men, "but always [refers] to the religious trust that reposes on God, or Christ, or divine things. . . . It would seem that the pregnant sense of *pistis* as self-abandoning trust was so fixed in Christian speech," that Warfield adds, "it had already become a Christian technical term, which needed no further definition that it might convey its full sense of saving faith in Jesus Christ to the mind of every reader."[21]

Another point needs to be made regarding the use of the terminology in James's epistle. According to Warfield, "it was to James that it fell to rebuke the Jewish tendency to conceive of the faith which was pleasing to Jehovah as a mere intellectual acquiescence in His being and claims."[22] James does not contradict Paul, since he with Paul and the early church indicates that belief in Christ is essential (1:1–3; 2:1) and is the only way that we can approach God (1:6; 5:15). The question that arises is, of course, the relationship between faith and works. "It is not faith as [James] conceives it which he depreciates," writes Warfield, "but that professed faith (2:14) which cannot be shown to be real by appropriate works (2:18), and so differs by a whole diameter alike from the faith of Abraham that was reckoned unto him for righteousness (2:23)." Abraham's trust in God was manifest in the action of raising the knife over Isaac. This is also "faith of Christians as James understood it (2:1; 1:3; 1:22)."[23] What James denies is that a mere profession of faith stands alone in the life of a Christian. Such a profession, which has resulted in justification, "shows itself in works . . . because a faith which does not come to fruitage in works is dead, non-existent."[24]

This voluminous biblical data leads Warfield to conclude,

> On the ground of such a usage, we may at least re-affirm with increased confidence that the idea of "faith" is conceived of in the New Testament as the characteristic idea of Christianity, and that it does not import mere "belief" in an intellectual sense, but all that enters into an entire self-commitment of the soul to Jesus as the Son of God, the Saviour of the world. . . . It is accordingly, solely from its *object* that faith derives its value. This object is uniformly the God of grace whether conceived of broadly as the source of all life, light, and blessing, on whom man in his creaturely weakness is dependent, or wherever sin and the eternal welfare of the soul are in view, as the Author of salvation in whom alone the hope of unworthy man can be placed.[25]

This survey of the biblical noun and verb forms *faith* and *believing* can only lead to the rather sad conclusion that both Hodges and MacArthur have failed to define faith in accordance with biblical and historic Protestant terminology. In fact, I must conclude that Hodges denies the Reformation (and I think utterly biblical) principle of *faith alone* (*sola fide*) by defining faith as mere assent, and MacArthur compromises the *sola* by adding moral obedience as an element of faith. Thus, it must be said that neither is wholly satisfied with the classical Protestant formulations on the subject of faith.

In comparing Hodges's definition of faith with the biblical data, we must conclude that he reduces faith to an intellectual act. And even though he uses the term *trust* in at least one instance, he does so only by equivocation. That Hodges defines faith as assent is proven to be true, when we include Hodges's assertion that once faith is exercised, it need not be sustained. This denies, altogether, the element of trust, which is part of the biblical terminology (*pisteuo* plus a preposition, such as *en* or *epi*) and which indicates something that is sustained. As Warfield asserts, faith in this sense includes "an absolute transference of trust from ourselves to another," Jesus Christ. It is simply ludicrous to assert, as Hodges does, that one can assent to true statements *about* Christ, without ever intending to obey him, and still possess "faith" in the biblical sense. It was our Lord, after all, and not MacArthur, who declared, "If you love me, you will obey what I command" (John 14:15). Thus Hodges's radical separation of faith from any of its fruits is an unbiblical formulation. It is, in fact, a most deadly form of antinomianism.

Hodges's notion that faith is the efficient cause of salvation is also in error. The Scriptures assign the role of efficient cause to God, not man (Heb. 12:2). And it has been argued that the biblical terminology supports the classical Protestant categories. Warfield's summary comments make the necessary point quite well:

> The *saving power* of faith resides thus not in itself, but in the Almighty Saviour on whom it rests. . . . It is not, strictly speaking, even faith in Christ that saves, but Christ that saves through faith.

The saving power resides exclusively, not in the act of faith or the attitude of faith or the nature of faith, but in the object of faith; and in this the whole biblical representation centers, so that we could not more radically misconceive it than by transferring to faith even the smallest fraction of that saving energy which is attributed in the Scriptures solely to Christ Himself. . . . The place of faith in the process of salvation, as biblically conceived, could scarcely, therefore, be better described than by the use of the scholastic term "instrumental cause."[26]

Hodges denies the Protestant doctrine of faith alone. He has not only redefined faith as assent, but has described faith as something other than what J. I. Packer presents as an "appropriating instrument, an empty hand outstretched to receive the free gift of God's righteousness in Christ."[27] It is now a work we perform, levering from God his grace, forcing God to give us the "gift" of the new birth. It need not be directed to the Christ of Scripture, who *is* Lord and who is to be obeyed, nor need faith be sustained. There is nothing "absolutely free" about a faith that cannot justify or a Saviour who cannot save without our help.

MacArthur, on the other hand, has a different problem with the biblical terminology for faith—a problem in many ways no less serious than that of Hodges. For, as we have seen, the terms *faith* and *believe* make *no* lexical or exegetical connection to repentance or obedience, in the sense in which MacArthur has imported them into *faith*. Repentance, obedience, yieldedness, and so on are not part of the biblical constructions. Faith is *not* repentance, nor obedience, nor does it include them as component parts. This is why Protestants have insisted upon faith *alone*. And this is why Protestants have been careful (unlike MacArthur) in how they have used the classical categories of knowledge, assent, and trust. Faith alone justifies, hence *sola fide*. The faith that saves is a faith that involves the mind, the heart, and the will. The whole person turns to Christ through faith. Thus, the type of "dead" faith that James is talking about is not lacking information, nor lacking orthodoxy, nor lacking obedience, but lacking genuine trust in Christ himself. This threefold distinction is supported by the biblical data, and its careful use in this debate would solve many of the problems raised.[28]

But, you may ask, don't Protestants insist that when people exercise saving faith they submit to Christ's lordship, are willing to obey Him in all things, and repent of their sins? Absolutely, yes! But notice that these categories are kept distinct. *Faith* links us to Christ. It is through faith that we are united to him. And thereby, we receive his saving benefits by grace through faith. The Reformed, then, have historically linked faith, repentance, and obedience together, not calling the latter two elements within saving faith itself, but understanding them as corollaries within the *ordo salutis*. That is, one who has exercised faith in Christ, and is united to Christ by that faith, will repent and will struggle to obey and yield. But these things are not conditions for nor component parts of faith itself. They are fruits of saving faith. They are the inevitable activity of the new nature. They are "effects"—signs that there has been an exercise of saving faith. They are not constituent parts of faith itself.

Indeed, the Reformed have been very careful as to how they link faith and repentance together. A. A. Hodge argues that repentance "presupposes faith, which is God's gift." Hodge adds that "repentance . . . expresses that hatred and renunciation of sin, and that turning unto God, *which accompanies faith as its consequent.*"[29] Berkhof makes the precise point that MacArthur omits:

> According to Scripture repentance is wholly an inward act, and should not be confounded with the change of life that proceeds from it. Confession of sin and reparation of wrongs are *fruits* of repentance. Repentance is only a negative condition, and not a positive means of salvation. . . . Moreover, true repentance never exists except in conjunction with faith, while on the other hand, wherever there is true faith, there is also real repentance. . . . Luther sometimes spoke of a repentance preceding faith, but seems nevertheless to have agreed with Calvin in regarding true repentance as one of the fruits of faith.[30]

Tragically, in struggling to combat the serious error of Hodges's antinomianism, MacArthur has produced some confusion regarding *sola fide*. For in MacArthur's system, faith has been combined with obedience to form a kind of *tertium quid* (third thing) that is neither faith nor obedience, but a combination thereof, a combination that implicitly denies the biblical essence of both faith and repentance. While avoiding the error himself, MacArthur is in danger of giving unintended aid to a kind of "neonomianism," a new legalism, wherein obedience, repentance, and submission all acquire a status that is a direct challenge to faith alone. In the Reformation system, repentance will never unite us to Christ, nor will repentance ever justify us. We cannot be saved without it, yet we are not saved by it. It is Christ who saves us, by grace through faith. Penitence, sorrow for sin, good works, and other "effects of faith" are the Holy Spirit's fruit to bear in our lives, not good works that we perform to earn God's favor or to assure ourselves that we have exercised saving faith.

Union with Christ

Michael Horton

Salvador was a Cuban spy, sent to Miami as a mole in order to learn military secrets from the United States government. However, Cuban nationalists with whom Salvador associated incognito eventually led the clever spy to renounce his loyalties to Castro. As a result, Salvador turned himself in to the United States government, and they offered asylum, protection, and a new identity. The government masterminded a "murder" of Salvador so Castro's officials would assume the death of their spy, and once this plan was carried out, Salvador was issued new documents, a new name, and a new life.

Paul appeals to this sort of language when he answers the question, "What shall we say then? Shall we continue in sin that grace may abound?" with his familiar response,

Certainly not! How shall we who died to sin live any longer in it? Or do you not know that as many of us as were baptized into Christ Jesus were baptized into His death? Therefore, we were buried with Him through baptism into death, that just as Christ was raised from the dead by the glory of the Father, even so we also should walk in newness of life. For if we have been united together in the likeness of His death, certainly we also shall be in the likeness of His resurrection. [Rom. 6:1–5 NKJV]

The apostle goes on to speak of the crucifixion and burial of our old identity, as the believer is raised with a new life. "Let us never forget that our old selves died with him on the cross that the tyranny of sin over us might be broken—for a dead man can safely be said to be immune to the power of sin" (v. 7 *Phillips*)

Israel had long sought its identity in conforming to the law. Many thought union with the law and with Moses by outward observance would lead to the identity that brought fulfillment, hope, and salvation. But Christ alone possessed in himself, in his essence as well as in his actions, the righteousness that God requires of humanity. Therefore, only through union with Christ can the believer enjoy the identity of belonging to God. "For sin shall not be your master—you are no longer living under the Law, but under grace" (v. 14 NIV).

This new identity is not something we achieve by converting ourselves or by trying to enter into it. It is given to us graciously by God, apart from and outside of ourselves. Just as Salvador could never again return to his former identity and owed his loyalty to those who had given him the new identity, so "released from the service of sin, you entered the service of righteousness" (v. 18 *Phillips*). Before, righteousness made no claims on us to which we could respond favorably, but now, because we are united to Christ, new affections and new loyalties produce new service.

It is important to realize that Christ does not come to improve the old self, to guide and redirect it to a better life; he comes to kill us, in order to raise us to newness of life. He is not the friend of the old self, only too happy to be of service. He is its mortal enemy, bent not merely on balancing it out by adding a new man, but on making a new man out of the old. Notice that the new birth is not the same as justification. The contemporary Wesleyan theologian John Lawson confuses justification and the new birth in precisely the same manner as medieval scholasticism did: "To be justified is the first and all-important stage in a renewed manner of life, actually changed for the better in mind and heart, in will and action." Further, "regeneration is an alternative word for the initial step in the life of saving faith in Christ. The legal term 'justification' has in mind this step. . . ."[1] This sort of confusion of legal and ethical categories has done great damage and even evangelicals who can endorse pristine definitions of justification can easily slip into just such a categorical confusion.

We are not justified by conversion; rather, conversion, or the new birth, is the gift of God given to those who are spiritually dead and, therefore, are unable to choose Christ. In the new birth, God grants the faith necessary to respond positively, and it is through this faith, not conversion itself, that one is accepted by God.

What Is "Union with Christ"?

If this doctrine is, as John Murray wrote, "the central truth of the whole doctrine of salvation," what does it mean and why is it so important?

First, union with Christ describes the reality of which Paul wrote in Romans 6. As a husband and wife are united through marriage and parent and child are united through birth, so we are united to Christ through the Spirit's baptism. Those who are familiar with the historical (if not the current) discourses of Reformed and Lutheran preaching will immediately recognize the emphasis on the objective work of Christ in history. Themes such as election, the incarnation, the substitutionary atonement, the active and passive obedience of Christ, justification, adoption, and the objective aspect of sanctification (that is, the declaration that we are already holy in Christ) form the diet of the best and most biblically faithful preaching. Each of these themes serves to remind the believer that his or her righteousness is found not within, but outside.

Nevertheless, there is a subjective aspect to our union with Christ that receives equal attention in Scripture, and, therefore, commands equal attention from us. Calvin wrote, "First, we must understand that as long as Christ remains outside of us, and we are separated from him, all that he has suffered and done for the salvation of the human race remains useless and of no value for us. . . . all that he possesses is nothing to us until we grow into one body with him."[2]

All of our righteousness, holiness, redemption, and blessing is found outside of us—in the person and work of Christ. This is the declaration of the Scriptures and, following the sacred text, of the Reformers, in the face of a doctrine of subjective righteousness located in the believer. And yet, as Calvin here points out, this "alien righteousness" belonging to someone outside of us would mean nothing if this Righteous One remained forever outside of us. An illustration might help at this point. In my junior year of college, I went to Europe with some friends and ran out of money. Happily, my parents agreed to deposit enough money in my account to cover my expenses. Was that now my money? I had not earned it. I had not worked for it. It was not my money in the sense that I had done something to obtain it. But it was in my account now, and I could consider it my own property.

While none of our righteousness is our own, Christ is! While none of our holiness belongs to us, properly speaking, Christ does! The devils know that Christ is righteous, but they do not, cannot, believe that he is their righteousness.

It is essential, therefore, to point unbelievers and believers alike to Christ, outside of their own subjective experiences and actions, but that is only half the story. The Christ who has done everything necessary for our salvation in history outside of us now comes to dwell in us in the person of his Holy Spirit. "To them God has chosen to make known among the Gentiles the glorious riches of this mystery, which is Christ in you, the hope of glory" (Col. 1:27). While our assurance is rooted in the objective work of Christ for us, it is also true that "We know that we live in him and he in us, because he has given us of his Spirit" (1 John 4:13).

John employs this language of union in his Gospel, where Jesus is referred to as a vine, with believers as branches (John 15). As the branch is dead apart from the life-giving nourishment of the vine, so humans are spiritually dead unless they are connected to Christ, the vine. Elsewhere, "Whoever eats my flesh and drinks my blood remains in me, and I in him" (John 6:56). As baptism is a sign and seal of our attachment to the vine (the beginning of our union), the Lord's Supper is a means of our perpetual nourishment from the vine.

Paul appeals to this doctrine as the organizing principle for his entire systematic theology. The first Adam–second Adam contrast in Romans 5 depends on this notion. "In Adam," we possess all that he possesses: original sin, judgment, condemnation, fear, alienation; "in Christ" we possess all of his righteousness, holiness, eternal life, justification, adoption, and blessing. Further, "God . . . made us alive with Christ even when we were dead in transgressions—it is by grace you have been saved. And God raised us up with Christ and seated us with him in the heavenly realms in Christ Jesus" (Eph. 2:4–6). "I have been crucified with Christ," Paul declares, "and I no longer live, but Christ lives in me" (Gal. 2:20).

Thus, this doctrine is the wheel that unites the spokes of salvation and keeps them in proper perspective. "In Christ" (that is, through union with him) appears, by my accounting, nine times in the first chapter of Ephesians. Chosen in Christ before the foundation of the world, God has thus "made us accepted in the Beloved" (NKJV). He cannot love us directly because of our sinfulness, but he can love us in union with Christ, because Christ is the one the Father loves. ("In him we have redemption"; "in whom also we have obtained an inheritance" [NKJV], and so on.)

Union with Christ and Conversion

This doctrine is another way of saying, "Christ alone!" All spiritual blessings in heavenly places are found in him. Even the gifts of the Holy Spirit are through and for the ministry of Christ the Mediator. No one is baptized in the Holy Spirit; everyone baptized is baptized by the Holy Spirit into Christ.

Regeneration, or the new birth, is the commencement of this union. God brings this connection and baptism even before there is any sign of life—God "made us alive . . . even when we were dead" (Eph. 2:5). The first gift of this union is faith, the sole instrument through which we live and remain on this vine. But this is a rich vine, filled with nourishing sap to produce an abundance of fruit. Though we are not attached to nor remain attached to this vine by the fruit (what branch depends on the fruit?), those who are truly members of Christ inevitably produce fruit. Through union with Christ, we receive his righteousness imputed (justification) as well as his righteousness imparted (sanctification). So conversion to Christ is one aspect of a prior work of God's grace in uniting us to his Son. At this point, then, it is essential to relate our understanding of conversion to contemporary concerns.

Two-Stage Schemes

Human-centered religion has always created two paths to life: one for the spiritually-gifted and another for those who settle for heaven, but do not choose the "abundant life." Roman Catholicism (medieval and modern) has offered these two paths in its distinction between "the secular," on the one hand, and the priesthood and others in the category of "the religious" on the other. Further, there are those who have indulged in venial sins (those which interrupt fellowship with God) and mortal sins (those which clear the board and make one start from scratch).

Evangelicals have created two paths, in part, by following the "Higher Life" interpretation of conversion and the Christian life, in which supersaints (often involved in "full-time Christian ministry") are "filled with the Spirit," while normal ("carnal") Christians make it to heaven, but without having any of the gifts of the Spirit or rewards.

"The Holy Spirit will fill us with His power the moment we are fully yielded," declares Bill Bright, founder of Campus Crusade for Christ. "God would be breaking His own spiritual laws if He forced man to do His bidding." It's a tragedy that "at the time of conversion the will of man is temporarily yielded to the will of God," but "after conversion, the heart frequently loses its first love" and therefore requires us to seek another filling. Just as the medieval believer required some ritual in order to fill up the bathtub of grace that had begun leaking from a venial sin, Bright urges, "If a Christian is not filled, he is disobedient to the command of God and is sinning against God." What is required is for the carnal Christian to follow the steps that would have been familiar to the medieval monk: First, "meditate"; second, "make it a practice to spend definite time each day in prayer for God's guidance. . . ." One must also confess each sin, since "unconfessed sin keeps many Christians from being filled with the Holy Spirit."[3]

Charles Finney is even quoted approvingly by Bright: "Christians are as guilty for not being filled with the Holy Spirit as sinners are for not repenting. They are even more so, for as they have more light, they are so much the more guilty." And Norman B. Harrison is cited: "The Spirit-filled life . . . is the only life that can please God." Of course, the heirs of the Reformation reply to today's heirs of the Middle Ages that there is only one life that can please God, and that is Christ's. And because his life is accepted and we are in him, hidden as it were, we are pleasing to God and are filled with the Spirit. Every believer possesses everything of Christ's.

What kind of father shares himself and his possessions with only a few favorite children and withholds his best from the others? Perhaps some would answer, "It's not a matter of the generosity of the father, but of the children's willingness to receive." While that is logically coherent, it reveals a fundamentally different theological perspective. Union with Christ is not the result of human decision, striving, seeking, yielding, or surrendering, but of Christ's. While we are called to be "filled with the Spirit" (Eph. 5:18), that is merely a figure of speech: "Do not get drunk on wine. . . . Instead, be filled with the Spirit." In other words, make sure you're under the right influence! Every believer is Spirit-filled and, therefore, a recipient of every heavenly blessing in Christ (Eph. 1:3–4).

Confusing Indicative and Imperative

Everywhere the Scriptures provide both the declaration of who we are in Christ (indicative) and the command to respond to that particular declaration in a certain way (imperative). For instance, Paul does not simply issue an imperative like, "Stop living with your boyfriend." He says, "How should we who have died to sin live any longer in it?" Paul does not call people to die to sin; he does not invite them to enter into a higher level of abundant life; there are not appeals to become something that the believer is not already. The believer has died, is buried, is raised, is seated with Christ in the heavenlies, and so on. These are not plateaus for victorious Christians who have surrendered all and willed their way to victory, but realities for every believer, regardless of how small one's faith or how weak one's repentance.

Thus, we must stop trying to convert believers into these realities by imperatives: "Do this." "Confess that." "Follow these steps," and so on. Union with Christ ushers us into conversion, and conversion ushers us immediately into all of these realities so that, as Sinclair Ferguson writes, "The determining factor of my existence is no longer my past. It is Christ's past."[4]

For those who speak as though the filling of the Spirit, the gifts of the Spirit, justification, the new birth, and union with Christ are things to be attained by "yielding," or by obedience to imperatives, Paul insists, "But of Him [God] you are in Christ Jesus, who became for us wisdom from God—and righteousness and sanctification and redemption—that, as it is written, 'He who glories, let him glory in the LORD'" (1 Cor. 1:30–31 NKJV).

Quietism and Legalism

Some Christians so emphasize a "let go and let God" passivity that even after conversion they act as though they believe they are still "dead in trespasses and sins" and do not "understand the things of the Spirit of God." Wanting to attribute everything to grace and God's work, they confuse justification and sanctification just as surely as those who want to underscore human involvement. In our conversion we are passive: acted upon rather than active, as Luther put it. We are justified through receiving what someone else has earned for us. But we grow in sanctification through *living out* what someone else has earned for us. Both are gifts we inherit from someone else, but the former is passively received and the second is actively pursued. If I were a pauper who had some benefactor deposit one billion dollars in my bank account, I would be regarded a billionaire. But I would feel a need to share this new wealth with old friends living on the street. The gift would be received passively, but in turn would be put to use for good actively.

If sanctification is confused with justification, it will lose the tension, reality, and rigor necessary for the battles of the Christian life; if justification is confused with sanctification, the product will be of no redemptive value. Therefore, we must clearly distinguish conversion from justification and realize that initial conversion is a passive reception of God's gracious acceptance of us in Christ, while the lifelong conversion process is an active pursuit of holiness and righteousness, the very thing the gospel promises that we already possess fully and completely in Christ.

In conclusion, let us meditate on the wonderful promise that in Christ we possess all of his riches, not just one or two of them. Do we try to imitate him? Yes—not merely as our moral example, the way Greek sailors may have venerated Neptune, or Greek philosophers venerated Aristotle's ethics, but as our indwelling Head. As the little brother stands in awe of his elder sibling, let us imitate our Elder Brother because of the fact that through his incarnation, death, resurrection, ascension, and meditation, we are flesh of his flesh and bone of his bone. For "both the one who makes men holy and those who are made holy are of the same family" (Heb. 2:11).

The call to the converted, therefore, is not, "Come to Christ; only he can give you the power to live the abundant Christian life!" Rather, it is, "Come to Christ; only he can be your abundance," as the Father has only "blessed us with every spiritual blessing in the heavenly places *in Christ*" (Eph. 1:3 NKJV, emphasis added).

Part **2**

Lessons from the Past

Calvin and the Council of Trent 5

W. Robert Godfrey

Justification has long been known among Protestants as the article of faith by which the church stands or falls. With the authority of Scripture and the nature of the Lord's Supper, the doctrine of justification was at the center of debates between the Reformers and the Roman Catholic church. Vast amounts of energy and ink were devoted to clarifying and defending it. All the great Protestant confessions state the Reformation doctrine.

This study will examine the doctrine of justification from the perspective of John Calvin's response to the decisions of the Roman Catholic Council of Trent. This perspective illumines the essential debate between Rome and the Reformers on justification.

Why the History Lesson?

Today such a historical reflection is especially needed. It is needed first because Christians must continually meditate on and be renewed in the truths of the Savior's work on their behalf. And second, because an understanding of history can help us to evaluate the new controversies that have arisen in the evangelical community in our time.

119

One of the significant modern debates has come to be known as "the lordship controversy." Can one have Jesus as Savior and not have him as Lord? Can one be saved without any change in one's life? Must one achieve a certain level of holiness to be saved? Such questions have been debated intensely, with Zane Hodges and John MacArthur emerging as principal antagonists in the latest phase of this dispute. The controversy at root is a new debate on the doctrine of justification.

How could major disagreement arise on a subject like justification, which has been studied exhaustively for centuries and about which there has been a clear consensus among evangelical Protestants? Part of the answer is that evangelical Christians on the whole have become very ignorant about church history. With what can only be called pride, many have thought that they could dig all of God's truth out of the Bible by themselves. They have neglected the treasures of insight into God's Word that have accumulated from the labors of brothers and sisters over the centuries. They have insisted on reinventing the wheel in our generation—and they have not managed to make it round.

A second part of the answer is that many evangelicals have developed a bias against theology and theological systems. They do not want theology; they want "the simple gospel." They believe that systems are artificial and are forced on the Bible. The Bible is their only creed. But they themselves end up with a system that is implicit, unexamined, and sometimes ruthlessly imposed on Scripture.

A third part of the answer as to how such a controversy could arise comes from the history of evangelical Protestantism. To summarize, albeit too briefly, from the seventeenth century on, many evangelicals have seen the greatest threat to true faith coming from formalism. Especially in the state churches of Europe, many people have called themselves Christians and have been willing to sign the formal confession of their church on the dotted line, but have shown no effect of the work of the Spirit in their lives. Therefore, Puritans, pietists, and later revivalists of many sorts focused on the need for greater life in the churches. This concern manifested itself in calls for conversion, for holiness, for revival, for decision. While this concern was valid—there was great formalism in the churches—some of the attempted solutions created more problems than they solved.

Some of the solutions tainted the gospel with legalism, implying or teaching that one could be right with God—could be justified—only by acquiring a certain amount of holiness. Such legalism tended to evoke a reaction to the opposite extreme of saying (or living as if) holiness was irrelevant to the Christian life. The pendulum swing between moralism and antinomianism continues to our day, and the extremes on either end of the swing are neither theologically correct nor spiritually profitable. Hodges clearly represents an antinomian extreme in the lordship controversy. While John MacArthur's position seems much more balanced, occasionally he slips into moralistic expressions.

The lordship controversy itself illustrates how theology is intensely practical. What is the gospel message? What are Christians to believe, and how are they to live? These theological questions are not abstract or peripheral, but are essential for Christians.

The Council of Trent

When the Reformation began and Luther trumpeted justification by faith alone, the Roman Catholic church was not in a strong position to respond. In the course of the Middle Ages much had been written on justification, and a consensus had emerged on the doctrine. But when discussion turned to the specifics of the nature and cause of justification, very significant differences of opinion were expressed; no comprehensive teaching on justification had been adopted officially by the church. Many leaders of the old church recognized their weakness on this point and called for an ecumenical council that could rule on justification (in addition to a variety of other issues). This council, after many delays, finally convened at the city of Trent in 1545, as the Reformation was in full swing. The Council of Trent established a definitive Roman Catholic position on justification.[1] For our purposes, we can summarize the key elements of that position in six points:

1. The Christian is justified by grace, but human free will, although weakened by sin, can and must cooperate with grace. Trent taught that grace is necessary and even primary in the

process of salvation, but human dignity and responsibility require that the human will also has a role. Grace enables the will to cooperate, but ultimately the will must act to make grace effective and saving. Trent sought to sound Augustinian in its stress on grace, but actually compromised with Pelagianism in the determinative function that it gave to the human will for salvation. (It is amazing how many evangelicals today share with Trent this understanding of grace.)

2. Faith was defined as a matter of the intellect, consisting of knowledge and assent to truth. Such faith, known as *unformed faith*, cannot justify. However, when faith is linked to love, it becomes *formed faith* and does justify. Faith alone does not justify, but faith and love (which produces good works) justify.[3] Trent rejected any idea that "head knowledge" alone saves. The Christian must link intellectual conviction with moral transformation for salvation. Love gives life to faith, just as the soul gives life to the body. Faith without love is dead, just as the body without the soul is only a corpse. Since God loves only the lovely, we must be changed morally by love in order to be acceptable to God.

Understanding Trent's definition of faith is crucial for any effective communication with knowledgeable Roman Catholics. When evangelicals speak of "faith alone," the Roman Catholic is likely to hear us saying that we are justified by the intellect alone. We must carefully define what we mean by faith to avoid that misunderstanding.

The tragedy of Hodges's position is that he very nearly defines faith the same way that Trent did—as assent to the truth. The difference between Trent and Hodges is that Hodges maintains that such assent is saving. This means that Hodges is even more unbiblical than Trent, missing the historic evangelical understanding of faith.

3. Justification is not solely by the imputation or crediting of Christ's righteousness to the Christian, but by the infusion of Christ's righteousness into the Christian so that he actually becomes righteous.[4] This point follows necessarily from Trent's discussion of faith. If the Christian must be morally transformed to be saved, then it is not enough for the righteousness of Christ to be counted as his. The righteousness of Christ must actually

live in him and *change him* so that he can be justified. Luther's idea of an "alien righteousness" is useless and, in fact, seriously misleading, according to Trent (and not a few evangelicals today). The Christian needs a morally renewing righteousness. That righteousness flows into the believer especially through the sacraments.

4. Justification finally rests on the Christian acquiring and maintaining a certain level of sanctification.[5] For Trent, grace was seen in rather quantitative terms. One needs a certain *amount* of grace to be acceptable. The moral transformation must reach a certain level. Certainly no mortal sins can be allowed to remain unconfessed and unforgiven, or salvation is impossible.

5. The Christian can fulfill the commands of God.[6] Again, moral responsibility and human dignity require the freedom and ability to obey all the commands of God—at least as a theoretical possibility.

6. The Christian cannot be certain, except by special revelation, that he is presently in a state of grace, or that he is elect, or that he will finally persevere and be saved.[7] Since sanctification is necessary for justification and the whole life of the Christian is in process, the Christian can have no assurance of salvation in this life. Trent went even further, however, and said that such assurance would not be spiritually profitable, but would produce spiritual pride and moral indifference. A measure of insecurity produces humility, piety, carefulness, and hard work.

Again, at this point evangelicals hoping to communicate effectively with knowledgeable Roman Catholics need to understand that we must not assume that everyone wants and is looking for assurance of salvation. Trent would see our assurance as arrogance. For Roman Catholics, the assurance taught by Hodges that if we once believe we are saved, even if we fail to bear any fruit or to continue to believe, seems to prove their worst fears.

Calvin's Response to Trent

In 1547 Calvin responded in a work entitled *Acts of the Council of Trent with the Antidote*,[8] analyzing and refuting the positions of Trent chapter by chapter. With careful theological reflection and scriptural evidence, he dismantled the Roman Catholic doctrine and stated his own. Let us look at the alternatives that Calvin offered to the essential points of Trent:

1. Calvin begins with the matter of grace in relation to justification. He acknowledges that man after the fall has a will, but insists that that will is dead in sin. The will can make decisions and take actions, but it is not free to cooperate with the grace of God. The will is so twisted and corrupted—what later Calvinism calls total depravity—that it has no ability or desire to choose for God or for salvation. The will is in rebellion against God. The only hope for man and his will lies in God's regenerating grace. God's sovereign and irresistible grace makes man willing. Anything good found in the human will is not earned by cooperation, but is a gift of grace. "The whole may be thus summed up—Their error consists in sharing the work between God and ourselves, so as to transfer to ourselves the obedience of a pious will in assenting to divine grace, whereas this is the proper work of God himself."[9]

Calvin especially appeals to Augustine and shows that Augustine on grace stands against Trent and with the Reformers. In doing so, Calvin demonstrates that Rome's claim to antiquity for its teachings is false. The Reformers have not produced a theological novelty, but stand with the Bible and the best tradition of the church.

2. Faith is a crucial topic for Calvin. He rejects the Roman distinction between formed and unformed faith, insisting that biblical faith is never just a matter of the intellect. Faith is not just knowledge and assent for Calvin; it is also trust. Faith justifies as it trusts the promises of God and rests in the righteousness of Christ. The true believer is not one who simply accumulates truths in his head, but one who relies upon Jesus. "Faith brings nothing of our own to God, but receives what God spontaneously offers us. Hence it is that faith, however imperfect, nevertheless possesses a perfect righteousness, because it has respect to nothing but the gratuitous goodness of God."[10] True faith, however small or weak, trusts Christ and so is the instrument that connects us to Christ and the fullness of his blessings. It is not imperfect faith that justifies, but the object of faith, the perfect righteousness of Christ.

Calvin insists that true faith is living and fruitful. It certainly produces a Christian life of love and good works, but the love and good works are not part of justification. Faith alone justifies, but true faith is never alone in the justified.

3. Calvin attempts to be absolutely clear about faith so that a proper distinction between imputation and infusion can be maintained. Christ's perfect righteousness is imputed or reckoned to us as the basis of our justification. Faith looks outside itself to Christ and his work as the only hope and strength: "But when they say that a man is justified when he is again formed for the obedience of God, they subvert the whole argument of Paul . . . (Rom. 4:14). . . . so long as we look at what we are in ourselves, we must tremble in the sight of God, so far from having a firm and unshaken confidence of eternal life."[11]

Calvin maintains that Christ does infuse his grace to change and sanctify the Christian. The Spirit does morally transform Christians. But that infusion or transformation has no part in justification. Calvin follows the Scriptures in seeing that perfection alone—not good intentions, heartfelt striving, or humble cooperation—is acceptable to God: "Be holy, because I am holy" (Lev. 11:44; 1 Pet. 1:16). Only a perfect righteousness can stand in the judgment, and the Christian can have such righteousness only outside of himself and in the perfection of Christ. The most sanctified Christian who ever lived was not perfectly holy—only Jesus met that standard. And the perfection of Jesus' righteousness reaches us untainted only as it is imputed to us and received by faith.

4. A key error of Rome is to confuse justification and sanctification. Calvin writes,

Justification and Sanctification, are constantly conjoined and cohere; but from this it is erroneously inferred that they are one and the same. For example: The light of the sun, though never unaccompanied with heat, is not to be considered heat. . . . We acknowledge, then, that as soon as any one is justified, renewal also necessarily follows: and there is no dispute as to whether or not Christ sanctifies all whom he justifies. It were to rend the gospel, and divide Christ himself to attempt to separate the righteousness which we obtain by faith [justification] from repentance [sanctification].[12]

Calvin teaches that justification and sanctification must be distinguished, or one slips into the moralism or legalism of Rome. At the same time he insists that they cannot be separated, or one slips into antinomianism. Justification is not sanctification, but sanctification always follows justification.

Calvin captures the biblical balance here beautifully. The second chapter of James's epistle shows that real faith produces works, and where works are absent, faith is not real. The Great Commission demonstrates the same thing. Jesus sent his disciples to make disciples, that is, followers who *are* justified and are *being* sanctified. The apostles in the Book of Acts preach both faith (justification) and repentance (sanctification) as the whole message from God. Hodges's distinction between "believers" who are saved but not sanctified and disciples who are saved *and* sanctified is completely without biblical basis. The one Jesus is justifier and sanctifier; he is Savior and Lord. The Westminster Larger Catechism (question 77) captures Calvin's thought exactly:

Wherein do justification and sanctification differ?

Although sanctification be inseparably joined with justification, yet they differ, in that God in justification imputeth the righteousness of Christ; in sanctification his Spirit infuseth grace, and enableth to the exercise thereof; in the former, sin is pardoned; in the other, it is subdued; the one doth equally free all believers from the revenging wrath of God, and that perfectly in this life, that they never fall into condemnation; the other is neither equal in all, nor in this life perfect in any, but growing up to perfection.

5. No one can keep any of the commands of God perfectly. All our best efforts are tainted with sin. Calvin writes, "It is too plain, however, that we are never animated and actuated by a perfect love to God in obeying his just commands. . . . In short, the seventh chapter of the Romans disposes of this controversy. There Paul, in his own person and that of all the godly, confesses that he is far from perfection, even when his will is at its best."[13] The

sinfulness of the best Christians makes it clear why only the perfect righteousness of Christ, received by faith alone, can justify.

The reality of our imperfection does not imply that we can be content with our sin. Rather it places clearly before us our agenda and goals. The Christian life is a constant war with sin and a desire to see more and more of the holiness of Christ manifested in us.

6. Certainty is an important theme for Calvin. Faith in Christ brings a certainty of sonship to the Christian. Faith brings joy and assurance that we are right with God. The Christian can and must be certain that he is in a state of grace. Calvin insists that there is no virtue or humility in doubt. The many and glorious promises of Jesus should produce great confidence. Because by faith we possess the perfect righteousness of Christ, we can have real assurance. Calvin writes:

> When, then is that boldness of which Paul elsewhere speaks, (Eph. iii.12,) that access with confidence to the Father through faith in Christ? Not contented with the term confidence, he furnishes us with boldness, which is certainly something more than certainty. And what shall we say to his own occasional use of the term certainty? (Rom. viii.37.) This certainty he founds upon nothing but a mere persuasion of the free love of God.[14]

Calvin also insists that the Christian can be certain of his election:

> I acknowledge, indeed, and we are all careful to teach, that nothing is more pernicious than to inquire into the secret council of God, with the view of thereby obtaining a knowledge of our election—that this is a whirlpool in which we shall be swallowed up and lost. But seeing that our Heavenly Father holds forth in Christ a mirror of our eternal adoption, no man truly holds what has been given us by Christ save he who feels assured that Christ himself has been given him by the Father, that he may not perish.[15]

And he argues a certainty of perseverance:

> For certainly, he whose expectation of eternal life is not founded on absolute certainty, must be agitated by various doubts. This is

not the kind of hope which Paul describes, when he says that he is certainly persuaded that neither life, nor death, nor things present, nor things to come, will dissolve the love which God embraces him in Christ. He would not speak thus did not the certainty of Christian hope reach beyond the last hour of life.[16]

Calvin asserts in his response to the Council of Trent that the Scriptures encourage a true Christian to certainty because of the rich promises of Jesus. Fear, doubt, and temptation must be resisted with trust and confidence in God. Rather than promoting moral indifference and spiritual laxity, assurance gives us the confidence and strength to love God and pursue holiness.

Conclusion

Calvin's response to Trent is so valuable that it should be read in its entirety. This brief summary should encourage us, however, to keep the doctrine of justification clear in our minds and central to our Christian life. Spiritual balance and power flow from this doctrine when it is rightly understood and rightly related to other elements of Christian truth.

In our day, when the church is weak and confused in many ways, we must not be led astray into thinking that either moralism or antinomianism will help us. *Moralism* destroys the glorious liberty we have through the work of Christ. It draws attention away from Christ and his grace. *Antinomianism* misses the call to holiness in Scripture and reinforces the serious erosion of morality in our society generally and in our churches. Awareness of the work of Christ and the holiness of God is at stake in understanding justification properly. Meditating on justification will draw us closer to Christ "who became for us wisdom from God—and righteousness and sanctification and redemption" (1 Cor. 1:30 NKJV).

Christ Crucified between Two Thieves

Michael Horton

When the ancient church was faced with heresies concerning Christ's person, the church father Tertullian described the situation as, "Christ crucified between two thieves." Like the hero in *Indiana Jones and the Temple of Doom*, the church steps cautiously, and sometimes nervously, between equally disastrous stones, forming a checkered path to the treasure.

Historically, the "two thieves" on either side of the biblical testimony to justifying and sanctifying grace have been antinomianism ("against law," from *nomos*, meaning "law") and legalism. In the current debate between Zane Hodges and John MacArthur, Jr., many of the same questions are raised as have been part and parcel of the debate throughout church history. However, make no mistake about it. While the Hodges position, in my estimation, is an antinomian "thief," the presentation one finds in MacArthur's *Gospel According to Jesus* is not, strictly speaking, legalistic. The Hodges/Ryrie position is self-consciously antinomian, while MacArthur's presentation, though confusing on some important points we will discuss, is trying to grapple with the Reformation interpretation of Scripture. For instance, while Hodges praises "free grace," he in fact has a lower view of grace than MacArthur does, as the former embraces Arminian *synergism* (human cooperation in regeneration) and the latter defends a *monergistic* scheme (God alone regenerates and justifies). Where MacArthur seems confusing at important points, Hodges and Ryrie are all too clear. Much of the ambiguity apparent in the recent discussions about justification and sanctification can be credited to a lack of interaction with past debates. Therefore, in this chapter I want to give a brief overview of the history of this debate and then focus specifically on the so-called antinomian controversy of the 1630s in New England.

Pelagius versus Augustine

In the late fourth century, a British monk visiting Rome was appalled by the decadence of Christendom's capital. Surely, he reasoned, the decline was due to the popularity of a certain African bishop. The monk was Pelagius, and the bishop was Augustine. The message Augustine made famous more than anyone else since the apostles was *salvation by grace*, though the bishop's thinking was not as precise on this matter as that of the sixteenth-century Reformers would be. "Command what you will, and give what you command," Augustine prayed in his famous *Confessions*. This line led Pelagius to accuse Augustine of antinomianism. After all, if everything depends on God's grace, no one will expend any effort. If grace precedes my willing and running, he reasoned, I can always blame God for not giving me the grace.

Thus, Pelagius reacted by teaching that we are born into this world morally neutral and only become warped by our social environment and the example of Adam. Notice, I said the *example* of Adam, as Pelagius denied original sin. We are affected by the father of our race only insofar as we choose to follow in his poor footsteps, but we are not in bondage to sin, nor is our nature predisposed to evil. How could God command holiness if humans were incapable of it? As would be a recurring feature of heresy, the disciples of Pelagius generally turned out worse than the mentor. A middle-ground, however, was achieved by one disciple, Coelestius, but Pelagianism *and* Coelestius's semi-Pelagianism were both roundly condemned by more church councils than any other heresy in history.

The Reformation

While the Middle Ages were full of recurring debates over this issue, the controversy erupted singularly in the sixteenth century. The monk Martin Luther was so scrupulous about confessing his sins that the other monks began making fun of him!

Ironically, Luther described the monasteries as dens of license. But this should not really surprise us. One of the first lessons we learn from church history is that legalism always breeds license. Wherever legalism rears its head, antinomianism is not far behind. Luther realized that one had to be schizophrenic to be a good monk. Mental health required a purging of the sense of guilt, yet Luther knew God was strict and demanding in his justice. The only way out was the biblical teaching, especially highlighted in Paul's letters, that God is in the business of justifying *the wicked*, not the righteous. In other words, a sinner is *declared* righteous apart from his own moral status. Luther used to secretly hate to hear words like *righteousness* or *holiness*, because they always meant for him the righteousness and holiness God *is* and *demands* from us, but which we are unable to meet. But Luther the monk, in his studies, stumbled onto Romans 1:17: "For in it [the gospel] the righteousness of God is revealed from faith to faith; as it is written, 'The just shall live by faith'" (NKJV). Righteousness became for Luther not only a description of God's character by which he judges us, not merely a demand made upon the sinner, but now also a *gift* that God graciously donates to those who trust Christ and his righteousness alone.

Without going into the details, suffice it to say that the Roman Catholic reaction was severe. While learned cardinals and bishops debated the issues—some siding with Luther and Calvin—the Council of Trent in 1563 condemned the doctrine of justification by faith alone as heresy on the grounds that it denied the necessity of moral transformation as a condition of acceptance before God. While the Reformers affirmed the necessity of moral transformation (sanctification), they insisted that obedience or growth in holiness were not conditions of justification. God imputes to the sinner the thirty-three years of Christ's active obedience to the law and his passive obedience to death on the cross as satisfaction and payment for all offenses. Furthermore, this "alien righteousness" (that is, the righteousness that is not one's own) is imputed to one's account upon the sole condition that it be received and embraced by the sinner. *Knowledge* of the gospel's content and object, *assent* to the truth of that message, and *trust* in the saving efficacy of Christ and his work form the definition of faith, by which alone we are promised our right standing with God.

Luther, Calvin, and the other Reformers spent much time and energy defending their position not only against the legalism of those who taught that justification and sanctification could be confused, but against the antinomianism of those who thought justification and sanctification could be divorced.

The Reformation way of putting it was this: We are justified by faith alone, but not by faith that is alone.

The Puritans (Late Sixteenth to Early Seventeenth Centuries)

There is no question that a difference in emphasis exists between the Reformers and the English and New England Puritans over the question of assurance.[1] The Reformed tradition in Europe, in agreement with Calvin's exegesis, argued that assurance is the essence of faith. In other words, to trust in Christ is to have the assurance that "there is therefore now no condemnation." If saving faith is more than the conviction that Jesus Christ died on the cross and rose from the dead, but that he did this *for me*, then that conviction is synonymous with assurance. To trust in Christ alone for salvation is to be assured that he will fulfill his promise. If we are not assured, we are not trusting.

Of course, this was never to suggest that assurance is complete, any more than faith. Our faith and assurance may be weak, sometimes barely distinguishable, but it is impossible to truly exercise a justifying faith that does not contain the assurance that Christ's saving work has guaranteed what has been promised in one's own case.

In the Puritan context, however, the Reformed doctrine of assurance underwent a slight shift in emphasis. The Reformation had been a biblical response primarily to legalism, as justification in the medieval church was confused with sanctification and assurance was impossible because being rightly related to God depended on whether one cooperated with grace from day to day. The Reformers rightly emphasized the objective character of the gospel: Christ crucified outside of my own personal experience and behavior, two thousand years ago, as a once-and-for-all satisfaction of divine justice in my place. But before a generation passed, there were those who had embraced the Reformation because they saw in it an opportunity to be saved by what we today might call "easy-believism." All they had to do was assent to the teachings of the Reformed or the Lutheran churches, just as they had to the Roman church, and they could be "safe and secure from all alarm." Although the Reformers protested that this was merely "devil's faith," the stuff of which hypocrites were made, it seemed that the profession of these growing ranks of hypocrites risked proving Rome's point, that the evangelical doctrine promotes license and presumption.

It was in this setting that the English Puritans pastored, convinced that the believer's inner life, the ministry of the Holy Spirit, and the concerns of piety had been almost abandoned by those who, in fleeing Rome for the Reformation, had merely leaped from the frying pan into the fire. Even though the Puritans shared an identical theological system with the Reformed on the continent of Europe, the former insisted that it is a mistake to say that assurance is of the essence of faith. In one case, it encourages presumption among the hypocrites who think they are justified even though there are no fruits; in the other, it creates anxiety among those who, instead of worrying about whether they have enough works, are now wondering if they have enough assurance! Calvin insisted that it is not the *degree* of faith or assurance that secured justification, but even the weakest grasp of faith, like the father of the demon-possessed son, who replied to Christ's invitation to believe with moving honesty: "Lord, I believe; help my unbelief!" (Mark 9:24).[2] Nevertheless, the pastoral setting provided for a variety of applications and Puritanism on this score was a deviation, not from the theology of the Reformation, but from the practical pastoral counsel on the matter of assurance. For instance, few leaders from the Continental Reformed side of the assurance question were as intimately associated with the English Puritans as Zacharias Ursinus (1534–83), principal author of the Heidelberg Catechism. And yet, Ursinus, following Calvin's line, argued from a number of texts, "No man can indeed know, or judge with certainty, from second causes [i.e., the fruit of conversion], or from events whether good or evil; for the external condition of men furnishes no safe criterion either of the favor of disaprobation of God. . . . We may therefore be ignorant of our salvation, as far as it is dependent upon second causes, but we may know it in as far as God is pleased to reveal it unto us by his Word and Spirit."[3]

This did not mean that one could not use evidences of true conversion to support one's assurance; nor did it mean that one could never be without such evidences. Even in committing great sinful acts, the truly converted man or woman is sorrowful and repentant. Nevertheless, it is always dangerous to build one's assurance on a foundation of works, even though one denies the place of works in justification.

As the Heidelberg Catechism is the most important representative document from the Continental consensus, so the Westminster Confession and Catechisms is the principal document from the Puritan and Presbyterian side of the assurance question. Again, this is not a matter of doctrine so much as of practical pastoral application of doctrine. Nevertheless, the shift from warning believers against introspection in an effort to discern evidences to encouraging it was very important practically. If assurance is not of the essence of saving faith, and it can be lost because of sin, sensitive persons will inevitably scrape their consciences raw until they find clues and, as Calvin warned, there will be no satisfaction with evidences; there will never be enough to secure the soul's confidence. One of the commissioners of the Westminster Assembly, from Scotland, George Gillespie, complained, "I hear much (will the perplexed soul say) of the nature of faith, of free justification, of the things sealed in baptism, etc.; but I cannot see that *I* have any interest for my part in these things" (emphasis mine).[4] In other words, the question was not, "Are we justified by faith alone, or by faith *and* its fruit?" but rather, "Since people are justified by faith alone, how can I know that I have exercised *saving* faith?"

MacArthur appears to be concerned about this same issue. He looks around and sees a church that is "populated with people who have bought into a system that encourages shallow and ineffectual faith." Listen to "the typical gospel presentation nowadays," MacArthur says:

> You'll hear sinners entreated with words like, "accept Jesus Christ as personal Savior"; "ask Jesus into your heart"; "invite Christ into your life"; or "make a decision for Christ." You may be so accustomed to hearing those phrases that it will surprise you to learn none of them is based on biblical terminology. They are the products of a diluted gospel. It is not the gospel according to Jesus. The gospel Jesus proclaimed was a call to discipleship, a call to follow Him in submissive obedience, not just a plea to make a decision or pray a prayer.[5]

Although Luther had his Agrigolas and Calvin his Libertines, the Reformers' mission was to break the grip of subjective, inward-looking legalism and to point believers outside of themselves to Christ. The Puritans, while retaining this emphasis on justification and objective redemption, wanted to flesh out what it meant for a justified believer to go on to maturity and growth in Christ. Again, it is hardly the case that the Reformers did not talk about sanctification and the Puritans did not talk about justification, but that the emphasis fell on different syllables in each case, because of the situation.

Having said all of this, it is important to point out that the Puritans nevertheless always reiterated the objective character of salvation, the graciousness of grace and the freeness of justification. As stern a critic of antinomianism as Gillespie was, he nevertheless made sure that he kept well within the evangelical parameters:

> We must first remember these three things: First, Our best marks can contribute nothing to our justification, but only to our conso-

lation; cannot avail to peace with God, but to peace with ourselves. . . . Faith cannot lodge in the soul alone, and without other graces, yet faith alone justifies before God. Secondly, Beware that marks of grace do not lead us from Christ, or make us look upon ourselves as anything at all out of Christ. Thou bearest not the root, but the root bears thee. Christ is made of God unto us sanctification as well as righteousness. . . . It is Christ's by propriety, thine only by participation.[6]

Gillespie also urges the Puritan notion of "the judgment of charity," that is, the idea that we must give other believers the benefit of the doubt when they say they are regenerate. We ought not to become "fruit police," dusting their outward behavior for the marks. "If they [Christians] could see into the hearts of others, to be sure of the sincerity and soundness of their graces, they could have a judgment of certainty concerning them; but this they cannot, for who knows the things of a man save the spirit of a man which is in him?"[7] The English Puritan, Thomas Goodwin, sent disturbed consciences back to the Word and sacraments (baptism and Holy Communion), "not to begin grace, but to confirm it,"[8] a piece of sound Reformation counsel. While assurance may be difficult, justification is an instantaneous act of God: "God pardons not the debt by halves, nor bestows Christ's righteousness by parcels."[9] While leaving no comfort for the impenitent, Goodwin assures the believer struggling with sin, "My ways of mercy are both above your ways of sinning and they also exceed all the thoughts of mercy which the best natured of you can have in pardoning others."[10] Goodwin preaches the gospel to comfort even Christians as sinners—not casting doubts on whether they are truly regenerate, but declaring,

> That God will pardon your sins of ordinary infirmities that you commit, that you think easily the covenant of grace doth reach and extend to; ay, but here is a proviso (you call them so in acts and wills) which is attached to this covenant of grace upon the supposition of the worst of cases, of the worst of those who are under the covenant of grace: 'If his children forsake my law, and walk not in my judgments' (Ps. 89:30–38). You see the amplitude of the covenant of grace (what hath God to do to run out to this?),

and you shall see the largeness of the covenant of grace, how far it extends.

After all, the "if" in the verse implies that it is a possible case for a Christian, says Goodwin.[11] Then notice his further counsel:

> He [God] repeats it [his willingness to forgive even great sins] over and over; for, as Calvin says, it is the hardest thing in the world to believe it, and whoever lives in great sins, it is the hardest thing in the world to believe that God will pardon him. But doth he speak of the members of Christ, is it of those that are actual members of Christ that he speaks this? Is it not of their sins *before* conversion rather? Nay, but it is after: 'If his sons forsake my law,' says the 30th verse. Those that are his sons and children are actually in the state of grace. At the day of judgment, says he, Heb. ii.13, 'Lo I and the children which God hath given me;' and he is called an 'everlasting Father,' Isa. ix.6. . . . Water may be so heated, that anybody that puts his hand into it may say, There is no cold in it; but yet, though it scalds, let it stand a while and all the heat will be gone. Let men in a state of grace be inflamed with lusts, that one would think there is nothing of grace, yet there is a principle of grace which will reduce them at last. So much for the greatness of sin![12]

Of course, God is not an indulgent father, but disciplines his children. Nevertheless, even that discipline is a sign of God's fatherly goodness. Goodwin was also anxious to send doubters back to the cross first, rather than fixing their eyes on their outward marks of discipleship:

> For what is the great hindrance in believing? The greatness of your sins, your hearts clearly misgiving you in that. Now it is conscience that is the subject of them; and it is the conscience raiseth and conjures them up, as I may so express it, against thee; for all the sins that lie in that dark cell thy heart, are made by conscience to appear and stare in thy face. . . . Conscience hath not learned its lesson from faith, it hath not gone and dipped itself in the blood of Christ by faith; for if it had, it would be quiet, and not always suggesting to a man what his sins are, so as to discourage and hinder him from believing. . . . There is nothing then that can satisfy

the conscience in respect of the guilt of sin, but the blood, and death, and resurrection of Jesus Christ.[13]

Goodwin warned against making the call to receive Christ or determine one's justification by its fruits a difficult matter by "turning the very gospel into a legal way." These "holy duties," the fruit of saving faith, writes Goodwin, can sometimes not only fail to give us assurance, but actually lead us away from Christ. Therefore, he says, "we cry out against this resting in duties, and shew the vanity and emptiness of all you can do to save you, or obtain Christ and God's favour, and bid men, as Luther, take heed not of their sins only, but of their good works also," as a possible means of distraction from Christ.[14]

The Congregationalist Puritan, Thomas Hooker, is sometimes considered one of the strictest and sternest among them, and his book, *The Poor Doubting Christian Drawn to Christ*, is one of the warmest pieces of pastoral comfort in print. Notice his advice, in the form of a dialogue:

> You must not come and think to buy a husband. The Lord looks for no power or sufficiency from you, of yourselves; nor of yourselves any power against corruption, or enlargement to duties. . . . 'As many as received him, to them he gave power to become the sons of God, even to them that believe on his name.' He doth not say, to as many as had such enlargement to duties, and such power against corruption; but if thou wilt take Christ upon those terms on which he offers himself. . . . And is it not plain then that it is thy pride and thy self-conceitedness that hinders thee? Thou thinkest thou must have thus much grace and holiness; and Christ must not justify the ungodly, but the godly man. But I tell thee, that, upon such terms, he will never justify thee, or any man while the world stands.[15]

To the poor, doubting Christian who wonders if his or her life's evidences extinguish all grounds for hope, Hooker writes, "The best Christians are most suspicious of themselves, and none fuller of doubts and fears than those that have least cause to fear or doubt that their estates are broken and bad."[16]

In one of the most sensitive and moving sermons one could read, "The Bruised Reed and Smoking Flax" (Matt. 12:20), the great Puritan, Richard Sibbes, preached that this is not merely a description of the unbeliever, but of the Christian, since "grace is not only little, but also mingled with corruption; whereof it is, that a *Christian* is said to be smoking flax." Our faith is like a candle whose flame sometimes looks as if it is extinguished, and with it, the fruit of faith. There sometimes seems to be no observable sign of life, but this text, says Sibbes, is there "to force us to pitch our rest on justification, not sanctification, which, besides imperfection, hath some soil."[17]

None of these examples ought to provide the Hodges camp with the slightest room for claiming support from the evangelicals of past centuries, for much more could be said from the writings of the Puritans and Reformers alike concerning the "devil's faith" that the "no-lordship" position is peddling. Furthermore, just because one's faith may burn low, and the evidences may seem barren, the former is never completely extinguished and the latter is never true in fact, though perhaps in one's own experience. Nevertheless, the rest of us—MacArthur included—can all learn something from the Puritans, not only about the inseparable connection between faith and repentance, but also about the mature balance illustrated in these brief samples. It is a balance that one sees lacking at times in some of the presentations of the classical evangelical view. By sending believers back to their fruit as evidence of their conversion, without also emphasizing the reality and depth of remaining sin, we do risk undoing the Reformation's call to "fix our eyes on Jesus Christ, the author and finisher of our faith" (Heb. 12:2).

As I look out on the horizon, I am not one of those who sees the greatest threat to the health of the church to be antinomianism by itself, but the deadly combination of antinomianism *and* moralism. Having rejected the divine law, we have merely put our own taboos in its place. Many, this writer included, have not found the churches influenced by Lewis Sperry Chafer's "Higher Life" dispensationalism places of spiritual rest. The same spirit that condemns others so quickly excuses itself so readily. Unlike the antinomians among the English Puritans, who so emphasized

God's activity in election, justification, adoption, effectual calling, and preservation that they denied the biblical teaching concerning human responsibility, today's antinomians (Hodges, Ryrie, Cocoris, et al.) are spurred on by an emphasis on *human* activity in salvation. This will just as surely throw people back onto themselves for salvation as their greatest fears of "lordship salvation." If the working of God depends at every moment on our will, or decision, our "letting him have his way," there will be no end to our anxiety.

I have seen a spirit of self-righteousness in churches representing both positions. In some "lordship" churches (i.e., historic, evangelical bodies), I have seen soul-killing legalism, where the law is still given power to condemn the believer, when the gospel is supposed to have silenced its threats. And in the "no-lordship" groups of my youth, I have seen and experienced anxiety over whether we were letting God have his way with us, whether we were Spirit-filled and Spirit-led because we didn't have a "quiet time" today. Were we, after all, second-class, carnal Christians who would be ashamed in heaven and lose our rewards? Both groups would do well to heed the warning of Sibbes about "moderation":

> Men must not be too curious in prying into the weaknesses of others. We should labour rather to see what they have that is for eternity, to incline our heart to love them, than into that weakness which the Spirit of God will in time consume, to estrange us. Where most holiness is, there is most moderation, where it may be said without prejudice of piety to God and the good of others. We see in Christ a marvellous temper of absolute holiness, with great moderation. What had become of our salvation, if he had stood upon terms, and not stooped thus low unto us? We need not try to be more holy than Christ. . . . The Holy Ghost is content to dwell in smoky, offensive souls. O that the Spirit would breathe into our spirits the like merciful disposition![18]

It must be remembered, however, that Puritanism was a diverse movement. The leading figures—Perkins, Owen, Ames, Goodwin, Sibbes, and Hooker, were Reformed pastors who simply wanted to breathe new life into "dead orthodoxy," by showing how the objective work of Christ *for* us related to the subjective work of Christ *in* us. Nevertheless, some of the later Puritans moved steadily away from the centrality of Christ's objective work. For example, Joseph Alleine terrorized his congregations with the threat that, ". . . if you are not a holy, strict, and self-denying Christian, you cannot be saved."[19] God "has declared that they that shall enter into His hill must be of clean hands and a pure heart (Ps. xxiv 3,4)."[20] And yet, even Alleine warns, "Beware of this, O professing Christians; you are much in duties, but this one fly will spoil all the ointment. When you have done most and best, be sure to go out of yourselves to Christ; reckon your own righteousness as filthy rags (Phil iii 9; Is lxiv 6)."[21] But this is sandwiched in between such statements as the following: "Oh what a misery is this, to be out of the favour, yea, under the hatred of God; that God, who can as easily lay aside His nature and cease to be God, as not be contrary to you and detest you, *except you be changed and renewed.*"[22]

The Reformation staked its whole claim on the biblical doctrine of justification and every other truth followed as handmaidens, but for some of the Puritans, Alleine for one, the key element of reconciliation with God seems to be moral renewal. There is every reason to believe that many of Alleine's parishioners could have experienced a degree of assurance no more certain or lasting than Roman Catholic believers experienced. For the Reformers, and for the better Puritans, the accent fell on judicial verdict, not moral renewal, although both were clearly taught as inseparable acts of God. To preach to parishioners as if they were unconverted, in spite of the fact that they attended to the means of grace (Word and sacrament) created a growing suspicion in some Puritan churches that comfort was beyond the reach of the average Christian. One hoped to attain to this assurance someday, but it was too difficult a thing to expect all at once. Those who stressed preparation for conversion and the difficulty of attaining assurance did not deny a single evangelical doctrine; they simply moved the accent from Christ's doing and dying to the believer's, all the while denying any merit in human activity.

The Antinomian Controversy

At long last, we come to the debate that bears closest resemblance to the current controversy. We could, of course, refer to others: the Marrow controversy in Scotland and the threat of the Sandemanians, for instance. But we find in the so-called antinomian controversy of the 1630s in America an instructive parallel.

First, remember that the most decisive difference between the Reformers' view of assurance and the Puritans' was on the question of whether assurance is of the essence of faith. Calvin, for instance, did not assert that the believer never doubted; nor did he argue that everyone had the same degree of confidence in the promise of forgiveness. Nevertheless, he said, weak faith is still saving faith, and saving faith brings with it a certainty that Christ's righteousness has been imputed to my charge. The Puritans, however, wanted to give more room to Christian experience, it seems. Assurance could be attained and lost, depending on one's moral and spiritual condition. There were things one could do, methods that could be employed to build assurance. The question was never, *How* am I saved? They were perfectly evangelical and Protestant on that one. Rather, it was, How can I *know* that I'm saved? The question was not, Must a person have works if he claims he has faith? With Paul and James, both the Reformers and the Puritans were certain that works are necessary consequences of saving faith. But the Puritans' question was whether works were necessary conditions of the *assurance* of saving faith.

After the collapse of an intense revival in 1633, the New England Puritans were despondent. How could the marvelous preaching and moving of the Spirit dissipate so quickly? they wondered. The end of the revival "engendered a mood of acute religious anxiety," wrote David D. Hall. "How could they tell if they were saved or not?"[23] The spiritual depression, lasting from 1633 to 1636, led some New England pastors to preach moralism, introspection, and preparation for conversion and revival instead of preaching Christ-centered sermons directing the faithful from the threats of judgment to the gospel of grace. In fact, Massachusetts Bay colony governor John Winthrop, himself a supporter of introspective piety, nevertheless reported a dramatic effect of such preaching during this time: "A woman of Boston congregation, having been in much trouble of mind about her spiritual estate, at length grew into utter desperation, and could not endure to hear of any comfort, etc., so as one day she took her little infant and threw it into a well, and then came into the house and said, now she was sure she should be damned, for she had drowned her child."[24]

It was into this spiritual depression that the English Puritan John Cotton sailed as he assumed the pastorate of the distinguished Boston Church in 1633. Alister McGrath notes Cotton's own theological development: "In an early discussion of Revelation 3:20, he argued that conversion consists of an act of God, knocking at the door of man's heart, followed by an act of man, opening the door in order that God may enter. Once man has performed this necessary act, he may rest assured that God will do the rest." But Cotton began to rethink things shortly before he left for America:

> What if man's depravity is such that he could not prepare himself? In a development which parallels that of Luther, Cotton appears to have arrived at the insight that there is no saving preparation for grace prior to union with Christ. . . . Christ is given to the sinner on the basis of an absolute, not conditional, promise. As a result, Cotton makes faith itself the basis of man's assurance, rather than preparation or sanctification. Cotton's rejection of sanctification as the basis of assurance was based upon his conviction that this was to revert to the covenant of works from the covenant of grace.[25]

It is fascinating to see, as we do in Cotton's earlier thinking, an Arminian group within English Puritanism. The diversity within the Puritan movement, for example, can be seen in the duel between John Owen and Richard Baxter. They are both considered Puritans, and yet one was a staunch Calvinist, the other somewhat of a neonomian. As German pietism was a movement of some Lutherans from an objectively-oriented faith to a more introspective piety, so too a good number of Puritans could scarcely be recognized as successors to the Reformed legacy.

In America, however, Cotton found a lethargic populace regularly scourged with threats and calls to excessive self-examination. Despairing of ever attaining assurance of God's favor, many of the people gave up entirely, and New England fell into quite a secular period. Again the lesson was demonstrated: legalism produces antinomianism. Most of the New England pastors believed that there were things a person could do to prepare himself or herself for grace. Conversion was synergistic—that is, it came about as the human will cooperated with divine grace. One could not actually be regenerated by an act of the will, but the emphasis in preaching fell on human activity toward conversion. Faith was viewed more as an activity, whereas the Reformers viewed faith as a passive (reception).

For whatever reasons, John Cotton had become more aligned with the thinking of the Reformers (and, I think, the New Testament) after his move to Boston. One of his devoted parishioners, Anne Hutchinson, followed the trail of her pastor to Boston the following year. Distressed over what she characterized as the "legal preaching" of the "covenant of works instead of the covenant of grace" by the New England clergy, Anne gathered groups together to discuss the Scriptures. Eventually, she began to claim divine inspiration equal to Scripture, and it was this that caught the attention of the ministers. As she increasingly came under fire for her "revelations," Anne stepped up her heated attacks on the "works-righteousness" of the New England gospel. Now it must be said that Anne Hutchinson, in addition to being a strange person, was certainly an antinomian. Very often, charges of antinomianism by legalists are not seaworthy, but Anne clearly denied the necessary connection between faith and repentance, justification and sanctification, and relegated the latter to "works-righteousness." Every command, every requirement in Scripture, was viewed by Anne as a form of legalism.

John Cotton, however, remained a respected minister even though the controversy was quite disturbing to the peace. The principal pastors on the other side of the debate were Thomas Shepard, Thomas Hooker, and Peter Bulkeley. "The answer to anxiety," wrote Shepard, "lies in constant activity."[26] At times the New England Puritans appeared to be following a system more akin to the medieval penitential system, with assurance of God's favor being granted through successive stages of contrition, purgation, illumination, and finally union. For Cotton, again following the Reformers, union with Christ was not the *goal* of the Christian life, but the *source*. Cotton argued, quite traditionally, that we do not attain union through a series of stages; rather we are united to Christ immediately by the Holy Spirit through faith. His opponents, however, like many of their English contemporaries, followed a line closer to the medieval scheme. Mystical tendencies always have been influenced by a shift from the centrality of Christ to that of the Holy Spirit, and some of the pastors evidenced this. Shepard wanted Cotton to answer whether a person is *de facto* in Christ, or *in fieri* in Christ—in other words, in Christ immediately upon faith in him, or in process of becoming "in him." Cotton answered that it was the former. Of course, to hold the latter, as Shepard and company in fact did, was to desert Geneva for Rome on a very key point.

Cotton agreed that the fruit of repentance could be used as evidence of saving faith, but insisted that the basis of assurance must always be objective and external to us, with the exception of the internal witness of the Holy Spirit, and even that witness is attached to the objective Word. Again and again, in addition to Scripture (his ultimate authority), Cotton cited Calvin, such as this line from the *Institutes*: "The grace of God and the certainty of salvation and faith neither arise from nor depend on our obedience." In fact, Cotton constantly cited Calvin to defend his own position while quoting Bellarmine (the Roman Catholic defender of the Counter-Reformation) as an authority for the position of the opposing pastors.

Against Cotton, the pastors were almost unanimously agreed that the promise of salvation was conditional, like the land promise of the Old Testament: "Do this and you shall live." This, of course, was an unmistakable departure from Reformation theology, and Cotton declared,

> To give my Sanctification for an evident ground and cause, or matter of my Iustification, is to build my Iustification upon my Sanctification, and to go on in a Covenant of Works. This is the foundation of Popery. If my Iustification lyeth prostrate, that is altogether dark and hidden from mine eyes, I cannot prove my

selfe in a state of Grace by my Sanctification: For whilst I cannot beleeve that my Person is accepted in Iustification how then shall I be the more releeved by my Sanctification?[27]

In other words, if my faith is too weak to have full assurance based on an unconditional promise, how on earth can I expect to get any better handle on my assurance by turning inward and taking inventory?

It must be stated, too, that Cotton never did deny the necessity of self-examination. Nor did he ignore the person and work of the Holy Spirit in human experience. But, like the Reformers, he required that the person and work of Christ and the objective promise, held forth in Word and sacrament, be the court of appeals for comfort and assurance. How do I know I'm saved? Not because I've made a decision, nor because I see the evidence of moral improvement in my life, nor even because I believe. Rather, I know that I have been saved, that I am being saved, and that I will one day be saved because God has promised Christ and his righteousness to me. He is the object of my hope—that body crucified and risen, my guard against doubt and fear. Not only is Christ sufficient for my justification; he is sufficient for my assurance of being justified. And this has been the gospel embraced by evangelical men and women throughout the centuries. To ignore the past is, as has been often quoted, to be doomed to repeat it.

Like Anne Hutchinson's, the Dallas position is clearly what its critics insist it is: nothing short of the antinomian heresy. The gospel is distorted in some bizarre ways by Hodges, Ryrie, Cocoris, and the like. Terms are redefined. Salvation is called "free," then, in fact, they deny that faith is the gift of God. Not only is faith for them mere assent; they assert that it is not even necessary for a believer to continue giving his assent. Presumably, men or women moved by a rousing chorus of "Just As I Am" can later become atheists and still end up in heaven because they performed the one "little work" necessary for God to be stuck with them. Though I hesitate to use such strong language, the more I read from the Dallas side, the more I wonder how it is possible for professing evangelicals to deny the reality of the new birth and the efficacy of God's sovereign grace and to affirm the possibility of salvation apart from persevering faith in Christ, without recognizing their radical departure from biblical and historic Protestantism.

MacArthur's treatment is much closer to what I would recognize as *The Gospel According to Jesus*. And yet, it is odd to find perfectly solid, evangelical, and Reformed definitions of justification with marvelous statements about salvation being the work of God alone and then, on the next page, to run into what appear to be implicit contradictions of those statements. At least the solid evangelical language is there, however, whereas one hardly knows where to begin with the Hodges position.

We will not settle for either moralism or antinomianism—for the confusion of faith and works or for their divorce. And may God steady us as we climb onto the shoulders of our predecessors to gain a perspective of the vista behind us, so that we can participate in rightly dividing the Word of truth for a new generation.

An American Tale 7

Paul Schaefer

Some people who have read with great interest the recent debate between John MacArthur and Zane Hodges (among others) over the concept of "lordship salvation" may be surprised to learn that this controversy has been an ongoing concern among Evangelicals in America throughout the twentieth century.[1] Indeed, a vast body of literature exists that argues the one side or the other, some of it quite acrimonious and vitriolic in tone, as proponents of the one label adherents of the other "heretics" and peddlers of "another gospel." Quite often throughout the century, this argument over the relationship between Christ's call to discipleship and his forgiving and justifying work has engaged some of the key leaders of what can be termed "confessional Reformed" Evangelicalism (so called because of their adherence to the Reformed confessions of faith) against key evangelical leaders influenced by Keswick teaching (also often dispensationalists). Interestingly, the latest blasts come from within dispensationalism itself.[2] Why such acrimony? Why such hostility?

In order to get a handle on these questions, this chapter will detail two earlier disagreements over Christ's lordship as it relates to salvation and will briefly survey the approach taken by the opposing sides in some of their training materials on Christian growth before moving to an analysis of the MacArthur/Hodges conflict. Evangelicalism today and historically offers a number of views on Christian growth other than the confessional Reformed or Keswick and/or dispensational ones (Lutheran, contemplative, Wesleyan, and Pentecostal, for example), and no slight is intended in not discussing these traditions.[3] The debate as it concerns the lordship question has most often arisen when Reformed confessionalists and Keswickians and/or dispensationalists argue with and respond to one another.

The names involved will be quite familiar to many readers of Christian literature—B. B. Warfield, Lewis Sperry Chafer, Steven Barabas, John Murray, Bill Bright, Francis Cosgrove, Jerry Bridges, John MacArthur, and Zane Hodges. When discussing the debates (Warfield/Chafer, Barabas/Murray, MacArthur/Hodges), this essay will refer to only those books or articles that touched off the disputes. The goal is to show the primary motivations behind each speaker's position and what troubles him most about his adversary's stance.

I hope to be as dispassionate as possible in my presentation of the relevant history. Nevertheless, although I grew up amidst teaching most closely aligned to the dispensational variety, my present sympathies lie both personally and pastorally with the spokespersons for the confessional Reformed approach. I believe this theology more truly expresses the viewpoint of Scripture than does the theology of my dispensational brothers and sisters. That said, I seek to be fair to both sides, for this is a debate between Christians, and undue vitriol merely exacerbates the tension.

Two points should be noted before moving directly into the tale. The first has to do with theological foundations. Although those of the confessional Reformed stripe tend towards the use of the "covenant" model and those from the dispensational camp speak of "dispensations" when approaching the lines of demarcation in God's plan for humanity,[4] both groups claim strong adherence to the Reformation dicta *sola gratia, sola fide,* and *sola scriptura.* In other words, both affirm that salvation is by *grace alone* received through *faith alone* and that God reveals this salvation in *Scripture alone,* which is inerrant and "the only infallible rule of faith and practice."

It should be noted, secondly, that this debate is far more than simply an American matter. Rather, it must be seen in an even greater historical context. In the history of Christian thought, particularly Protestant Christian thought, the relationship between the believer's faith and his good works has been debated hotly time and again. One merely needs to think of Luther refuting Agricola, Calvin blasting the Libertines, or the Puritans of both old and New England encountering people with "antinomian" leanings in order to place the present difficulties in a much needed historical perspective.[5] In other words, the road has been traveled before, and there really is "nothing new under the sun" (Eccles. 1:9).

Protestant Christianity at its most orthodox has always proclaimed the assuring and comforting doctrine "justification by grace alone because of Christ alone, received through faith alone" as well as the caveat that a true faith will be fruitful in good works. Indeed, a truly biblical Christianity always stands poised between two soul-destroying heresies of an *antinomianism* on one side that says one can be a Christian without saving grace causing any real effective change in one's life and a *legalism* on the other that tells us we need more than Christ for salvation. The one tears apart justification and sanctification as the twin blessings of union with Christ, and the other adds an ingredient (under various guises) to reliance on the Savior and his work alone for our redemption. The apostle Paul certainly knew this; just take a brief glance at Romans 6 and Colossians 2. And so with all this in mind, we come to our "American Tale."

Not All Quiet on the Western Front: The Uneasy Alliance

As the "guns of August" fell silent in Europe, marking the end of the First World War, a fierce battle raged among the proponents of what has come to be known historically as fundamentalism. The term *fundamentalism,* not coined until the 1920s (that is, late in the movements' own history), refers to that coalition of "conservative evangelicals" that began to emerge in the closing years of the nineteenth century and gathered force as a critic of "modernism," both theological and social, in the first three decades of the twentieth century.[6] This coalition, comprising people and groups with divergent theological traditions and interpretations of the Bible, all stood firm in their denunciation of antisupernaturalism and of attacks on biblical fidelity, and all affirmed certain points of "fundamental" doctrine, such as the inerrancy of Scripture, the reality of biblical miracles, the virgin birth of Christ, the substitutionary atonement and physical resurrection of Christ, and the reality of a literal second coming.[7]

But all was not unity and felicity among these allies. While they waged war against the true foe of modernism, dissension continually broke out among the ranks and even among the leaders of the fundamentalist alliance. Points of contention included divergent views on the relationship between Christianity and culture and differences over particular eschatological details,[8] but a major rupture occurred whenever those inspired by Keswick teachings,[9] usually also those with dispensational leanings, locked horns with confessionalist Reformed, most notably the Princetonians,[10] on the doctrine of the Christian life.

One such eruption occurred in 1918 when Lewis Sperry Chafer, a dispensational Bible teacher who was later to be a founder, president, and professor of systematic theology at Dallas Theological Seminary, penned the practical handbook *He That Is Spiritual*.[11] The critique came in *The Princeton Review* of April 1919 from none other than the "lion of Princeton" himself, B. B. Warfield.[12] Thus, the debate offered here engaged two significant figures in this uneasy alliance of co-belligerents to modernism.

Chafer opened his discussion directly with one point that would continue to disturb the confessionalist Reformed throughout the century—the doctrine of the "carnal Christian." He arrived at a basis for classifying all humans as under three categories, "natural," "spiritual," and "carnal," through his reading of 1 Corinthians 2:9–3:4—an explanation made famous largely by the notes of the original *Scofield Reference Bible*.[13] Though saved, Chafer wrote, carnal Christians walk according to the dictates of the world and show little appetite for true spiritual meat, only being able to bear milk. He concluded, "the 'carnal' Christian is . . . characterized by a walk that is on the same plane as that of the 'natural' man. . . . The objectives and affections are centered in the same unspiritual sphere as that of the 'natural' man. In contrast to such a fleshly walk, we read: 'This I say then, Walk in the Spirit, and ye shall not fulfill the lusts of the flesh.' This is spirituality."[14]

Chafer continued, "there are two great changes which are possible to human experience—the change from a 'natural' man to the saved man, and the change from the 'carnal' man to the 'spiritual' man." He also admitted that when one is saved through faith in Christ, he "may at the same time wholly yield to God and enter at once a life of true surrender." Yet, for Chafer, this was not an immediate, necessary consequence, for the two changes describe separate events in the Christian life. Indeed, he contended, "many Christians are 'carnal,'" and are in need of finding the biblical "steps" toward a "real adjustment to the Spirit."[15]

Even though he demanded two classes of Christians, Chafer harshly repudiated some traditional perfectionist terms like "second blessing" and "higher life" as "man-made" and "perverted statements of the doctrines of sanctification and perfection." Such ideas, he argued, lead believers down the unfortunate road of looking for experiences rather than knowing the "exact conditions" upon which the "transformation" from carnal to spiritual comes as recorded in the "exact words of revelation."[16] All true believers, he noted, are regenerated, indwelt, baptized, and sealed with and by the Spirit.[17] Nevertheless, one need not "abide in Christ" or "walk by the Spirit" to be a true Christian, for while the Holy Spirit is "in" all believers, he is not "upon" all. So then, how, according to Chafer, does one make the transition from carnal Christianity to "true spiritual living"?[18]

The reality of Spirit-filled life, Chafer contended, arises in the believer, "not by struggling" but by "the outflow of the limitless life of God." Chafer distinguished between those who try to *imitate* the Christian life, an unspiritual characteristic, and those who know the joy of divine power *imparted*. At this point his dispensationalism came into play as he sought to warn those in the "age of grace" to abandon "living by rules":

Grace teachings which anticipate *all* the walk and warfare of the believer will be found in portions of the Gospels and The Acts and throughout the Epistles of the New Testament. It is a complete system and requires no additions from the law. It incorporates many of the principles which were in the law, but these are always so restated as to be in exact harmony with the position and liberty of the one who is 'inlawed to Christ.' . . . No Christian is under the law as a rule of life.[19]

Lest he be accused of an absolute antinomianism, for indeed this goes far in jettisoning the classic Reformation teaching on the third use of the law,[20] Chafer advocated standards that would place the Spirit-filled Christian (but hence not the carnal Christian) "in a position wherein he cannot do the things which he otherwise would." Nevertheless, he also believed that such standards must be viewed as "another complete system" in "exact harmony with the positions of grace," for "in the demands of the law there is no consideration of the most vital activities which are anticipated under grace—prayer, a life of faith, and soul-winning service." Divine enabling is needed, and the law cannot provide that.[21]

This divine enabling comes, Chafer held, as one is filled with the Spirit. And so at this point, after defining the problem of "carnal Christianity" and describing what true spirituality is not, Chafer introduced the "three conditions" necessary for "a right adjustment to the Spirit": confession of known sin, yielding all of oneself to God, and walking in or by the power of the Holy Spirit. He rejected any view that told Christians to wait for a personal filling or that described the filling as happening after a period of intense prayer. Rather, "It is the *normal* work of the Spirit to fill the one who is rightly adjusted to God. The Christian will always be filled while he is making the work of the Spirit possible in this life."[22]

Chafer supplied his first condition, "confession of known sin," as the remedy for "grieving the Spirit." Since, he argued, no person "can deal intelligently with unknown sin," God calls only for a confession of "known sin" in order for a person to move from the carnal state to the spiritual state: "The issue is . . . a well-defined wrong, about which the child of God has been made conscious by the Spirit."[23] Carefully avoiding calling all conditions of mental, physical, or emotional distress or unhappiness "known sin," Chafer advised praying for "greater understanding" when such things occur. Again, the issue for Chafer was confession of "known sin" as revealed by the "exact direction of the Word." He summarized, "The blessing [of Spirit-filling] does not depend upon sinless perfection; it is a matter of not grieving the Spirit. It is not an issue concerning *unknown* sin: it is an attitude of the heart that is willing always instantly to confess every *known* sin."[24]

The second condition the Christian needs to fulfill to be spiritual, Chafer contended, deals with the problem of "quenching the Spirit." Such quenching comes, he remarked, when one refuses to "yield" to the revealed will of God and continues to "resist" and "say no" to God. His proposed cure consisted of a "full dedication": ". . . we cannot be rightly adjusted [to the Holy Spirit], or be *spiritual,* until we have yielded to the mind and will of God."[25] Continuing his theme of not only distinguishing but separating justification from sanctification, Chafer stressed that such yielding is not commanded by God; instead, "it is something we *should* do because we are saved."[26]

As believers yield to God, Chafer held, God then consecrates them for spiritual service. Indeed, before one can really serve God, Chafer exhorted, one must yield, for "yieldedness" consists in "willing," not "doing." "The issue, it is clear, is not that of resolving to *do* anything: it is rather that of an attitude of willingness that Another may do according to the last degree of His blessed will."[27] Indeed, it means following Jesus' own example: willing to *go* wherever God sends, willing to *be* whatever God wants, and willing to *do* whatever God commands.

Such heavy demands, he explained, could never be carried out without yielding: "There can be no true spirituality until surrender is made." We can never produce our own spirituality, he demanded, "but we can '*let*' it be done in us by another." According to Chafer, "in this little word '*let*' is compressed the whole Bible teaching concerning the believer's responsibility toward the possible manifestation of Christ in the daily life by the Spirit."

Once yielded, and only then, the believer, now Spirit-filled, experiences effectual prayer, celestial joy, and perpetual fruit.[28]

Chafer explained his third condition for true spirituality under the positive rubric of "walking in the Spirit." While the believer ceases to quench and grieve the Spirit by confession of known sin and by yielding all of himself to God, he walks spiritually by fully relying on the Spirit's power. Interestingly, Chafer described this as something the believer must "do." This doing, however, arises only in yielding, for only the Spirit can provide the power for spiritual walking: "[Walking] is an unbroken reliance upon the Spirit to do what He has come to do and what He alone can do."[29] Thus, while Chafer admonished believers to be active in the "fight of faith," he contended that this fight stands in contrast to a fight whereby the believer tries to live the Christian life under his own strength: "Its [the fight's] realization is never by a human resolution or struggle or the resources of the flesh. . . . The child of God has an all-engaging responsibility of *continuing* in an attitude of reliance upon the Spirit."[30]

This is necessarily so, Chafer continued, because God's standards of spiritual conduct are so high and because the believer faces three great enemies in the spiritual fight: the world, the flesh, and the devil. After detailing this battle, Chafer began the longest section of his treatise, an exposition of his understanding of the doctrine of sanctification.[31] Two main points in this examination are germane to our discussion of the controversy over lordship in twentieth-century American evangelicalism.

First, Chafer separated salvation into two parts: a salvation to "safety" from the "penalty" of sin and a salvation into "sanctity of daily life." Both, he demanded, are conditional through a person's "faith"; yet, here faith also is distinguished. Faith for "safety," he taught, implies an "act" whereas faith for "sanctity" implies an "attitude":

> Salvation from the guilt and penalty of sin is wrought for us the *moment* we believe. . . . We are saved from the power of sin as we believe. The one who has been justified by an act of faith must now *live* by faith. . . . there are a multitude of saints whose sin nature has been judged and every provision made on the divine side for

a life of victory and glory to God who are not now realizing a life of victory. They have only to enter by faith into the saving grace from the power and dominion of sin. This is the reality of a "walk," a "race," a "warfare." It is a *constant* attitude. . . . Sinners are not saved until they trust the Savior, and saints are not victorious until they trust the Deliverer.[32]

In making this Savior/Deliverer distinction, Chafer showed the way he interpreted Romans 6:1–8 on the believer's union with Christ. He believed his to be a *positional* union, whereby the "sin nature" is judged as dead to us: "The old nature must be judged in order that God may be free to deal with it in the believer's daily life. . . . The 'old man' is said to have been 'crucified with him,' and we are 'dead with him,' 'buried with him' and are partaking in his 'resurrection life.' . . . In that new sphere and by that new power the Christian may now walk."[33]

The key word there is *may*, because Chafer strongly rejected any notion that argued eradication of the disposition to sin: ". . . the 'old man' will remain active, apart from sufficient control."[34] Chafer thus understood union to be *positional* because it provides a "possible deliverance": "We are already cojoined to Christ by the baptism of the Spirit . . . which places us positionally beyond the judgments of sin and we are therefore free to enter the experience of the eternal power and victory of His resurrection. . . . Believing this, we will fearlessly *claim* our position in His boundless grace and dare to enter the life of victory." The believer makes this claim by "reckon[ing that] the divine requirements for our deliverance . . . have been met perfectly [through Christ's substitutionary death] and [by] believ[ing] that, because of this, we can now 'walk in newness of life.'"[35]

The definition of the heretofore mentioned "old man" leads to the second key point in Chafer's exposition of sanctification. Chafer argued, "The unregenerate have but one nature, while the regenerate have two. There is but one fallen nature, which is from Adam, and one new nature, which is from God." Lest he be accused of some type of spiritual schizophrenia, Chafer added, "Personality—the Ego—remains the same individuality through all the operations of grace, though it experiences the greatest possible advancement, transformation and regeneration from its lost estate in Adam, to the positions and possessions of a Son of God in Christ."[36]

If a believer were to ask Chafer, "Who am I in reality?" he would answer with a *positional/experiential* dialectic: "*Positionally*, the 'old man' has been put off forever. *Experientially*, the 'old man' remains as an active force in the life which can be controlled only by the power of God." Chafer understood the conflict described in Romans 7:14–25 this way. He took it as a picture of a conflict between the two natures in the believer and concluded that it portrayed defeat, because the "new 'I'" is "isolated from the enabling power of the Spirit." Although he did not use its language, one gathers that he would have concurred with the saying that a believer must get "self off the throne" and move out of the defeat of Romans 7 to "put Christ on the throne" (be Spirit-filled) and so come into the victory of Romans 8.[37]

Chafer, so strongly repudiating any notion of eradication of the old nature, supplied the notion of "control" as God's means to deal with the sinful nature still in the believer: "This it may be stated is one of the most important undertakings of the Spirit *in* and *for* the believer. He proposes both to *control* the old nature and to *manifest* the new."[38] While Chafer's whole notion of being filled emphasizes some type of "lordship decision" separate from "the decision to be saved" (to use revivalist parlance), he concluded with an exhortation that such filling was just the beginning of a progressive sanctification. The two natures, he taught, stand side by side until death. The believer is not to seek to eradicate the old man but rather to have a "definite reliance" on the Spirit and from there to "walk." He concluded:

> [This] walk is step by step and this demands *constant* appropriation of the power of God. . . . It is a "walk," a "race," a "fight." All this speaks of continuation. . . . What then is true spirituality? It is the unhindered manifestation of the indwelling Spirit. These blessed realities are all provided for in the presence and power of the Spirit and will normally be produced by the Spirit in the Christian who is not grieving the Spirit, but has confessed every *known* sin; who is not quenching the Spirit, but is yielded to God; and who is walk-

ing in the Spirit by an attitude of dependence upon His power alone.[39]

Warfield responded to *He That Is Spiritual* with a substantial, six-page review. (Most reviews in *The Princeton Theological Review* were one or two pages long.) He asserted right at the beginning that Chafer's teaching on the Christian life tried to combine elements from two incompatible theological systems. This clash of systems, he thought, resulted from Chafer's intermingling of the teachings from his background in the Southern Presbyterian Church (hence, confessional Reformed or what Warfield called "evangelicalism") with those from his "long associat[ion] . . . with a coterie of . . . 'Bible Teachers.'" From the latter he learned "that curious religious system (at once curiously pretentious and curiously shallow) which the Higher Life leaders of the middle of the last century brought into vogue. . . ."[40] Warfield contrasted the origins of these two systems by calling the first a "product of the . . . Reformation . . . know[ing] no determining power in the religious life but the grace of God," while the second in "all its forms—modifications and mitigations alike" seemed to be coming "straight from the laboratory of John Wesley" and was "incurably Arminian, subjecting all gracious workings of God to human determining."[41]

Chafer's rejection of some of the terminology of former Higher Life advocates,[42] Warfield contended, "hew[s] . . . a rather narrow line, for he does teach that there are two kinds of Christian, . . . and he does teach that it is quite unnecessary for spiritual men to sin and that the way is fully open to them to live a life of unbroken victory if they choose to do so."[43] Warfield even listed a large number of places where Chafer used the "vocabulary [of] . . . his Higher Life friends" with expressions like "claiming it," "unbroken victory," "realize *at once*," and "moment by moment triumph." Warfield's conclusion: even with Chafer's rejection of some terms, his "teaching is indistinguishable from what is ordinarily understood by the doctrine of a 'second blessing,' 'a second work of grace,' 'the higher life.'"[44]

Warfield vigorously attacked Chafer's notions of "double salvation" and of "two natures" in the saved person. He did so, first, by asserting that Chafer's whole idea of a double salvation from the penalty and power of sin, both salvations to be claimed by faith, was itself Arminian in flavor:

> No doubt what we are first led to say of this [Chafer's exposition of double salvation] is that here is the quintessence of Arminianism. God saves no one—He only makes salvation *possible* for men. Whether it becomes *actual* or not depends absolutely on their own act. It is only by their act that it is made *possible* for God to save them. But it is equally true that here is the quintessence of the Higher Life teaching, which merely emphasizes that part of this Arminian scheme which refers to the specific matter of sanctification.[45]

Second, Warfield contended that Chafer's teaching on "two natures" in the regenerate arose from his allergic reaction to anything smacking of an "eradication" theory. The either–or mentality of Chafer in arguing for either the eradication of the old man or the control of the old man by the filling of the Spirit, Warfield believed, was unjustified:

> In point of fact, both "eradication" and "control" are true. God delivers us from our sinful nature, not indeed by "abruptly" but by progressively eradicating it, and meanwhile controlling it. For the new nature which God gives us is not an absolutely new somewhat, alien to our personality, inserted into us, but our old nature itself remade—a veritable recreation, or making of all things new.[46]

In the end, Warfield contended, Chafer left the reader with a great paradox. He might call it two natures in one person, but according to Warfield, Chafer presented two people—an old man from nature who can never be saved and a new man from outside nature who is the object of God's grace. Warfield wrote: "[Chafer with his 'two natures' idea] does not seem to see that thus the man is not saved at all: a different, newly created, man is substituted for him. When the old man is got rid of—and that the old man has to be ultimately got rid of [Chafer] does not doubt—the saved man that is left is not at all the old man that was to be saved, but a new man that has never needed any saving."[47]

As much as anything else, the whole conception of the so-called carnal Christian disturbed Warfield. He felt, in fact, that Chafer could have been "preserved . . . from his regrettable dalliance with the Higher Life formulas" and the splitting of Christians into two types, by following something Chafer himself had written ("not well expressed it is true"):[48]

> In the Bible, the divine offer and condition for the cure of sin in an unsaved person is crystallized into one word, *"believe"*; for the forgiveness of sin with the unsaved is only offered as an indivisible part of the whole divine work of salvation. The saving work of God includes many mighty undertakings other than the forgiveness of sin, and salvation depends only upon *believing.* It is not possible to separate some one issue from the whole of His saving grace, such as forgiveness, and claim this apart from the indivisible whole. It is, therefore, a grievous error for the unsaved person to seek forgiveness of his sins as a separate issue. A sinner minus his sins would not be a Christian; for salvation is more than subtraction: it is addition. . . . Thus the sin question with the unsaved will be cured as a part of, but never separate from the whole divine work of salvation, and this salvation depends upon believing.[49]

In concurring with this statement, Warfield added (even using certain terms of Chafer's), ". . . salvation is a unit, and . . . he who is united to Jesus Christ by faith receives in Him not only justification—salvation from the *penalty* of sin—but also sanctification—salvation from the *power* of sin—both 'safety' and 'sanctity.'"

To a degree, Warfield must have been baffled at how someone who argued as Chafer had could then turn around and teach that there are two kinds of Christians. Yet, Chafer did just that. Warfield responded, "It is a grievous error to teach that a true believer in Christ can stop short in 'carnality.'" Indeed, Warfield continued, Chafer's characterization of the carnal man actually "assigns to the lower class [of Christians] practically all the marks of the unregenerate man."[50] Warfield recognized that Chafer loyally taught progressive sanctification, but Chafer also held strongly to his two types of Christians. The final statement in Warfield's review encapsulates the confessional Reformed problem with the concept that there are two types of believers:

. . . the remainders of the flesh in the Christian do not constitute his characteristic. He is in the Spirit and is walking, with however halting steps, by the Spirit; and it is to all Christians, not to some, that the great promise is given, "Sin shall not have dominion over you," and the great assurance is added, "Because ye are not under the law but under grace." He who believes in Jesus Christ is under grace, and his whole course, in its process and in its issue alike, is determined by grace, and therefore, having been predestined to be conformed to the image of God's Son, he is surely being conformed to that image, God Himself seeing to it that he is not only called and justified but also glorified. You may find Christians at every stage of this process, for it is a process through which all must pass; but you will find none who will not in God's own good time and way pass through every stage of it. There are not two kinds of Christians, although there are Christians at every conceivable stage of advancement. . . .[51]

Chafer responded to Warfield in a quite extended footnote covering pages 78–80 of the 1919 edition of *He That Is Spiritual.* He reproached Warfield on two levels. First, he contended that Warfield's strong emphasis on the sovereignty of God could lead to a "fatalism, wherein there is no place for prayer, no motive for the wooing of God's love, no ground for condemnation, no occasion for evangelistic appeal, and no meaning to very much Scripture. . . ."[52] The will, Chafer agreed, must certainly be "moved" by God for someone to come to Christ; nevertheless, he asserted that "believing" and "yielding" (or salvation 1 for "safety" and salvation 2 for "sanctity") both "depend upon divinely enabled human choice." Warfield's criticism of Chafer's emphasis on "well-defined human acts and attitudes" brought Chafer's scorn. These acts and attitudes, he felt, were "evidently Biblical"; to reject them left a person with an "arbitrary theological theory."[53]

His second objection to Warfield came as he replied to the long statement at the end of Warfield's review (quoted above). He agreed with Warfield that "there are varying degrees of carnality as there are varying degrees of spirituality," but further criticized Warfield for failing to take full note of what Chafer termed the "two well-defined classes of believers." Castigating Warfield for confusing the "change from carnality to spirituality" with "Christian growth [which] is undoubtedly a process," Chafer argued that "spirituality" is an "immediate" possession of any believer who has responded to God with the previously mentioned three conditions. However, such a one might still be quite "immature." He concluded, "Christian experience bears unfailing testimony to two outstanding facts: (1) There is an abrupt change from the carnal to the spiritual when the Biblical conditions are met. And (2) there is an abrupt loss of spiritual blessing whenever there has been a yielding to sin."[54]

But frankly, does this statement not sum up Warfield's concern? The continual burden in Chafer's whole scheme is put on individual choice. Power from God is only *possible* according to him. Indeed, the quotation leads to an intriguing question: Can a person pop back and forth from the "spiritual man" to the "carnal man"? A person once told me (and this is an extreme, but an actual, example), "I was a 'carnal Christian' for an hour today; then I confessed my sin, yielded to God, and I am now a 'spiritual Christian,' walking in the Spirit." As Mr. Spock would say, "Fascinating."

Also, Warfield did not deny human responsibility; he merely asserted the *actual* triumph of grace in the believer's life. He believed both that every true Christian is "the spiritual man"— even the most immature—and that progressive sanctification is an accurate description of the way in which the Christian enters the fray in God's power against the world, the flesh, and the devil. What he rejected was the need for a "crisis event" whereby a Christian passed from one category, "carnal," to another category, "spiritual." It must be added that Chafer's rebuke to Warfield that Warfield should support his teaching with more biblical exposition is quite unfortunate. Just proof-texting, as Chafer frequently did, does not constitute exegesis.[55]

In reality, both men sought to undergird their ideas from Scripture, but both also approached the matter of Christian spirituality through the lens of certain theological principles. Chafer spoke of the need to avoid "arbitrary theological theory" and the need to follow the "exact words of Scripture." Nevertheless, his dispensationalism, his "two natures" theory, and his focus on meeting "exact conditions" and "claiming spirituality" all affected his reading of the Bible as much as Warfield's emphasis on divine sovereignty and on regeneration meaning that God both controls by the power of the Spirit the remnants of indwelling sin and progressively eradicates them in the one whom he has remade, as that person grows in faith.

The amount of time and space taken here to review the Chafer/Warfield debate, although considerable, is easily justifiable. The issues contested encapsulate the warp and woof of the continuing controversy as it has come down to us in America. Let us turn now to a debate that marks a second round in the controversy.

From Fundamentalism to Evangelicalism: The Tale Continues

By the mid-1930s, the old fundamentalist coalition began to disintegrate and redefine itself. The break-up of old Princeton and the subsequent forming of Westminster Seminary; splits in the Northern Presbyterian and Baptist denominations, with some conservatives leaving and others staying to try to stem the modernist tide; ruptures even among the newly formed conservative denominations; the rise of new and the strengthening of existing independent and interdenominational parachurch groups and schools—all these factors pose difficulties when trying to define the nature of modern conservative evangelicalism.[56] Since the 1930s, "conservative evangelical" has usually been the term used as a catch-all label for those who have maintained a concern for biblical authority, the historical Jesus and his substitutionary death, the necessity of conversion, the need for Christians to grow in faith, and the "blessed hope" of a literal second coming.

The debate on Christ's lordship has taken some interesting turns in the last five decades as well. In our media age Christians have been exposed to so many varieties of teaching on the Christian life that a demarcation of where exactly an individual teacher or group stands gets quite muddied. On the other hand, some debates have become clearer. Before moving to the difficult job of assessing current evangelical positions on our subject, a presentation of a second debate which has clarified the controversy, that between

Steven Barabas of Wheaton College[57] and John Murray of Westminster Seminary,[58] might help to show further the tensions over "lordship."

Barabas, essentially writing a history of the Keswick movement in *So Great Salvation* (1952), provided a thoughtful and sensitive description of the Keswick teaching which, although it has English roots, has so influenced many American Christians. But Barabas's intent was not merely to describe what he called "one of the most interesting religious phenomena of our time."[59] He also commended the Keswick teachings: "We find . . . that both in teaching and in practice Keswick proceeds on scriptural lines. It tells us that practical holiness is *possible*. God has made it so."[60] At times his enthusiasm for Keswick led to unfortunate exaggeration. For example:

> It must be granted that in its doctrine of sanctification by faith Keswick has restored to the Church an emphasis that is strictly Biblical. . . . [T]he doctrine of sanctification by faith was allowed to lie dormant for centuries, unknown and unappreciated except by a few . . . Christians. *It remained for Keswick to call the attention of the Church to it.*[61]

No mention was made of dispensationalism by Barabas, for not all Keswick teachers have been dispensationalists.[62] Indeed, at one point Barabas commended Charles Hodge's definition of sin (following the Westminster Shorter Catechism, question 14) as one that "every Keswick speaker I know of would subscribe to without question."[63] Chafer also made use of the same definition, but whereas Hodge had spoken of transgression or lack of conformity to *divine law*, Chafer's dispensationalism forced him to make a slight, but important, change: "Sin has been well defined, from a study of the whole testimony of the Word of God, to be 'any violation of, or want of conformity to, *the revealed will of God*.'"[64]

Even without the dispensationalism, however, Barabas's teachings maintained much of the same flavor as Chafer's. He asserted that there are two types of Christians, acknowledging that "defeat and failure" rather than "victory" are the "usual experience of most Christians."[65] Barabas, of course, abhorred this situation and desired "defeated Christians" to use Keswick teachings for the remedy, since Keswick regards itself as a "spiritual clinic" instructing "that a life of victory over conscious sin is the rightful heritage of every child of God. The *normal* experience of every Christian should be one of victory instead of constant defeat."[66] The question is, How does one move from this "defeat" to the "normalcy of victory"?

Like Chafer, Barabas focused on Romans 6:1–8, but he preferred the term "imputed sanctification" to "positional." Nevertheless, he also spoke of possibly needing to be actualized, rather than something more definitive, when describing this faith union of the believer with Christ:

> It is not enough for us just to *know* by our union with Christ in His death upon the cross we have been freed from the dominion of sin. That freedom is only potential. It must be progressively realized in daily experience, and this is done by walking in the Spirit. Christ is our sanctification . . . and all sanctification is dependent primarily upon His work. The Holy Spirit is our sanctifier. He renders real and operative our death to sin and life to God. Unless the Holy Spirit is given His rightful place in the life of the Christian, then even though historically and judicially he was crucified with Christ, the experience of the "wretched man" in Romans vii will be the result.[67]

Barabas made much of the doctrine of "progressive sanctification," which he defined as "a process, . . . that gradual transformation, by the Holy Spirit, of the believer into the likeness of Christ." He contrasted it with regeneration from whence "it begins" by arguing that "regeneration is not capable of degrees; no one is more or less regenerate than another. Sanctification, on the other hand, does admit of degrees."[68] Yet, Barabas also taught that the "experience" of sanctification begins with a "crisis" decision:

> This decision marks the greatest crisis in a person's life. To cease directing one's own life . . . : to say to God, "Lord I abdicate the throne of my life in order that Thou mayest rule in every detail of

my life"—this is life's greatest decision. It is the major, the supreme
decision of life, and it cannot be but a crisis, a turning point in life.
Anyone who goes through this experience with a full realization
of all that it means, will very likely go through an agonizing crisis.
For many people the crisis is prolonged—perhaps even over years—
and the decision is piecemeal; for some there are stages in the crisis and in the decision; and then for a few, of course, there is hardly
any struggle in making the decision. . . . Such a decision should
normally be made at regeneration, but frequently it is not; but if
it does not come then, it must come later. The decision is the
inescapable condition of progressive sanctification.[69]

Murray began his review of Barabas by congratulating him on
a book well-written, with a "useful survey" and a clear enuncia-
tion of the "Keswick message." Murray also stated several areas
of appreciation of the Keswick teaching: its recognition of "the
once-for-allness of the victory over sin secured for the believer in
virtue of his union with Christ," its emphasis on the progressive
nature of sanctification "in connection with which the believer's
responsibility is to be fully exercised," and its stress on the work
and presence of the Spirit in the believer's life. He concluded, "We
need only elementary appreciation of the claims of Christ upon
his disciples to understand how significant was the rehabilitation
of such truths as these in an age when evangelical fervour had
fallen to a very low ebb."[70]

Murray, however, had grave reservations about Keswick's claim
to be a "convention 'for the promotion of *scriptural* holiness.'" He
contended that Keswick teaching actually reflects a "defective
view of holiness and of its demands."[71] These concerns he laid out
quite systematically as (1) an inadequate view of indwelling sin
in the believer; (2) a misunderstanding of the whole question of
eradication, suppression, or counteraction to sin; (3) a failure to
do full justice to Romans 6; (4) a corresponding failure to do justice to Romans 7:14–25; and (5) altogether too great an emphasis on the need for a "crisis." Because Murray expressed himself
so clearly,[72] the reader is here offered some of his own statements
on each point:

(1) While Keswick stresses the gravity of sin, there is still an underestimation of the consequence for the believer of remaining indwelling sin. . . . If sin still dwells in the believer, if there is still a tendency to sin . . . , then we ought always to be conscious of that sin. . . . To fail to be conscious of it amounts either to hypocrisy or self-deception. To have sin in us and not be conscious of it is itself grave sin; it is culpable ignorance or culpably ignoring. . . . [I]ndwelling sin is defiling and it defiles the holiest of the believer's thoughts, words, and actions.

(2) . . . [I]t is by progressive eradication of inward corruption that we are progressively conformed to the image of Christ. . . . [I]t is only as we are sanctified within that we can be sanctified in what is more overt and voluntary. [This] eradication, of course, . . . will not be complete until sanctification is complete. . . . Barabas' averment to the effect that on Warfield's position [on eradication] "it should be practically, if not entirely, impossible to sin" . . . towards the end of the believer's life evinces again the failure to assess the gravity and liability of any remaining corruption, a gravity of which Warfield took full account.

(3) The freedom from the dominion of sin which Paul speaks of [in Romans 6] is the *actual* possession of every one who is united to Christ. It is not merely *positional* victory which every believer has secured. . . . This victory is received by faith in Christ and in effectual calling. . . . But it is not simply positional, far less is it potential; it is actual. And because it is actual it is experimental. To speak of freedom from the dominion of sin in terms other than the actual as . . . experimental is to indulge in an abstraction. . . . It is true there are differing degrees in which the "reckoning" to which Paul exhorts in Romans 6 is applied and brought to expression in the life and experience of believers. But the victory over sin is not secured by the "reckoning"; it is secured by virtue of union with Christ in that initial faith comprised in effectual calling and is therefore the position of every believer, however tardy may be his advance in the path of progressive sanctification. . . . If we fail to make account of this basic and decisive breach with sin, specifically with the rule and power of sin, which occurs when a person is united to Christ in the initial saving response to the gospel, it is an impoverished and distorted view of salvation in Christ that we

entertain and our doctrine of sanctification is correspondingly impaired.

(4) It is a bold assertion to describe the struggle of Romans 7:14ff. as one of defeat and that categorically and without qualification. . . . Anyone imbued with sensitivity to the demands of holiness and who yearns to be holy as the Father in heaven is holy must experience the contradiction which Romans 7:14ff. portrays. A believer without this tension would be abnormal. . . . It is only by ignoring the reality of the contradiction that we can get away from the *necessity* of this inner conflict. . . . There is no need or place for a contrast between the exultant confidence of Romans 8 and the struggle of Romans 7:14ff. The more intense the conflict of Romans 7, the more the apostle gloried in the triumphing grace of Romans 8 and of Romans 7 itself. . . . It is only by evading the realities of sin and grace that we can escape from the stern realism of the conflict of Romans 7. There is grand candour in this passage, the candour of inspired utterance.

(5) Keswick insists upon the distinction between the . . . continuous process by which we are conformed to . . . Christ and the definite decision for holiness . . . which is a point of crisis. But must we not bear in mind that decision for holiness or dedication to God is itself something to which progressive sanctification must be applied?[73]

A Brief Interlude: Taking the Message to the Campus

As mentioned at the beginning of the last section, with the disintegration of the old fundamentalist alliance after 1929, conservative Christians of varying persuasions began to reassess and redefine the movement of which they were a part. The catch-all term that probably best describes the alliance as it now stands, "conservative evangelical," includes Christians with a great variety of beliefs; for example: separatist fundamentalists (who are usually dispensationalists), confessional Reformed, neo-evangelicals, conservative Lutherans (often Missouri Synod), Southern Baptists (of both stripes—"fundamentalist" and "moderate"— although the one might deny the right of the other for inclusion), the evangelical "left" ("left" socially and politically, not theologically), conservative Wesleyans, Pentecostals, neo-Pentecostals, and even many who might say "I don't know and I don't care, I'm just a Christian" (these we might call "the great unaligned"). With all of them filling the airwaves and flooding the markets with books, pamphlets, and tracts, what has happened to the "lordship" issue?

Answering that question is a tall order, well beyond the space allotted for a chapter. One way to get a handle on how some conservative evangelicals have dealt with the issues since the Barabas/Murray conflict (1954), however, is to glance briefly at some of the training materials supplied by two of the largest organizations for college campus ministry: Campus Crusade for Christ and the Navigators.[74] Both have influenced and helped many Christians, not only at colleges and universities; through their presses (Here's Life and NavPress) and other ministries (e.g., Crusade's *Here's Life* campaigns and Nav's *2:7* program for local churches), they have introduced their emphases to many non-students as well.

Bill Bright,[75] president and founder of Campus Crusade, has explained his basic understanding of the "Spirit-filled life" in a number of books, tracts, and pamphlets, the best known being the booklet *Have You Made the Wonderful Discovery of the Spirit-Filled Life?*[76] In this, Bright draws three circles representing the "three kinds of people" the Bible describes: the "natural man," the "spiritual man," and the "carnal man." He uses as his text, of course, 1 Corinthians 2:14–3:3. After describing the spiritual man and admonishing all Christians to remember that "the degree to which these traits are maintained . . . depends upon the extent to which the Christian trusts the Lord with every detail of his life, and upon maturity in Christ" (in other words, progressive sanctification), Bright asks, "Why is it that most Christians are not experiencing the abundant life?"

The reason, he argues, is that most Christians are "carnal Christians." Bright portrays such Christians as trusting in their "own efforts" to live the Christian life and in this supplies Romans 7:14ff. as one of his proof-texts. The answer? Be filled with the Spirit, which Bright interprets as being "controlled and empowered" by the Holy Spirit. How? Three steps: desire to be controlled and empowered, confess sins, and ask by faith.

The booklet then encourages the reader to pray a prayer in faith, not to depend upon feelings, and to continue a "walk by faith." Bright concludes with two possible scenarios for the now "Spirit-filled" Christian: (1) The person in a "continuous walk" may be confronted by an area of life displeasing to the Lord. That person should "thank God that He has forgiven all your sins— past, present, and future—on the basis of Christ's death" and "claim" God's love and forgiveness. The walk continues. (2) It is also possible to "retake the throne" of one's life through sin, "a definite act of disobedience." In such a case, he exhorts the offending person to "breathe spiritually," or "confess your sin" (exhale) and "surrender the control of your life to Christ" (inhale).

To a large degree, this sounds very much like both Chafer and Barabas. Indeed, Bright's "Fact (the engine)–Faith (the coal car)–Feeling (the caboose)" train diagram towards the close of the booklet comes quite close to what a Keswick speaker once said. Compare:

BRIGHT: Do not depend upon feelings. The promises of God's Word and not our feelings, is [sic] our authority. The Christian lives by faith (trust) in the trustworthiness of God Himself and His Word. The train diagram illustrates the relationship between fact (God and His Word), faith (our trust in God and His Word), and feelings (the result of our faith and obedience). . . . The train will run with or without the caboose. However, it would be futile to run the train by the caboose. In the same way, we, as Christians do not depend upon feelings, but place our faith (trust) in the trustworthiness of God and the promises of His Word.

EVAN HOPKINS, *Keswick teacher*: Do not wait for feeling. I used to put it before my working-men . . . in this way. Here are three men walking in procession—Mr. Fact goes first, Mr. Faith follows him, and Mr. Feeling follows Mr. Faith. Supposing the middle man turns around and looks at Mr. Feeling, everything goes wrong. His business is to fix his eye upon Mr. Fact, and Mr. Feeling follows him.[77]

Bright more explicitly shows his close ties to Keswick-type teaching in a pamphlet, "Ye Shall Receive Power." He writes, "What is wrong? Recently, Dr. Billy Graham stated on a nationally televised broadcast that at least 90 percent of all Christians in America are living defeated lives. . . . It is quite likely, dear friend, according to the law of averages that you are one of these." Bright relates this experience of defeat to Pilgrim's wallowing in the "slough of despond" in Bunyan's *Pilgrim's Progress*; the problem with this, of course, is that Pilgrim at this point is not yet a Christian![78] He then gives his textual support for the concept of the "defeated Christian": "Romans 7:13–24 is your experience. . . ."[79]

The need is to be filled with the Spirit, Bright proclaims. Before examining the idea of filling, he proceeds by relating that "at the time of spiritual birth" the Holy Spirit regenerates, indwells, seals, and baptizes the new believer into the body of Christ" (see Chafer's remarks on p. 153). This, Bright contends, "is a positional relationship," which gives *"every Christian the potential to witness with power and live a life of victory over sin. This potential power . . . is released by faith as the Christian surrenders the control of his life to the Holy Spirit."* Bright commends the experiences of such former Higher Life teachers as John Wesley, Charles Finney, G. Campbell Morgan, Reuban Torrey, Andrew Murray, and Hudson Taylor as examples of some who understood the filling.[80]

"Basically, the problem," Bright notes, *"is that of the will. . . .* At the time of conversion the will of man is temporarily yielded to the will of God. . . . However, after conversion, the heart frequently loses its 'first love.'" The answer: "The Holy Spirit will fill us with His power the moment we are fully yielded." Bright admonishes that "up until the moment" when a Christian "completely surrenders" his will to God's will, "'the Holy Spirit has been a guest in your house'" but One who has been "locked up in a small closet, while you used the rest of your house for your own pleasures."[81]

Bright continues with some careful caveats, nonetheless. He contends that such yielding, resulting in the walk in the Spirit, is not an "ecstatic experience," that the filling comes to different Christians in different ways, and that after being filled there is a need to continue to mature and grow in Christ.[82] Yet, even with the caveats—caveats, it must be added, to which both Chafer and

Barabas would agree—Bright's overall presentation corresponds well to that of the dispensationalist Chafer and the Keswick proponent Barabas on the issues of two types of Christians and the doctrine of sanctification.

The reason for this extended discussion of Bright is that the Reformed confessional teacher R. C. Sproul, professor of theology at Reformed Theological Seminary in Orlando, has written,

> On the surface, it appears as if Dr. Bill Bright is teaching an absolute distinction between two kinds of Christians. I am confident, however, that this is not the intention of the booklet [*Have You Made the Wonderful Discovery . . .*] or of its author. Rather, in a pastoral way, Dr. Bright is discussing the classic struggle here between the flesh and the Spirit that every genuine Christian faces. The point of the booklet is to call us to exercise the power of the Holy Spirit in our lives in order to keep the evil tendencies of the old man in check.[83]

How is this possible when so much of Bright's teaching sounds like it came directly from Chafer or from Keswick? Part of the answer may lie in Bright's place in the lordship question. His famous booklet *The Four Spiritual Laws*[84] very clearly makes a "lordship decision" a part of becoming a Christian (law 4: "We must individually receive Jesus Christ as Saviour and Lord"). In the booklet, Bright introduces the reader to only two of his three circles: the natural man and the spiritual man, or as he calls them here, the "self-controlled life" and the "Christ-controlled life." When someone wishes to come to Christ, he or she is asked to pray a simple prayer, which not only includes thanksgiving for forgiveness but also says "make me the kind of person you want me to be." To be sure, this is a "willingness," and according to Bright a Christian can "retake the throne" through disobedience. But it is also a call to commitment to Christ's lordship as part of becoming a Christian.

The dispensationalist leader Charles Ryrie, former professor of theology at Dallas Theological Seminary, understood this. Not writing directly of Bright, but certainly of this kind of evangelism, in *Balancing the Christian Life*, he argues, "Recently there has been a modification of this position [on lordship salvation] to say that *willingness* to be controlled by the Lord at the time of salvation is all that is required in addition to faith in order to be saved. That is, there must at the time of salvation also be a moment of willingness to commit one's life absolutely to the Lord even though the practice of a committed life may not follow completely."[85] Of course, Ryrie got it wrong. Bright does not say to "add this to faith" (nor do Warfield and Murray, the two so-called lordship teachers examined thus far). But rather he calls the prayer for forgiveness, cleansing, *and* commitment a prayer of faith. Nevertheless, Ryrie is right to point out that this teaching varies from the "Saviour only" school.

Another possible explanation for Sproul's reluctance to place Bright among those who make a hard-and-fast categorization of two kinds of Christians can be found in the *Have You Made the Wonderful Discovery . . .* booklet itself. There, Bright warns "the individual who professes to be a Christian but who continues to sin" that "he may not be a Christian at all." Thus, one should never feel safe if one *desires* to be a carnal Christian.[86]

Yet, even with Sproul's statement in mind and Bright's own emphasis on lordship, warnings to the careless, and strong belief in the progressive nature of sanctification, it must be seen that Bright's teaching, in overall tenor and spirit, lies much closer to that of Chafer and Barabas (especially Barabas) than it does to Warfield or Murray. In fact, in a training manual put out by Crusade with Bright as editor, *Ten Basic Steps Toward Christian Maturity, Teacher's Manual,* Bright quotes extensively from Andrew Murray, Charles Trumball, and other Keswick and Higher Life advocates to support his understanding of the spiritual life.[87] What can be said in summation is that Campus Crusade, being an interdenominational organization with a large staff, probably has advocates of both views using the Crusade materials in different ways. Nevertheless, the overall thrust of Bright's foundational materials for the movement seems to fall, Sproul's comments notwithstanding, on the Keswick side.

When reviewing materials from the Navigators for this chapter, I must confess that I began to think of a "Navigator paradox." Two books issued by NavPress in 1978, illustrate this point. On the one hand, the training manual by the Navigators' Director of Church Life, Francis Cosgrove, *Essentials of New Life*[88] (interestingly, written while he was serving on the staff of a church which is now in the Reformed confessional Presbyterian Church in America), demonstrates some definite affinities to Keswick-type teachings, with a lordship view similar to Bright's. On the other hand, the practical exposition on the Christian life *The Pursuit of Holiness*[89] by Jerry Bridges, the Navigators' secretary-treasurer, bears striking similarities to doctrines espoused by Warfield and Murray (especially Murray, whom he quotes abundantly).

Why? It is hard to say, but, again, like Crusade, the Navigators maintain an interdenominational status, and thus the staff members live and breathe in a broadly defined evangelical framework. A brief examination of Cosgrove and Bridges will hopefully show this paradox.

Like Bright, Cosgrove rejects a "Savior-only" approach to salvation: "If we claim to have received Christ as Saviour and Lord and continue to live in sin, we are only deceiving ourselves."[90] He also emphasizes both progressive sanctification and some type of "crisis event" of "yielding it all":

> . . . submission to the Lordship of Christ is not once-for-all. We may make an initial commitment to submit to Him when we first discover that He is worthy of our allegiance. But there must also be a day-by-day recommitment to His authority. . . . [T]he issue of the Lordship of Christ is the most critical of any Christians' life. . . . We must give Him our life—our future, our present, our past. We must live only for Him daily. Only then do we experience the full life He has promised.[91]

From speaking on lordship, Cosgrove moves to an explanation of discipleship. Whether fully conscious of it or not, he here develops the concept of two types of Christians. His choice of words is not "carnal" and "spiritual," but "mediocre" and "disciple": "Jesus Christ lays the claims of Christian discipleship before every one of us who belongs to Him. He confronts us with a choice: the path of discipleship or the path of mediocrity." Again: "God wants all Christians to be His disciples, but the choice is up to us. . . . Becoming a disciple doesn't happen by osmosis. It comes through a commitment to the terms of discipleship."[92] The path of mediocrity puts a person "on the shelf":

> Many Christians sitting in the pews of churches Sunday mornings have faced that crossroad and have chosen to go the route of . . . mediocrity. Yes, they know Jesus as Saviour; they have eternal life. Once they faced some choices about following Him, but perhaps did not fully understand what they were, and chose to go in the wrong direction. As far as being used by God in evangelism, being in the army of Christ and having an impact on the world, they are out of the picture.[93]

This path of mediocrity can be exited, Cosgrove admits, to go to the path of discipleship. But if these paths really exist, could they not cause many earnest God-fearing Christians to ask regularly which on-ramp they are on? Cosgrove has been quite influenced by long-time Navigator leader, Walter Henrichsen. Henrichsen's most famous book title sums up Cosgrove's approach: *Disciples Are Made—Not Born*.[94] A Reformed confessionalist response might be titled: "Disciples Are Born [Again] and Build as Being Built Up by the Spirit."

Jerry Bridges, unlike Cosgrove, chooses not to speak of paths of discipleship and mediocrity. Indeed, he asserts, ". . . we may say that no one can trust in Christ for true salvation unless he trusts Him for holiness. This does not mean the desire for holiness must be a conscious desire at the time a person comes to Christ, but rather that the Holy Spirit who creates within us saving faith also creates within us the desire for holiness. He simply does not create the one without the other."[95] Bridges sees personal holiness as grounded in Christ's holiness, as something in which we grow, and even alerts the Christian to the fact of God's gracious discipline to lead a person to greater holiness.

Focusing on Romans 6 and 7, he argues that in our union with Christ "we have been delivered out of the realm of sin and placed in the kingdom and realm of righteousness." This hardly means, according to Bridges, that we cease battling sinful inclinations. Quite the contrary, "We may not like the fact that we have a lifelong struggle with sin, but the more we realize and accept it, the better equipped we will be to deal with it." Bridges, however, sounds a decisive note: although indwelling sin remains, it is "dethroned." Of course, the flip side remains true: though dethroned, it still attacks—"it wages guerrilla warfare against us."[96]

For help in the "daily battle," Bridges draws the believer's attention to deliverance from the reign of sin, to union with Christ, and to the indwelling Holy Spirit who reveals sin, creates the desire for holiness, and strengthens the Christian in the struggle.[97] Bridges moves from this to a very strong statement of the believer's responsibility:

> It is time for us Christians to face up to our responsibility for holiness. Too often we say we are "defeated" by this or that sin. No, we are not defeated; we are simply disobedient! It might be well if we stopped using the terms "victory" and "defeat" to describe our progress in holiness. Rather we should use the terms "obedience" and "disobedience." When I say I am defeated by some sin, I am unconsciously slipping out from under my responsibility. I am saying something outside me has defeated me. But when I say I am disobedient, that places the responsibility for sin squarely on me. . . . We need to brace ourselves up, and to realize that we are responsible for our thoughts, attitudes, and actions. We need to reckon on the fact that we died to sin's reign, that it no longer has any dominion over us, that God has united us with the risen Christ in all His power, and has given us the Holy Spirit to work in us. Only as we accept our responsibility and appropriate God's provisions will we make any progress in our pursuit of holiness.[98]

As we move to round three of the Hodges/MacArthur bout, it is helpful to note that the debates over lordship, union with Christ, and sanctification have been with us continually and probably will remain so.

A Battle Royal

Paul Schaefer

Although the various protagonists of the two sides in the "lordship salvation" debate surveyed in chapter 8 have had serious problems with one another's views, the tone has generally been measured and often irenic. With John MacArthur's *The Gospel According to Jesus* versus Zane Hodges's *Absolutely Free!*, however, the gloves come off. They engage not only in polemic (something apparent in Chafer/Warfield and Barabas/Murray), but also hyperbole (note the titles!)[1] and severe attacks on their adversaries. This battle constitutes the most recent salvo in our "American tale."

Interestingly, neither writer thought it necessary to make many references to Romans 6, what has been seen so far as the *textus classicus* in the Warfield/Chafer and Barabas/Murray debates and in the expositions of the Christian life by both sides.[2] Both may feel that they have sufficiently covered this ground elsewhere, but since the issues in the debate are serious, careful reflection on that Scripture passage would have been helpful.

MacArthur could argue that his set purpose was to exegete the so-called hard sayings of Jesus, but with chapter titles like "He Calls for a New Birth," "He Demands True Worship," "He Opens Blind Eyes," and "He Condemns a Hardened Heart," surely he could have added "He Unites Us to Himself by Grace through Faith" and done an exegesis of John 15 and Romans 6. Hodges does, at least, exegete John 15 in his chapter with the homey title "Dining with Jesus" and rightly criticizes MacArthur for not allowing that Scripture passage to instruct his polemic (pp. 134–40, 222 n. 1).[3]

Yet, in his criticism, Hodges caricatures rather than analyzes what he calls "the lordship position" on this text: ". . . in most lordship teaching, 'not abiding' is not really possible for a truly regenerate person. Thus, the command to Christians to abide once again reduces itself to a charade " (p. 136). It is quite difficult to know just who he includes in "most lordship teaching." Warfield, Murray, and Bridges, "lordship teachers" all, told Christians to take seriously the commands given to them; they believed in progressive sanctification. Listen to another so-called lordship teacher, Sinclair Ferguson of Westminster Theological Seminary, on John 15:

> The Christian . . . bears fruit by maintaining his relationship to Christ, so that Christ's life may be in him and may release through him God's grace and love. . . . [The] twin truths [from John 15 and Romans 6], that we have been grafted by the grace of God into Christ, and that our union with Christ gives us a new relationship both to *sin* and to *God*, form a fundamental growth point in Christian understanding and living. . . . We are all tempted to quick routes and short-cuts to the truth of these passages making lasting impressions upon us, and transforming our lives. But the great lessons, like the best fruit, take time, care, thought, and patience to really learn. . . . Here in John 15, Jesus reveals [God's pattern for spiritual growth]. It is based on our union with Him. It is furthered by the Father's pruning. It depends on the disciple's abiding in Christ.[4]

Hodges's overriding concern for the "simple" (a favorite word in his text) gospel message about faith in Christ for salvation (pp. 27–33),[6] his stress that the Christian life is growth in grace and often a struggle (pp. 67–71), and his sensitivity to those who are spiritually hurting (pp. 93–95) are all to be commended. Nevertheless, he also dabbles in obfuscation and even states things in such a way that might have made his forebears like Chafer cringe.

For example, after saying that the path of discipleship is a choice that not all saved people will follow (hence, two types of Christians, something to which Chafer would agree), he states, ". . . it is our responsibility to make the issues clear: Salvation is absolutely free; discipleship most certainly is not" (p. 88).

From what we saw earlier of Chafer, he would concur that discipleship is a process in which we are involved; but he stressed that we are involved through faith and by "walking in the Spirit." It may just be fuzziness on Hodges's part, but it sounds here as if Hodges is saying that salvation is free but sanctification is by works. That may not be his intended meaning, but it is hard to say.

What does Hodges mean by "salvation"? Possibly "justification," or maybe "going to heaven"? He writes, "Simply put, we may say this: the call to faith represents the call to eternal salvation. The call to repentance is the call to enter into harmonious relations with God" (p. 145). But does not Paul say that "peace with God" and "reconciliation to God," both of which must surely include "harmonious relations with God," are the present possessions of *all* true believers in light of their justification by grace through faith? (Rom. 5:1, 10–11). Indeed, does not Paul throughout Romans 5:1–11 describe salvation as a unit with past, present, and future aspects? As Warfield might say to Hodges (as he did to Chafer): ". . . . salvation is a unit, and . . . he who is united to Jesus Christ by faith receives in Him not only justification—salvation from the *penalty* of sin—but also sanctification—salvation from the *power* of sin—both 'safety' and 'sanctity.'"[5]

In his exposition of James 2, "The Choice Is Yours" (a strange exposition in itself, for Hodges seems to teach that those with "dead faith" are truly saved), he makes the rather cryptic remark: "If [James's] readers would lay aside any besetting wickedness, and if they would meekly receive God's Word, *their lives could be spared from a premature and untimely death through sin. . . .* It is not enough merely to hear [the Word's] instruction. To benefit from it—*to prolong one's life by means of it*—one must also do it" (p. 121, emphasis mine). Is the reader to assume from this then that all Christians who go to an early grave have not been "spiritual"? Maybe he means something else, but if so, he does not develop it clearly, and the implications are pastorally insensitive, confusing, and without scriptural merit.

As noted, it is quite distressing how Hodges simply makes straw men out of those he calls "lordship teachers." In another example of Hodges's false characterization of "them," he writes, "Today there exists in part of the evangelical church a wholly unrealistic view of the nature of Christian experience. According to those who hold this view, effective Christian living is virtually an inevitable result of new birth" (p. 69). Who is he talking about here? He cites no one specifically. And if he means the Reformed confessionalists, which of those whom we have treated so far ever said anything like this? It is easy to win points when you have no opponent.

Interestingly, in one of his other blasts against "lordship salvation," where he contends that it "throws a veil" over the New Testament and "differs only insignificantly from official Roman Catholic" dogma (pp. 19–20), he mentions approvingly (p. 206 n. 5) an article by Robert Godfrey, a confessional Reformed and one of the contributors to this volume. It must be queried whether, if Hodges took time to examine, for instance, Godfrey's teachings on divine sovereignty, union with Christ, and sanctification, he might not call Godfrey's position "Roman Catholic" as well? Whatever Hodges would call it, one imagines, he would dislike it.

Hodges also castigates lordship salvation for promoting a "judgmental and pharisaical spirit" among God's people: "How tempting it is to our sinful flesh to believe that we have a right to say to a failing professing believer, 'You really are not good enough to be on your way to heaven'!" (p. 19). I am sure one exists somewhere, but I have yet to find any proponent of lordship salvation, at least as it has been taught by Reformed representatives, who would ever dare say such a thing. Their own battle with indwelling sin and appropriation of Luther's famous dictum *simul iustus et peccator* (simultaneously justified and sinful) would prevent it. Indeed, this whole criticism could easily be turned on its head against the teachers of the concept of two kinds of Christians. As Ernest Reisinger asserts:

This teaching [two types of Christians] breeds Pharisaism in the so-called "spiritual Christians" who have measured up to some man-made standard of spirituality. There ought to be no professed "spiritual Christians," much less "super-spiritual" ones! George Whitefield, a man who lived very close to his Saviour, prayed all his days, "Let me begin to be a Christian." And another Christian has truly said: "In the life of the most perfect Christian there is every day renewed occasion for self-abhorrence, for repentance, for renewed application to the blood of Christ, for application of the rekindling of the Holy Spirit."[6]

While MacArthur misquoted Berkhof in support of the former's contention that faith is knowledge, assent, and "the determination of the will to obey the truth" (MacArthur, p. 173), Hodges can lay no claim to a full concurrence with Berkhof's definition of saving faith either, for Berkhof's includes coming to Christ as both justifier and sanctifier, Saviour and Lord. Nevertheless, MacArthur does move away from this classic Reformed conception with his constant emphasis on obedience. MacArthur asserts such things as: "faith encompasses obedience." "The real believer will obey." "Clearly, the biblical concept of faith is inseparable from obedience. 'Believe' is synonymous with 'obey' in John 3:36. . . ." And (quoting Kittel's *Theological Dictionary of the New Testament*), "'To believe' is 'to obey'" (pp. 173–75). Where is the notion of "reception and appropriation of Christ as the source of pardon and of spiritual life" in this? The whole idea seems as centered on the human agent as the conception of faith advocated by Hodges is.

It could be that MacArthur is going to these extremes because of his deep distaste for "Savior only" theology (like that of Hodges). For, in the same section quoted in the previous paragraph, he qualifies some of his stronger remarks: "no one will obey perfectly, . . . but the desire to do the will of God will be ever present in true believers." "True faith always manifests itself in obedience." "Righteous living is an inevitable by-product of real faith." And, "this is not to say that faith results in anything like sinless perfection" (pp. 174–76). All his statements placed together, however, force this dilemma: Is obedience a "manifestation" and "by-product" of a resting in and reliance on Christ as Lord and Saviour, or as he seems to say at some points, is it actually a constituent part of the *definition of faith?*

These two ideas differ widely. The first shows the believer the comfort and assurance of salvation in Christ as well as the very real cost of coming to Christ *and* the resources for the daily battle against sin, while the second could easily mire believers in moralism and a constant questioning of whether they have true faith, since they are certainly not obedient *enough*. MacArthur would do well to clarify by exegeting a passage like Romans 7 instead of leaving this key text to a footnote (p. 174 n. 14).

As with Hodges, MacArthur sometimes draws unfortunate conclusions from his exegesis, such as those, for example, in his chapter on the rich young ruler (Matt. 19) entitled "He Challenges an Eager Seeker." MacArthur rightly contends that "the issue here was clearly this man's salvation, not some higher level of discipleship subsequent to conversion" (p. 78) and proceeds from there to supply both a strong criticism of much of today's evangelistic methods and tactics and a reminder of the scriptural emphases on the depth of sin and the need to confront people with God's standard in the law:

> Jesus' answer took the focus off the young man's felt need and put it back on God: "There is only One who is good." Then He slammed him up against the divine standard, not because *keeping* the law would merit eternal life, but so that he would see how far he fell short. . . . [T]he emphasis in Jesus' teaching from the beginning had been to define all the law in such a way that no one—even those who adhered strictly to the law's external requirements—could look at the commandments and feel justified. [pp. 84–85]

Then comes the part that concludes with a slightly odd turn. From a Reformed point of view, the problem centers not on anything MacArthur says that is overtly false (he teaches justification by grace alone through faith alone)[7] but rather on his emphasis. MacArthur speaks of the "ultimate test" given to the young man as, "will this man obey the Lord?" Is that what is going on here? Or, was Jesus breaking him by the law in order that this man might see his absolute need and fly to Christ alone for salvation from both the power and penalty of sin?

MacArthur realizes that Jesus was not telling people they must give up all they possess in preparation for becoming Christians, but he adds, ". . . we *do* have to be willing to forsake all . . . , meaning we cling to nothing that takes precedence over Christ" (p. 87). Pastorally, such advice could be disastrous. There are indeed times when we must warn the presumptuous, as Jesus did here, but at other times comfort must be given. In both cases, the solution must always be centered on Christ alone. Christ is the answer for either presumption or despair. MacArthur's focus seems to be on "my willingness" instead.

In a debate against Roman Catholic teachings on salvation, John Calvin drew attention to the same passage and also spoke of the need to show people the divine standard. But his conclusions differ from MacArthur's.

[The young man] is rightly sent back to the law wherein there is a perfect mirror of righteousness.

With a clear voice we too proclaim that these commandments are to be kept if one seeks life in works. And Christians must know this doctrine, for how could they *flee to Christ* unless they recognized that they had plunged from the way of life over the brink of death? . . .

To sum up, if we seek salvation in works, we must keep the commandments by which we are instructed unto perfect righteousness. But we must not stop here unless we wish to fail in midcourse, for none of us is capable of keeping the commandments. Therefore, since we are barred from law righteousness, we must betake ourselves to another help, that is, to faith in Christ. For this reason, as the Lord in this passage recalls to a teacher of the law whom he knew to be puffed up with empty confidence in works, in order that he may learn he is a sinner, subject to the dreadful judgment of eternal death, so elsewhere he comforts with the promise of grace without any mention of the law others who have already been humbled by this sort of knowledge: "Come to me all who labor and are heavy-laden, and I will refresh you . . . and you will find rest for your souls" [Matt. 11:28–29].[8]

With all this in mind, it must be stated, however, that MacArthur's doctrinal formulations contain many of the same concerns that have characterized the Reformed position encountered in Warfield, Murray, and Bridges. For example, he concludes his first chapter, "A Look at the Issues," with this strong summation:

> Faith and works are not incompatible. There is a sense in which Jesus calls even the act of believing a work (John 6:29)—not merely a human work, but a gracious work of God in us. He brings us to faith, then enables and empowers us to believe unto obedience (cf. Rom. 16:26).
>
> It is precisely here that the key distinction must be made. Salvation by faith does not eliminate works *per se*. It does away with works that are the result of human effort alone (Eph. 2:8). It abolishes any attempt to merit God's favor by our works (v. 9). But it does not deter God's foreordained purpose that our walk of faith should be characterized by good works (v. 10).
>
> We must remember above all that salvation is a sovereign work of God. Biblically it is defined by what it produces, not by what one does to get it. Works are *not* necessary to earn salvation. But true salvation wrought by God will not fail to produce the good works that are its fruit (cf. Matt. 7:17). We are God's workmanship. No aspect of salvation is merited by human works (Titus 3:5–7). Thus salvation cannot be defective in any dimension. As a part of His saving work, God will produce repentance, faith, sanctification, yieldedness, obedience, and ultimately glorification. Since He is not dependent on human effort in producing those elements, an experience that lacks any of them cannot be the saving work of God.
>
> If we are truly born of God, we have a faith that cannot fail to overcome the world (1 John 5:4). We may sin (1 John 2:1)—we *will* sin—but the process of sanctification can never stall completely. God is at work in us (Phil. 2:13), and He will continue to perfect us until the day of Christ (Phil. 1:6; 1 Thess. 5:23–24). [p. 33]

This statement is so clear that it seemed necessary and proper to quote it in full. Many other segments could be cited as well, such as MacArthur's relation of the account of the thief on the cross as "A Picture of Grace" (pp. 147–48) and his response to a person who had listened to him on the radio and then accused him of confusing justification with sanctification.[9] The conclusion: MacArthur surely stands among the Reformed when he explains his understanding of the biblical view of salvation.

So, why all this emphasis on "my willingness" and "faith as obedience"? Primarily, of course, MacArthur wishes to preserve the biblical emphasis on the need for a human response to God's call to turn from sin and to turn to Christ. But there are two other possible reasons as well. First, MacArthur still clings to his dispensationalist past (cf. p. 25). As discussed in chapter 8, classic dispensationalists lay great stress on "yielding all" to Christ in order to "walk in the Spirit." To be sure, they repudiate the idea that this must come at the moment of conversion, although it may. Could it be, and this is a query only MacArthur can answer, that he has retained this dispensationalist emphasis and simply moved the "crisis event" of "obediently yielding all" up the ladder of his *ordo salutis* to conversion itself?

A second possible cause could be the way MacArthur reads the Puritans.[10] Demonstrating a respect and admiration for that "spiritual brotherhood" of seventeenth-century divines from both old and New England, he quotes them extensively and enthusiastically.[11] Yet, he does so quite uncritically. Puritanism, as a movement of revival,[12] was far from a monolithic religious grouping. There existed a spectrum, so to speak, of theological opinion. And, as with all movements of revival in the history of the church, exaggerated emphases occurred among some adherents. One should read with discrimination so as to pick the most theologically sound thinkers, if one wishes to emulate them. (I would start with John Owen.)[13]

While MacArthur shares with many Puritans similar points in exegesis and their uninhibited call (which, it should be remembered, was to an established church in England which they believed to be only "halflie reformed") that true believers will "exercise themselves in godliness," he makes a few unguarded definitions in systematic theology that most of them would not have countenanced. Although he does quite well to quote from the *Westminster Standards* (albeit not from the original but from Vincent's exposition of the Shorter Catechism), for these documents present Puritanism in its most mature theological form and in its most careful expression, he does not seem to have fully assessed their positions. For example, he cites question 86 from Vincent's exposition of the Shorter Catechism (which I will quote a little more fully than MacArthur does in his appendix).

> LXXXVI Ques. What is faith in Jesus Christ?
> Answer: Faith in Jesus Christ is a saving grace whereby we receive and rest upon him alone for salvation, as He is offered in the gospel.
> Q.1. How is faith a saving grace?
> A. Faith is a saving grace, not by the act of believing, as an act, for then it would save as a work—whereas we are saved by faith in opposition to all works; but faith is a saving grace as an instrument apprehending and applying Jesus Christ and his perfect righteousness, whereby alone we are saved. . . .
> Q.2. Who is the author of faith in Jesus Christ?
> A. The author of faith in Jesus Christ is God, whose gift it is, and who works this grace of faith in the soul by his Spirit. . . .
> Q.4. What is the object of this grace of faith?
> A. The object of this grace of faith is the Lord Jesus Christ, and his righteousness, and the promises which are made through him in the covenant of grace. . . .
> Q.8. How is Jesus Christ offered to us in the gospel?
> A. Jesus Christ is offered to us in the gospel, as priest, prophet, and king; and so we must receive him, if we would be saved by him.
> Q.9. When doth the soul rest upon him for salvation?
> A. The soul doth rest upon Christ for salvation when, being convinced of its lost condition by reason of sin, and its own inability, together with all the creatures' insufficiency, to recover it out of this estate, and having a discovery and persuasion of Christ's ability and willingness to save, it doth let go hold of all creatures, and renounce its own righteousness, and so lay hold on Christ, rely upon him, and put confidence in him, and in him alone, for salvation.[14]

Since he quotes it approvingly, MacArthur apparently concurs with this; nonetheless, one does not discover the same clarity and tight definitions in MacArthur that are found in both the catechism and in Vincent's exposition of it. With his emphasis on "surrender" and on "faith as obedience," MacArthur opens himself up to the criticism of de-emphasizing faith as complete trust "in Christ and him alone" as both justifier and sanctifier in favor of a much more moralistic and human-centered focus. While MacArthur clearly professes that a Christian's obedience in no way merits salvation, his real distaste for all antinomianism sometimes seems to lead him to make unfortunate inferences.

This said, however, when MacArthur dips into the past to prove a point, he does so with far more overall care than Hodges does. For instance, in another of his polemical blasts at the "lordship view," Hodges contends:

> Saving faith is taking God at His Word in the gospel. . . . The effort to make it more is a tragic blemish on the history of the Christian church. The roots of this effort run deep into certain types of post-Reformation thought. And in the English-speaking world, this radically altered concept of saving faith can with considerable fairness be described as Puritan theology. Lordship salvation, in its best known contemporary form, simply popularizes the Puritanism to which it is heir. [pp. 32–33][15]

And so, with a flick of his pen, Hodges assigns the teachings of generations of English evangelicals to the trash heap of history. Yet he makes not one specific reference to any of these Puritans who so "radically altered" the "concept of saving faith." How then can he state that he has come to such a conclusion with "considerable fairness"? Instead of offering even a single quotation from a single one of these nameless "Puritans," he directs the reader to his endnotes, where one finds references to two modern scholars, R. T. Kendall and M. Charles Bell.[16] He states that they have "effectively analyzed" this "change from John Calvin's view of faith to the view we encounter so frequently in post-Reformation Calvinism" (p. 208 n. 8).

Kendall's thesis, the older of the two and to which Bell is indebted (though not uncritically), has been criticized sharply by a number of scholars of both Reformation and post-Reformation studies, so extreme care must be taken to decide whether or not its analysis is "effective."[17] It most definitely is not the final word. Interestingly, Kendall, after taking over the pulpit of Westminster

Chapel in London, became embroiled in a "lordship controversy" of his own.[18] When Hodges chastises MacArthur for seeming "unaware of the current literature, which has demonstrated that Puritan theology, especially in the area of faith and assurance, did not at all reflect the doctrine of John Calvin himself and is a distinct departure from Reformation thought" (p. 208 n. 9), and then simply cites Kendall and Bell, one has to wonder how *aware* of the current literature Hodges is.

To engage in historical theology is enjoyable and rewarding. But if one is to do it, one must do it responsibly and fairly. Hodges does give a few citations from Calvin and Luther, it is true, but these are almost exclusively read through Kendall's and Bell's spectacles.[19] And whether Luther or Calvin would agree with Hodges that "[t]he Bible never affirms that saving faith per se is a gift" (p. 219 n. 1), the reader is left to judge for himself.[20] Right after Hodges makes this claim, he says of MacArthur's view of Ephesians 2:8–9 (see p. 186), "As all perceptive theologians will recognize, what MacArthur has done is to impose his own theological grid on Ephesians 2:8–9" (p. 219 n. 1). Is Hodges telling us that when he exegetes Scripture, he is theologically neutral? Apparently so, for after his absolute dismissal of Puritanism, he pleads for the church to "permit" the Scriptures "to speak for themselves" (p. 33). And, of course, what he expects us to find is the message he espouses.

Finally, if Hodges is going to make grand claims about post-Reformation theologians both from the Continent and from England, he should show his readers that he has an acquaintance with them and with the scholarship on them (certainly more than two books which themselves have been criticized strongly!). He certainly has the right to come to similar conclusions to Kendall's and Bell's after some study, but he should show some sign of knowing the issues. To this reviewer, Hodges has in no way demonstrated such knowledge. Rather his dips into the pool of historical theology have never gone beyond the shallow end. And so when he writes, "Lordship salvation, in its best known contemporary form, simply popularizes the Puritanism to which it is heir," he makes a rather meaningless abstraction.

A Story, Some Questions, and a Quotation: The Tale's End

A story (the names have been omitted to protect the innocent): While I was serving as director of college ministries on the pastoral staff of a large urban church, one of the students came into my office and related this story. He had just been involved in a week-long evangelistic campaign at a nearby university. After it was over, the group got together to share "war stories" (an absolutely dreadful term—What are we doing in evangelism, sharing good news to a sinful world in need of Christ, or lobbing "holy hand grenades"?). One of the students, a freshman and a new Christian, told of how, when he was sharing the gospel with someone and got to the "decision page" of his manual, he asked him which one of the "two circles" (self-directed life or Christ-directed life) represented his life. He responded, "Neither." The young Christian countered, "Which circle would you like to have represent your life?" The fellow responded, "Neither." The young Christian asked the group, "What should I have done?" One of the older students replied, quite seriously, "Well, why not share with him the 'third circle' [the 'carnal Christian']?" I was told by my student friend that the staff workers were appalled at such a notion and quickly told the young student that if a similar case ever came up again he was to tell the person that they were in one or the other of the two circles pictured in the gospel tract. Then the student who related this story to me asked me, "But, logically, if you believe that a Christian can choose to be either a 'carnal' or a 'spiritual' Christian, why can't you also present that same option to a non-Christian?"

Some questions: Our "American Tale" is just about at an end. But not really, for the debate rages on. Let us take a moment to review four significant issues in the debate as it has come down to us:

1. A theological issue: Both sides affirm that Jesus Christ is fully God and fully human. Both also agree that Jesus is Savior and Lord. But one side says that the call to discipleship is separate from the gospel call, indeed separate enough that

the calls may be given to believers at different junctures in their Christian life; the other side understands the two calls as intertwined.

2. First exegetical issue: Both sides agree that Romans 6 is the classic text on spiritual life. Both also affirm that every true Christian is united to Christ. But one side argues that this union is *positional* and needs to be actualized by "yielding," while the other side characterizes the union as *definitive*, with the human response of "reckoning" being a response to the work of God which is already powerfully transforming the believer.

3. Second exegetical issue: Both sides agree, with a few notable exceptions among some Reformed confessionalists,[21] that the man of Romans 7:14–25 is a Christian. But the one side interprets Paul's experience here as one of defeat, so that Paul needs to move out of Romans 7 into Romans 8 by appropriating the filling of the Spirit. The other side sees Paul's struggle here as normative, with Romans 7 and Romans 8 being flip sides of one another.

4. A soteriological issue: What is the relationship between justification and sanctification? Both sides affirm that justification and sanctification must be distinguished theologically. As to sanctification, both sides agree that it is progressive. But one side not only distinguishes the two events but allows for them to be separated, at least experientially, thus paving the way for a doctrine of two types of Christians. The other group distinguishes justification from sanctification but also views them as the two very real twin blessings of union with Christ, so that, as Warfield contended, ". . . the remainders of the flesh in the Christian do not constitute his characteristic. . . . He who believes in Jesus Christ is under grace, and his whole course, in its process and in its issue alike, is determined by grace, and therefore, having been predestined to be conformed to the image of God's Son, he is surely being conformed to that image, God Himself seeing to it that he is not only called and justified but also glorified. You may find Christians at every stage of this process, for it is a process through which all must pass. . . ."[22]

A quotation to ponder: In March 1760, William Grimshaw, a Calvinistic Methodist, wrote to Charles Wesley, the Methodist leader:

> My perfection is to see my own imperfection. My own comfort, to feel that I've the world, the flesh, and the devil to overcome thro' the Spirit and the merits of my dear Saviour. And my desire and hope is to love God with all my heart, mind, soul, and strength to the last gasp of my life. —This is my perfection. I know no other, expecting to lay down my life and my sword together![23]

Conclusion
Christ Died for the Sins of Christians, Too

Rod Rosenbladt

Any evangelical—indeed, any Christian—would probably say that the key issue of human life is that of a saving relationship with God through Jesus Christ. Those who are familiar with the Scriptures, who know what is described about the nature of the fall of the human race in Genesis 3, and, who have come to grips with the texts that plumb the true depths of that fall and its ramifications for every human being born after Adam and Eve, would probably not hesitate to say that humanity became at that point totally depraved.

Total depravity, of course, does not mean that the human race has become as bad as it can possibly be, but that every part of us is infected with a deep infection and that we cannot heal our own disease. This reality moves the evangelical to affirm, therefore, that the eternal Logos assumed to himself a particular human nature and had as his work to be our prophet, priest, and king and to solve our basic problem in our stead or in our place. The word that most evangelicals would use for this is a biblical word—*salvation*.

And so, in one way, our subject here is a simple one: How am I to be saved? And in a way, the answer to the question is as simple: Believe on the Lord Jesus Christ, and you will be saved! Or, to use two texts that Luther and Calvin cited with great frequency in their debates, "For we maintain that a man is justified by faith apart from observing the Law" (Rom. 3:28) and, "to one who does not work but trusts him who justifies the ungodly, his faith is reckoned as righteousness" (Rom. 4:5 RSV).

Two matters of history are crucial to our discussion: (1) The Reformers really believed that the popular (and, by the mid-sixteenth century, official) Roman Catholic position was self-salvation. By "Roman Catholic," I don't mean what's going on at your local Catholic church today. Rather, it is to the medieval position that I refer, the Roman Catholic theology that was represented in the Council of Trent in 1545–1563.

(2) When God gives orders and tells us what will happen if we fail to obey those orders perfectly, that is in the category of what the Reformers, following the biblical text, called *law*. When God promises freely, providing for us because of Christ's righteousness the status he demands of us, this is in the category of *gospel*. It is good news from start to finish. The Bible includes both, and the Reformers were agreed that the Scriptures taught clearly (contrary to many forms of dispensationalism) that the law (whether Old or New Testament commands) was not eliminated for the believer. Nevertheless, they insisted that nothing in this category of law could be a means of justification or acceptance before a holy God.[1]

The law comes, not to reform the sinner nor to show him or her the "narrow way" to life, but to crush the sinner's hopes of escaping God's wrath through personal effort or even cooperation. All of our righteousness must come from someone else—someone who has fulfilled the law's demands. Only after we have been stripped of our "filthy rags" of righteousness (Isa. 64:6)—our fig leaves through which we try in vain to hide our guilt and shame—can we be clothed with Christ's righteousness. First comes the law to proclaim judgment and death, then the gospel to proclaim justification and life. One of the clearest presentations of this motif is found in Paul's epistle to the Galatians.

For many in the German Higher Life movement, and those in the stream of Wesley generally, the motif, instead, has been law—gospel—law. B. B. Warfield, the great dean of "Old Princeton" Reformed theologians, was one of the clearest early critics of this trend, a trend that has now culminated in the vast literature on "victorious living" versions of the Christian life. Warfield argued that, at the bottom of it all, the Higher Life movement was nothing more than a revival of prominent Wesleyan–Arminian features. Warfield also stated that he was fairly convinced that the Arminians worshiped another God.[2] That's a deep criticism. Is it justified? To answer that, let us go back for a moment to the Reformation debate.

In the sixteenth century the issue of law and grace was more clearly dealt with than at almost any other time since the apostles. The lines were cut cleanly, and as the great Yale historian, Roland Bainton rightly noted, it was the only real issue of the century.[3] Anybody studying the sixteenth century primarily through the issue of economics, for example, is going to miss the whole point. It is impossible to understand the sixteenth century if you start with the categories of Marxism and revolution, or anything else.

Further, it is no exaggeration to say that Luther and Calvin dealt with the biblical passages about the way of salvation more clearly than anyone since the apostle Paul—although they would have been the last to say that they were speaking at the level of an inspired apostle. Throughout the Middle Ages, the Western church was discussing and debating the nature of justification. What then were the medieval positions on this doctrine?

Thomas Aquinas had a doctrine of justification, but for him it was just one doctrine among many.[4] Somewhere tucked behind, around, and under such subjects as regeneration, predestination, and sanctification was his position on justification. It was a doctrine of justification that involved God loving the sinner insofar as he or she was not a sinner. He did not love the sinner *as* sinner; how *could* a holy and just God love a sinner? But he loved sinners insofar as they had the potential to *not be* sinners.[5]

Duns Scotus spoke of the necessity of an absolutely selfless act of contrition (sorrow) and love for God by natural means if a person was to be saved. Think about that for a moment. At least once during your life, you would have to perform an utterly selfless act that had no vested interest for you whatsoever, or you would not be saved.[6] Luther believed that this way of justification prevented God from befriending publicans and sinners, and that if it were true, God was not truly free.

Of course, there were many other views. Strict Augustinians insisted on the priority of grace, which, because of predestination, rendered it absolutely certain that one would be justified—one day in the future. Even for the Augustinians—and there were not a few—justification was primarily moral transformation, not a legal declaration distinct from any prior moral conditions.

The medieval consensus that won out has come to be known by the technical name *semi-Pelagianism*—from the late fourth- to fifth-century debate between Augustine, defender of grace, and Pelagius, a monk who denied original sin and, therefore, the need for supernatural grace. While the Synod of Orange (529 A.D.) condemned both Pelagianism *and* semi-Pelagianism, the heresy of works-righteousness, erected on the foundation of free will, grew increasingly popular among the masses and even among theologians.

What the Reformers said of the position was that it was by necessity a theology of doubt, of fear, and finally of despair of ever being saved. One had to be sanctified enough first in order to merit justifying grace, and the essence of justification was a real change within the human heart. (We shall consider parallels to this in evangelicalism later on in this chapter.) Justification, in main-stream Roman Catholic theology, is primarily a real, empirical change in the human heart. Aquinas argued that justification involves a gradual change from unjust to just, thus justified. Grace amounts to an infused power to enable one to cooperate with the Spirit, to gradually move oneself from the category of "ungodly" to that of "righteous." And this would be evident in fewer and fewer sins by the believer.[7]

As if Aquinas were anticipating the Enlightenment, he seemed to have much more in common with Kant than with the New Testament when he offered a statement likely to be heard in any number of evangelical circles in our day: "God never asks of anyone something for which he does not first give them the power to perform it." The Reformers of course, had (and their followers still ought to have) tremendous problems with this theory that underestimates both the seriousness of sin and the greatness of grace.

What then is the doctrine of justification as taught by the Reformers? Justification is, they said, primarily a *forensic* declaration, that is, it comes from the world of law courts. In this transaction, we the guilty party stand before the judge who is righteous and are declared to be not only innocent, but perfectly righteous. (Notice how the popular phrase "just as if I'd never sinned" tells only half the story. We are not only forgiven; we are also credited with Christ's complete righteousness as though we had kept the law perfectly through the course of our lives.) The Reformers did not believe that this justification was an empirical change in the human heart; rather, it was external.

One of my favorite stories that illustrates this particular matter deals with a time when Luther, under the ban of the empire, was translating the Bible into German at the Wartburg castle and could only have contact with his colleague Melanchthon by courier. Melanchthon had a different sort of temperament than Luther. Some would call him timid; others of a less generous bent might call him spineless. At one time, while Luther was off in the Wartburg castle translating, Melanchthon had another one of his attacks of timidity. He wrote to Luther, "I woke this morning wondering if I trust Christ enough." Luther received such letters from Melanchthon regularly. He had a tendency, a propensity, to navel-gaze and to wonder about the state of his inner faith, and whether it was enough to save. Finally, in an effort to pull out all the stops and pull Melanchthon out of himself, Luther wrote back and said, "Melanchthon! Go sin bravely! Then go to the cross and bravely confess it! The whole gospel is outside of us."

This story has been told time and time again by less sympathetic observers than I in an effort to caricature Luther and the Reformation generally as advocates of licentious abandon. If we are not justified by our own moral conformity to the law, but by Christ's, surely there is nothing keeping us from self-indulgence. Of course, this was the criticism of the gospel that Paul anticipated in Romans 6: "Shall we go on sinning so that grace may increase? By no means!" Nevertheless, Luther's pastoral advice was calculated to jar Melanchthon out of morbid introspection. Great sinners know liberation when they have it, but Melanchthon had been a scrupulous, pious Catholic. Luther's words did not bring him assurance, but only doubts. For his assurance depended not so much on God's promise to the ungodly *as* ungodly (Rom. 4:5), but on his own ability to see growth and improvement in his "Christian walk." Luther's frustrated counsel was not an invitation to serve sin, but an attempt to shock Melanchthon into realizing that his only true righteousness was *external* to him. "The whole gospel is outside of us."

In order to define justification precisely, we ought to use the Reformers' full formula, taking the words of William Hordern:

> The Doctrine is properly called *justification by grace alone through faith alone*. Through the years a kind of shorthand has risen whereby we have spoken of justification by faith alone. In and of itself this is innocent enough and it avoids having to keep repeating the full formula. But the trouble with this abbreviation is that it can give a quite mistaken view of what the doctrine is really saying. When by grace alone is dropped from the phrase, the impression is that faith is the primary element in justification. But then faith begins to appear as something that we must perform. And so, ironically, the term justification by faith leads to a new doctrine of works. Faith comes to be seen as a work that we must accomplish in order to save ourselves.[8]

Ironically, even in the Lutheran church the concept that Hordern warned against is rife. A recent national survey in North America found out that an overwhelming percentage of Lutherans, across synodical lines, were functioning Roman Catholics. Many of them answered yes to questions such as, "I think I will be saved because I am trying harder to obey the Ten Commandments this week than last week."[9] A few years ago Will Herberg noted that a predominant aspect of North American religion was that we have faith in faith. One American evangelist, in fact, wrote a booklet entitled, "How to Have Faith in Your Faith." The idea is that to believe fervently is good, regardless of what it is we believe. No doubt this attitude is partly the result of the abbreviation *justification by faith alone.*

I mentioned that the Roman Catholic position was that we are saved by grace, and that grace is an infused power to lead a God-pleasing life. Luther did not agree that the word *grace* in the Bible means *an infused power to live a God-pleasing life,* as though grace were a substance. He said rather that grace is the opposite of merit: unmerited favor. We are saved by God's graciousness to us. God has decided to be gracious to sinners; we are saved by his graciousness.

Grace is not even a principle. It is an attribute, a disposition, of the living God. He is gracious. To be saved by God's graciousness is to give up on merit, or to use Luther's phrase, to "let God be God." Luther believed that to let God be God is to recognize that it is he who does the saving, and part of what is requisite in that is for us to quit trying to do the saving. The Roman Catholic position was that God and the believer working together can save, while the Reformation position insisted that God can save sinners only if they stop trying to save themselves. The cause of God's graciousness to sinners is not our faith, the Reformers insisted; the cause of God's graciousness to sinners is his graciousness. In other words, we do not leverage the love of God out of heaven. We do not have an Archimedean point for a lever to pry it down toward us. Our openness, our yearning for him, our longing to be part of his gracious plan—none of this justifies; none of these dispositions or desires on our part can pry open the gate of heaven.

If the Reformers were correct in interpreting what Paul was getting at in his epistle to the Romans, 100 percent of our salvation is due to God's graciousness, and 0 percent is due to anything in us. The Reformation's answer to the question, "Do I contribute anything to my salvation?" is, "Yes, your sin!" The value then of saving faith is only a value in virtue of the Object grasped. Faith itself has no virtue; it connects us to the One who is virtuous.

Along these lines, a book that has been a low point in the history of publishing in the West appeared in the 1950s entitled *The Magic of Believing.* Again, it's Charlie Brown's line: It doesn't matter what you believe, as long as you believe in something. Belief helps to keep your blood pressure down, and you will be less likely to have ulcers if you have faith in something, no matter what it is. This was not the Reformers' position. For them, faith had no virtue on its own. It is, they said, an empty hand grasping the free treasure of Christ. The old sermon illustration is worth remembering: If a person happens to be drowning, and someone throws out a life-preserver and pulls the person in, it would be bizarre for the rescued party to say, "Did you see how I grasped that ring? Why, just look at these hands!"

Luther said that faith in Christ to save allows God to be who he is. And so the Reformation affirmation is that we are saved *on account of Christ through faith,* not that we are saved on account of faith through Christ. It is the graciousness of God that saves us by his act in Christ, not our faith itself. If we say that our faith is something that we offer to God—like some sort of transaction in which God offers salvation in exchange for our act of faith or decision, we are functioning Roman Catholics.

I used to say to some of my evangelical students that they ought to find a priest and join the Roman Catholic Church, because they shared the same theology and the priest could say it more clearly than they could. What has become blurred and confused in evangelical circles is quite clearly and articulately spelled out in the dogmatic conclusions of the Roman Catholic magisterium.

Man, said Luther and Calvin, has no faith, and he cannot produce any faith. We are all helpless, impotent, and bankrupt by virtue of our participation in Adam and Eve's act, and we cannot pull ourselves up by our own bootstraps. The place we find this most clearly expounded by Luther is in *The Bondage of the Will.*

I hear the reader asking, "Well then, is saving faith just a matter of knowing facts?" Hardly, and the Reformers knew that. They distinguished between *historical faith* and *saving faith.* Historical faith has human speculations as its goal or end. It is an intellectual acceptance of facts concerning Jesus' life, work, and death; nevertheless, it comes only from the human mind, acknowledging the facts, but remaining basically uninvolved with the One that caused the facts to happen. And the key phrase that Luther used was that the person who just has historical faith believes that none of this is *pro me,* or for me. Once a person comes to accept that this whole action summed up in the Nicene Creed is *for me,* then, said Luther, we are talking about the kind of faith that saves. There we have an active embracing of the Son of God and his self-sacrifice. You may say, "Ah ha! Then there is something self produced in faith after all." The Reformers would answer, "Not at all. God gets all of the credit when someone trusts Christ." It is the power of the Holy Spirit through the gospel that gives that inclination to us against our own.

One primary theme in the New Testament, and in the Reformation, is that Christ's death was outside of me and for me. It is not primarily something that changes me. After one has been declared righteous by grace through faith, this grace *will* begin to change us (sanctification). Nevertheless, its changing us is certainly not what justifies us. In Roman Catholicism, and in John Wesley's work, the accent falls on actual moral transformation; what makes us acceptable to God is his *internal* work of renovation within our hearts and lives. Thus, through the influence of Arminianism and Wesleyanism, the situation in many evangelical churches is almost indistinguishable on these points from medieval Rome. Some of the preaching in evangelicalism—certainly some of the Sunday school material and some of the addresses by retreat speakers and Christian leaders—all taken together as the basic spiritual diet, tend to reinforce that old intuition that good people are the ones who are saved and that those who are not so good are the ones who are lost.

The bellwether test as to where a person stands on this issue is what he or she does with Romans 7, particularly passages such as, "For the good that I will to do, I do not do; but the evil I will not to do, that I practice. O wretched man that I am! Who will deliver me from this body of death?" (vv. 19, 24). Often, those who are not grounded in the Reformation say that this was Paul's experience *before* he met the Lord. Those of us from a Reformation perspective, however, would probably say there is no better description of the Christian life in all of the Bible than Romans 7. The Reformers really believed that the Christian life was a matter of being *simul iustus et peccator*—simultaneously justified and sinful—and that we would remain in this tension until death. They were eager to proclaim Christ as Savior *and* Lord and would never have tolerated the dichotomy expressed by Zane Hodges and other antinomian Bible teachers. Further, they were absolutely opposed to a self-salvation by self-surrender.

Any righteousness that we have, even in the Christian life, is a gift to us. The Reformers would not have been especially impressed with the teaching that has come from the Keswick movement in England, from the German Higher Life movement, from Ian Thomas, from the American Finneyites, from Andrew Murray, or from some of the writings of Lewis Sperry Chafer. Consider this comment from B. B. Warfield on Chafer:

> Mr. Chafer makes use of all the jargon of the Higher Life teachers. In him, too, we hear of two kinds of Christians, whom he designates respectively "carnal men" and "spiritual men," on the basis of a misreading of 1 Cor. ii. 9ff; and we are told that the passage from the one to the other is at our option, whenever we care to "claim" the higher degree "by faith." With him, too, thus, the enjoyment of every blessing is suspended on our "claiming it." We hear here, too, of "letting" God, and, indeed, we almost hear of "engaging" the Spirit (as we engage, say, a carpenter) to do work for us; and we do explicitly hear of "making it possible for God" to do things—a quite terrible expression. Of course, we hear repeatedly of the duty and efficacy of "yielding"—and the act of "yielding ourselves" is quite in the customary manner discriminated from "consecrating" ourselves. . . .

Many of the elements present in medieval theology are replicated in North American fundamentalism and evangelicalism. The family resemblances on the doctrine of justification, if you want to talk across the spectrum of Christian theology, are Luther and Calvin, Wesley and Rome.

Did the Reformers then have any doctrine of sanctification? Of course they did. We are all familiar with the biblical announcements as to what is involved in sanctification: the Word, the sacraments, prayer, fellowship, sharing the gospel, serving God and neighbor. And the Reformation tradition acknowledges that there are biblical texts that speak of sanctification as complete already. This is not a perfection that is empirical or observable, but a definitive declaration that because we are "in Christ," we are set apart and reckoned holy by his sacrifice (1 Cor. 1:30; Heb. 10 and so on). Anybody who is in Christ is sanctified, because Christ's holiness is imputed to the Christian believer, just as Jesus says in John 17:19, "For them I sanctify myself, that they too may be truly sanctified." God sees the believer as holy. That means that Wesley should not have terrified Christian brethren with texts such as, "Without holiness, no one will see the Lord." The Christian is holy; it is all imputed. And then there are texts such as, "Be holy as I am holy." What would the Reformers do with that? They would say we are called to be holy. But why should we be holy if we are already perfect in Christ? Because we are saved unto *good works*, not unto licentiousness, according to Romans 6; the question has been asked before. Good works are done out of thankfulness of heart by the believer who *has been saved*, not by one who is trying *to be saved*.

Clearly the Reformers had a doctrine of sanctification. They believed that the law in the Bible has three uses. First, it is a *civil* ordinance to keep us from stealing each other's wives, husbands, and speedboats. The civil use of the law applies to the whole culture. Second, the *theological* use of the law is to reveal our sin and drive us to despair and terror so that we will seek a savior. Luther believed that is a primary use of the law in all of Scripture. But the Reformers also believed in a third use of the law, and that is a *didactic* use, to teach the Christian God's will for holy living.

If a Christian is reading the law and says, "This is not yet true of me: I don't love God with all my heart, and I certainly don't love my neighbor as I love myself. In fact, just today I failed to help a poor man on the side of the road who was having car trouble. I must not yet be a Christian," here the Reformers would counsel, "You hurry back to the second use of the law and flee to Christ where sanctification is truly, completely, and perfectly located." After this experience, the believer will feel a greater sense of freedom to obey, and this is the *only* way that one will ever feel free to obey. The difference between all Higher Life movements and the Reformation perspective finally turns on the question of what Baptists call the assurance of salvation and what the Reformers called *fides reflexa* (reflexive faith). The answer of the Higher Life movement to the struggling Christian is, Surrender more, or,

What are you holding back from the Lord? The Reformation answer is different.

A friend of mine was walking down a street in Minneapolis one day and was confronted by an evangelical brother who asked, "Brother, are you saved?" Hal rolled his eyes back and said, "Yes." That didn't satisfy this brother, so he said, "Well, *when* were you saved?" Hal said, "About two thousand years ago, about a twenty minutes' walk from downtown Jerusalem."

The most important thing to remember is that the death of Christ was in fact a death even for Christian failure. Christ's death saves even *Christians* from sin. There is always "room at the cross" for unbelievers, it seems. But what we ought to be telling people is that there is room there for Christians, too. This, then, is what was meant earlier by the motif of law—gospel—law in many evangelical circles. The law condemns, driving us to Christ the gospel, from whom we receive both instantaneous justification and progressive sanctification for the rest of our lives, according to the Reformation perspective. While the law still guides, it can never make threats. But in contemporary evangelicalism, the law can come back to undermine the confidence of the gospel. It can still make threats; it can still condemn. There is wonderful grace for the "sinner," and the evangelical is at his best in evangelism. But the question as to whether there is enough grace for the sinful Christian is an open one in many gatherings, and I have had many students tell me, "My last state is worse than the first. I think I've got to leave the faith because I feel worse now than I did before." I have had people come up to me after I had spoken and tell me, "This is about the last shot I've got. My own Christian training is killing me. I can understand how, before I was a Christian, Christ's death was for me, but I am not at all sure that his death is for me now because I have surrendered so little to him and hold so much back. My trouble really began when I committed myself to Christ as Lord and Savior." That perversion can be the result of pastoral teaching, Sunday school curriculum, and the declarations of evangelical Christian leaders.

Instead, there must be a clear and unqualified pronouncement of the assurance of salvation on the basis of the fullness of the atonement of Christ. In other words, even a Christian can be saved. The other "gospel," in its various forms (Higher Life, legalism, the "carnal Christian" teaching, and so on) is tearing us to pieces. I must warn you that the answer to this devastating problem is not available on every street corner. It is available only in the Reformation tradition. This is not because that particular tradition has access to information other traditions do not possess. Rather, it is because the same debate that climaxed in that sixteenth-century movement has erupted again and again since in less precise form. In fact, since Christ's debates with the Pharisees and Paul's arguments with the legalists, this has been *the* debate of Christian history. At no time since the apostolic era were these issues so thoroughly discussed and debated, as they were in the sixteenth century. To ignore the biblical wisdom, scholarship, and brilliant insights of such giants as the Reformers is simply to add to our ignorance the vice of pride and self-sufficiency. The Reformation position is the real evangelical position.

The only way out is an exposition of the Scriptures that has to do with *law* and *gospel*—an exposition of the Scriptures that places Christ at the center of the text for everybody, including the Christian. All of the Bible is about him. All of the Bible is even about him for the Christian!

I used to tell my students at an evangelical Christian college that they had never heard real preaching, with the exception of a few sound evangelistic appeals. Their weekly diet in the congregation was not, as it should have been, a proclamation of God's grace to them because of the finished and atoning death of Christ—God's grace for them *as Christians*. That emphasis is desperately needed. And the only way to find that kind of preaching is to go back to when it was done, and it was done in the sixteenth century. The real hope for the church in the West, humanly speaking, lies with evangelicals. Barring an unusual act of God, the mainline churches are not going to get the church back on its feet. Generally speaking, they simply do not have a high enough view of the inspiration of Scripture to listen to it anymore.

The evangelicals do. They believe that the Scriptures are true, but tend to read them as a recipe book for Christian living, rather than for the purpose of finding Christ who died for them and who is the answer to their unchristian living. We must have that kind of renewal, and it can only come from the evangelicals. The evangelical movement in America must begin reading from the Reformers instead of pretending that they are committed only to the Bible, without any system of doctrine, when it is clear what books, tapes, and sermons have shaped their faith and practice. Another thing we are going to have to re-examine in connection with Christian growth is the question of the sacraments—not sacramentalism, but the very nature of the sacraments (baptism and the Lord's Supper), which receives far more attention in the Scriptures than in contemporary evangelical discussion and piety. We are going to have to talk about them again. The major themes of the Reformers are precisely the ones the evangelical must be encouraged to recover.

Appendix 1

Ten Propositions

1. It is impossible that saving faith can exist without a new nature and thereby new affections (love, a desire for holiness, and so on).
2. Saving faith is nevertheless not the same thing as such affections or desires and does not include in its definition the effects of which the new birth is the cause.
3. It is not enough to say that we are justified and accepted by grace alone, for even Rome has agreed that it is only by God's grace that we can become transformed in holiness. We must add that we are justified by grace alone through faith alone, and it is a great error to change the meaning of faith to include acts of obedience and repentance in an effort to make a disposition other than knowledge, assent, and trust a condition of justification.
4. The definition of saving faith is: Knowledge, which we take to mean the intellectual grasp of the relevant historical and doctrinal facts concerning Christ's person and work and our misery; Assent, or the volitional agreement of our hearts and minds that these facts are true; and Trust, which is the assurance that these facts that are true are not only true generally, but true in my own case. In this way I abandon all

hope for acceptance with God besides the holiness and right-eousness of Christ.

5. Not only is the ground of our justification the person and work of Christ; the assurance, hope, and comfort that this salvation belongs to us must have Christ alone as its sufficient object and faith as its sufficient instrument.

6. While evidences of the new birth can be discerned by ourselves and others, such evidences do not have sufficient righteousness or holiness to form a ground of assurance or a clear conscience. For, as Calvin says, "A fine confidence of salvation is left to us, if by moral conjecture we judge that at the present moment we are in grace, but we know not what will become of us tomorrow!"

7. We affirm that, although no one will be justified by works, no one will be saved without them.

8. We affirm that it is contempt and presumption, not faith, that produces apathy with regard to the commands of God.

9. He seeks to tear Christ apart who imagines a savior without a lord. Christ offers no priesthood outside his prophetic ministry and kingly reign.

10. Those who are confident in this: that because they have exercised their will or mind in such a way that God is obligated thereby to save them, show contempt for God's holiness and Christ's cross.

Appendix 2

Benjamin B. Warfield on Lewis Sperry Chafer

A Review of *He That Is Spiritual*

Mr. Chafer is in the unfortunate and, one would think, very uncomfortable, condition of having two inconsistent systems of religion struggling together in his mind. He was bred an Evangelical, and, as a minister of the Presbyterian Church, South, stands committed to Evangelicism of the purest water. But he has been long associated in his work with a coterie of "Evangelists" and "Bible Teachers," among whom there flourishes that curious religious system (at once curiously pretentious and curiously shallow) which the Higher Life leaders of the middle of the last century brought into vogue; and he has not been immune to its infection. These two religious systems are quite incompatible. The one is the product of the Protestant Reformation and knows no determining power in the religious life but the grace of God; the other comes straight from the laboratory of John Wesley, and in all its forms—modifications and mitigations alike—remains incur-

211

ably Arminian, subjecting all gracious workings of God to human determining. The two can unite as little as fire and water.

Mr. Chafer makes use of all the jargon of the Higher Life teachers. In him, too, we hear of two kinds of Christians, whom he designates respectively "carnal men" and "spiritual men," on the basis of a misreading of 1 Cor. ii. 9ff (pp. 8, 109, 146); and we are told that the passage from the one to the other is at our option, whenever we care to "claim" the higher degree "by faith" (p. 146). With him, too, thus, the enjoyment of every blessing is suspended on our "claiming it" (p. 129). We hear here, too, of "letting" God (p. 84) and, indeed, we almost hear of "engaging" the Spirit (as we engage, say, a carpenter) to do work for us (p. 94); and we do explicitly hear of "making it possible for God" to do things (p. 148)—a quite terrible expression. Of course, we hear repeatedly of the duty and efficacy of "yielding"—and the act of "yielding ourselves" is quite in the customary manner discriminated from "consecrating" ourselves (p. 84), and we are told, as usual, that by it the gate is opened into the divinely appointed path (pp. 91, 49). The quietistic phrase, "not by trying but by a right adjustment," meets us (p. 39), and naturally such current terms as "known sin" (p. 62), "moment by moment triumph" (pp. 34, 60), "the life that is Christ" (p. 31), "unbroken walk in the Spirit" (pp. 53, 113), "unbroken victory" (p. 96), even Pearsall Smith's famous "at once": "the Christian may realize *at once* the heavenly virtues of Christ" (p. 39, the italics his). It is a matter of course after this that we are told that it is not *necessary* for Christians to sin (p. 125)—the emphasis repeatedly thrown on the word "necessary" leading us to wonder whether Mr. Chafer remembers that, according to the Confession of Faith to which, as a Presbyterian minister, he gives his adhesion, it is in the strict sense of the term *not necessary* for anybody to sin, even for the "natural man" (ix, 1).

Although he thus serves himself with their vocabulary, and therefore of course repeats the main substance of their teaching, there are lengths, nevertheless, to which Mr. Chafer will not go with his Higher Life friends. He quite decidedly repels, for example, the expectation of repetitions of the "Pentecostal manifestations" (p. 47), and this is the more notable because in his expositions of certain passages in which the charismatic Spirit is spoken of he has missed that fact, to the confusion of his doctrine of the Spirit's modes of action. With equal decisiveness he repels "such man-made, unbiblical terms as 'second blessing,' 'a second work of grace,' 'the higher life,' and various phrases used in the perverted statements of the doctrines of sanctification and perfection" (pp. 31, 33), including such phrases as "entire sanctification" and "sinless perfection" (pp. 107, 139). He is hewing here, however, to a rather narrow line, for he does teach that there are two kinds of Christian, the "carnal" and the "spiritual"; and he does teach that it is quite unnecessary for spiritual men to sin and that the way is fully open to them to live a life of unbroken victory if they choose to do so.

Mr. Chafer opens his book with an exposition of the closing verses of the second and the opening verses of the third chapter of 1 Corinthians. Here he finds three classes of men contrasted, the "natural" or unregenerated man, and the "carnal" and "spiritual" men, both of whom are regenerated, but the latter of whom lives on a higher plane. "There are two great spiritual changes which are possible to human experience," he writes (p. 8)—"the change from the 'natural' man to the saved man, and the change from the 'carnal' man to the 'spiritual' man. The former is divinely accomplished when there is real faith in Christ; the latter is accomplished when there is a real adjustment to the Spirit. The 'spiritual' man is the divine ideal in life and ministry, in power with God and man, in unbroken fellowship and blessing." This teaching is indistinguishable from what is ordinarily understood by the doctrine of a "second blessing," "a second work of grace," "the higher life." The subsequent expositions only make the matter clearer. In them the changes are rung on the double salvation, on the one hand from the *penalty* of sin, on the other from the *power* of sin—"salvation into safety" and "salvation into sanctity" (p. 109). And the book closes with a long-drawn-out "analogy" between these two salvations. This "analogy" is announced with this statement: "The Bible treats our deliverance from the bondservitude to sin as a distinct form of salvation and there is an analogy between this and the more familiar aspect of salvation which is from the guilt and penalty of sin" (p. 141). It ends with this fuller summary:

> There are a multitude of sinners for whom Christ has died who are not now saved. On the divine side, everything has been provided, and they have only to enter by faith into His saving grace as it is for them in Christ Jesus. Just so, there are a multitude of saints whose sin-nature has been perfectly judged and every provision made on the divine side for a life of victory and glory to God who are not now realizing a life of victory. They have only to enter by faith into the saving grace from the power and dominion of sin. . . . Sinners are not saved until they trust the Saviour, and saints are not victorious until they trust the Deliverer. God has made this *possible* through the cross of His Son. Salvation from the power of sin must be claimed by faith. [p. 146]

No doubt what we are first led to say of this is that here is the quintessence of Arminianism. God saves no one—He only makes salvation *possible* for men. Whether it becomes *actual* or not depends absolutely on their own act. It is only by their act that it is made *possible* for God to save them. But it is equally true that here is the quintessence of the Higher Life teaching, which merely emphasizes that part of this Arminian scheme which refers to the specific matter of sanctification. "What He provides and bestows is in the fullest divine perfection; but our adjustment is human and therefore subject to constant improvement. The *fact* of our possible deliverance, which depends on Him alone, does not change. We will have as much at any time as we make it possible for Him to bestow" (p. 148).

When Mr. Chafer repels the doctrine of "sinless perfection" he means, first of all, that our sinful natures are not eradicated. Entering the old controversy waged among perfectionists between the "Eradicationists" and "Suppressionists," he ranges himself with the latter—only preferring to use the word "control." "The divine method of dealing with the sin-nature in the believer is by direct and unceasing *control* over that nature by the indwelling Spirit." (p. 134). One would think that this would yield at least a sinlessness of conduct; but that is to forget that, after all, in this scheme the divine action waits on man's. "The Bible teaches that, while the divine provision is one of *perfection* of life, the human appropriation is always *faulty* and therefore the results are *imperfect* at best" (p. 157). God's provisions only make it *possible* for us to live without sinning. The result is therefore only that we are under no *necessity* of sinning. But whether we shall actually sin or not is our own affair. "His provisions are always *perfect*, but our appropriation is always *imperfect*." "What he provides and bestows is in the fullest divine perfection, but our adjustment is human. . . . The *fact* of our possible deliverance, which depends on Him alone, does not change. We will have as much at any time as we make it possible for Him to *bestow*." (pp. 148, 149.) Thus it comes about that we can be told both that "the child of God and citizen of heaven may live a superhuman life, in harmony with his heavenly calling by an unbroken walk in the Spirit,"—that "the Christian may realize *at once* the heavenly virtues of Christ" (p. 39); and that, in point of fact, he does nothing of the kind, that "all Christians *do* sin." (p. 111). A possibility of not sinning which is unillustrated by a single example and will never be illustrated by a single example is, of course, a mere postulate extorted by a theory. It is without practical significance. A universal effect is not accounted for by its possibility.

Mr. Chafer conducts his discussion of these "two general theories as to the divine method of dealing with the sin-nature in believers" on the presumption that "both theories cannot be true, for they are contradictory" (p. 135). "The two theories are irreconcilable," he says. (p. 139.) "We are either to be delivered by the abrupt removal of all tendency to sin, and so no longer need the enabling power of God to combat the power of sin, or we are to be delivered by the immediate and constant power of the indwelling Spirit." This irreducible "either–or" is unjustified. In point of fact, both "eradication" and "control" are true. God delivers us from our sinful nature, not indeed by "abruptly" but by progressively eradicating it, and meanwhile controlling it. For the new nature which God gives us is not an absolutely new somewhat, alien to our personality, inserted into us, but our old nature itself remade—a veritable recreation, or making of all things new. Mr. Chafer is quite wrong when he says: "Salvation is not a so-called 'change of heart.' It is not a transformation of the old; it is a regeneration, or creation, of something wholly new, which is possessed in conjunction with the old so long as we are in the body." (p. 113). That this furnishes out each Christian with two conflicting natures does not appall him. He says, quite calmly: "The unregenerate have but one nature, while the regenerate have two." (p. 116.) He does not seem to see that thus the man is not saved at all: a different, newly created, man is substituted for him. When the old man is got rid of—and that the old man has to be ultimately got rid of he does not doubt—the saved man that is left is not at all the old man that was to be saved, but a new man that has never needed any saving.

It is a temptation to a *virtuoso* in the interpretation of Scripture to show his mettle on hard places and in startling results. Mr. Chafer has not been superior to this temptation. Take but one example. "All Christian love," he tells us (p. 40) "according to the Scriptures, is distinctly a manifestation of divine love *through* the human heart"—a quite unjustified assertion. But Mr. Chafer is ready with an illustration. "A statement of this is found," he declares, "at Rom. v, 5, 'because the love of God is shed abroad (lit., gushes forth) in our hearts by (produced, or caused by) the Holy Spirit, which is given unto us.'" Then he comments as follows:

> This is not the working of the human affection; it is rather the direct manifestation of the "love of God" passing *through* the heart of the believer *out from* the indwelling Spirit. It is the realization of the last petition of the High Priestly prayer of our Lord: "That the love wherewith thou hast loved me may be in them" (John xvii, 26). It is simply God's love working *in* and *through* the believer. It could not be humanly produced, or even imitated, and it of necessity goes out to the objects of divine affection and grace, rather than to the objects of human desire. A human heart cannot *produce* divine love, but it can *experience* it. To have a heart that feels the compassion of God is to drink of the wine of heaven.

All this *bizarre* doctrine of the transference of God's love, in the sense of His active power of loving, to us, so that it works out from us again as new centers, is extracted from Paul's simple statement that by the Holy Spirit which God has given us His love to us is made richly real to our apprehension! Among the parenthetical philogical comments which Mr. Chafer has inserted into his quo-

tation of the text, it is a pity that he did not include one noting
that *ekgeo* is not *eiskeo,* and that Paul would no doubt have used
eiskeo, had he meant to convey that idea.

A haunting ambiguity is thrust upon Mr. Chafer's whole teaching by his hospitable entertainment of contradictory systems of
thought. There is a passage near the beginning of his book, not
well expressed it is true, but thoroughly sound in its fundamental conception, in which expression is given to a primary principle of the Evangelical system, which, had validity been given to
it, would have preserved Mr. Chafer from his regrettable dalliance
with the Higher Life formulas. "In the Bible," he writes,

> the divine offer and condition for the cure of sin in an unsaved
> person is crystallized into the one word, "believe"; for the forgive-
> ness of sin with the unsaved is only offered as an indivisible part
> of the whole divine work of salvation. The saving work of God
> includes many mighty undertakings other than the forgiveness of
> sin, and salvation depends only upon *believing.* It is not possible to
> separate some one issue from the whole work of His saving grace,
> such as forgiveness, and claim this apart from the indivisible whole.
> It is, therefore, a grievous error to direct an unsaved person to seek
> forgiveness of his sins as a separate issue. A sinner minus his sins
> would not be a Christian; for salvation is more than subtraction, it
> is addition. "I give unto them eternal life." Thus the sin question
> with the unsaved will be cured as a part of, but never separate
> from, the whole divine work of salvation, and this salvation
> depends upon *believing.* [p. 62]

If this passage means anything, it means that salvation is a unit,
and that he who is united to Jesus Christ by faith receives in Him
not only justification—salvation from the *penalty* of sin—but also
sanctification—salvation from the *power* of sin—both "safety" and
"sanctity." These things cannot be separated, and it is a grievous
error to teach that a true believer in Christ can stop short in "carnality," and, though having the Spirit *with* him and *in* him, not
have Him *upon* him—to use a not very lucid play upon prepositions in which Mr. Chafer indulges. In his attempt to teach this,
Mr. Chafer is betrayed (p. 29) into drawing out a long list of char-
acteristics of the two classes of Christians, in which he assigns to

the lower class practically all the marks of the unregenerate man. Salvation is a process; as Mr. Chafer loyally teaches, the flesh continues in the regenerate man and strives against the Spirit—he is to be commended for preserving even to the Seventh Chapter of Romans its true reference—but the remainders of the flesh in the Christian do not constitute his characteristic. He is in the Spirit and is walking, with however halting steps, by the Spirit; and it is to all Christians, not to some, that the great promise is given, "Sin shall not have dominion over you," and the great assurance is added, "Because ye are not under the law but under grace." He who believes in Jesus Christ is under grace, and his whole course, in its process and in its issue alike, is determined by grace, and therefore, having been predestined to be conformed to the image of God's Son, he is surely being conformed to that image, God Himself seeing to it that he is not only called and justified but also glorified. You may find Christians at every stage of this process, for it is a process through which all must pass; but you will find none who will not in God's own good time and way pass through every stage of it. There are not two kinds of Christians, although there are Christians at every conceivable stage of advancement towards the one goal to which all are bound and at which all shall arrive.

Princeton
Benjamin B. Warfield

Reprinted from the *Princeton Theological Review* 17 (April 1919), 322–27. The book being reviewed is, Lewis Sperry Chafer, *He That Is Spiritual* (New York: Our Hope, 1918).

Appendix 3

Select Doctrinal Statements from the Reformation

On Repentance

Luther spoke, in the Smalcald Articles, of "those fanatics" who separate justification and sanctification. "If sin does what it wishes, the Holy Spirit and faith are not present," he wrote, since the dominion of sin has been broken. Earlier in this Third Article, Luther wrote:

Here the fiery angel Saint John, the preacher of true repentance, intervenes. With a single thunderbolt he strikes and destroys both [Pharisee and Sadducee]. "Repent," he says. On the one hand there are some who think, "We have already done penance," and on the other hand there are others who suppose, "We need no repentance." But John says: "Repent, both of you. Those of you in the former group are false penitents, and those of you in the latter are false saints. Both of you need the forgiveness of sins, for neither of you knows what sin really is, to say nothing of repenting and shunning sin. None of you is good. All of you are full of unbelief, blindness, ignorance of God and God's will. For he is here present, and from his fullness have we all received, grace upon grace. No man can be just before God without him. Accordingly, if you would repent, repent rightly. Your repentance accomplishes nothing. And you hypocrites who think you do not need to repent, you brood of vipers, who has given you any assurance that you will escape the wrath to come?"

Luther's Basic Theological Writings,
ed. Timothy F. Lull (Minneapolis: Fortress, 1989), 525–26

On Good Works

Luther also praised good works, as long as they were not viewed as conditions for peace with God:

"By their fruits you shall know them" (Matt. 7:20). But here a question arises: Since we say that God saves us by faith alone, without regard to works, why does Saint Peter say that He judges, not according to the person but according to works? The answer is this: What we have taught with regard to the fact that faith alone justifies before God, is true and beyond a doubt; for it is so clear from Scripture that it cannot be denied. That here the apostle says God judges according to the works is also true. But we must certainly hold that where there is no faith, there can be no good works; and, on the other hand, that there is no faith where there are no good works. Therefore join faith and good works so that all Christian life is summed up in these two. As you now live, so it will be with you hereafter; for God will judge you according to your life.

Therefore although God does judge us according to our works, it still remains true that works are only the fruits of faith by which we perceive where there is faith or unbelief. Consequently, God will sentence and convict you in the light of your works [because] these reveal either that you have or have not believed. Similarly, you cannot more effectively convict and judge a liar than by his words. Yet it is evident that he is not made a liar by the words but became a liar before he spoke the lie, for the lie must rise from the heart into the mouth.

Therefore, very simply understand this passage in this way. Works are fruits and signs of faith, and God judges men according to such fruits. These must certainly follow faith that men may publicly see whether there is faith or unbelief in the heart. God will not judge by your name, whether you are called a Christian or have been baptized. But He will tell you: If you are a Christian, tell Me where the fruits are by which you can prove your faith.

From the Weimar edition, vol. 12, 289

Luther on the Nature of Faith

Faith, however, is a divine work in us. It changes us and makes us to be born anew of God (Jn. 1); it kills the old Adam and makes altogether different men, in heart and spirit and mind and powers, and it brings with it the Holy Ghost. Oh, it is a living, busy, active, mighty thing, this faith; and so it is impossible for it not to do good works incessantly. It does not ask whether there are good works to do, but before the question rises it has already done them, and is always at the doing of them. He who does not these works is a faithless man. . . . Faith is a living, daring confidence in God's grace, so sure and certain that a man would stake his life on it a thousand times. This confidence in God's grace and knowledge of it makes men glad and bold and happy in dealing with God and all his creatures; and this is the work of the Holy Ghost in faith. . . . Such righteousness, nature and free will and all our powers cannot bring into existence.

Commentary on Romans
(reprint; Grand Rapids: Kregel, 1954), xvii–xviii

Calvin on Regeneration

Finally, we acknowledge that this regeneration is so effected in us that, until we slough off this mortal body, there remains always in us much imperfection and infirmity, so that we always remain poor and wretched sinners in the presence of God. And, however much we ought day by day to increase and grow in God's righteousness, there will never be plenitude or perfection while we live here. Thus we always have need of the mercy of God to obtain the remission of our faults and offenses. And so we ought always to look for our righteousness in Jesus Christ and not at all in ourselves, and in him be confident and assured, putting no faith in our works.

Article 9, the Genevan Confession (1536)
Confessions and Catechisms of the Reformation, ed. Mark Noll (Grand Rapids: Baker, 1991), 128

Editor's Note:

For detailed summaries of the officially adopted positions of the Protestant churches, we refer the reader to the following:

1) Luther's Small and Large Catechisms
2) The Formula of Concord
3) The Heidelberg Catechism
4) The Westminister Confession of Faith and Catechisms

Endnotes

Introduction: *Don't Judge a Book by Its Cover*

1. Unless stated otherwise, all Hodges quotations are taken from Zane C. Hodges, *Absolutely Free!: A Biblical Reply to Lordship Salvation* (Grand Rapids: Zondervan, 1989).

2. Ibid., 228 n. 5.

3. Ibid., 145.

4. Ibid., 219 n. 1.

5. All Stanley quotations are taken from Charles Stanley, *Eternal Security* (Nashville: Oliver Nelson/Thomas Nelson, 1990), 121–29.

6. John Calvin, *Institutes of the Christian Religion*, 2 vols., ed. John T. McNeill, trans. Ford Lewis Battles (Philadelphia: Westminster, 1960), 3.18.2, 4, 6.

7. Ibid., 3.3.14.

8. Unless stated otherwise, all MacArthur quotations are taken from John F. MacArthur, Jr., *The Gospel According to Jesus* (Grand Rapids: Zondervan, 1988).

9. Calvin, *Institutes*, 3.3.5.

10. Ibid., 3.3.1.

11. Louis Berkhof, *Systematic Theology* (Edinburgh: Banner of Truth, 1958), 505.

12. Richard A. Muller, *Dictionary of Latin and Greek Theological Terms* (Grand Rapids: Baker, 1985), 116.

13. Calvin, *Institutes*, 3.11.14.

14. Ibid., 3.18.9.

15. John Calvin, *Commentaries*.

16. MacArthur argued in his first editions that "the Bible does not recognize faith that lacks this element of active repentance" (p. 32); that "repentance is a critical element of saving faith" (p. 162), and that "repentance is a critical element of genuine faith" (p. 172). However, when we discussed the confusion this might cause between faith and repentance, MacArthur changed the text to read "conversion." This is a substantial change that brings MacArthur into harmony with the Reformation interpretation of these key texts on this point. While faith and repentance are inseparable, and repentance is much more than a synonym for believing in Christ (contra Hodges), they are also distinct; repentance is not faith and faith is not repentance, even though both are certain fruits of conversion or effectual calling (John 1:12–13; Rom. 9:12–18; Eph. 2:1–5).

17. Calvin, *Institutes*, 3.3.1.

18. Ibid., 3.2.29.

19. Ibid.

20. Ibid., 3.19.2.

21. Timothy George, "The Spirituality of the Radical Reformation" in *Christian Spirituality: High Middle Ages and Reformation*, ed. Jill Raitt (London: Routledge and Kegan Paul, 1987), 346.

22. Calvin, *Institutes*, 3.13.3–5.

23. Ibid., 3.14.19–3.15.1.

24. Ibid., 4.1.8.

25. John Newton, *Works*, vol. 1 (Edinburgh: Banner of Truth, reprinted 1985), 348.

26. Ibid., 195.

Chapter 1 *Repentance in Romans*

1. Foreword to John F. MacArthur, Jr., *The Gospel According to Jesus* (Grand Rapids: Zondervan, 1988), xi.

2. Zane C. Hodges, *Absolutely Free!: A Biblical Reply to Lordship Salvation* (Grand Rapids: Zondervan, 1989), 27.

3. John Murray, *The Epistle to the Romans*, vol. 1 (Grand Rapids: Eerdmans, 1968), 212.

4. For a helpful refutation of this very popular but dangerously false use of Paul's statements in 1 Corinthians 3:1–4, see Ernest C. Reisinger, *What Should We Think of "the Carnal Christian"?* (Edinburgh: Banner of Truth, 1978).

5. See chapter 7, "Dropping Out," in Hodges, *Absolutely Free!* 79–88.

6. Anders Nygren, *Commentary on Romans*, trans. Carl C. Rasmussen (Philadelphia: Muhlenberg, 1949), 242–46.

Chapter 2 *The Law According to Jesus*

1. Unless stated otherwise, all MacArthur references are to John F. MacArthur, Jr., *The Gospel According to Jesus* (Grand Rapids: Zondervan, 1988).

2. *D. Martin Luthers Werke, Kritische Gesamtausgabe*, Weimar, 1883–, 40I, 336f., author's translation.

3. Luther, ibid., 36, 25, 29, author's translation.

4. If you are inclined to believe that the despair I describe is unlikely to result from MacArthur's teaching, look at his new book, *Saved Without a Doubt* (Wheaton, Ill.: Victor, 1992), pp. 7–8 especially. In his opening pages, MacArthur quotes a letter from a parishoner who said that he began to doubt his salvation on account of a growing conviction in his heart, his powerlessness against temptation, *and MacArthur's preaching*. He said that he felt like a "pile of manure on the white marble floor of Christ."

To be fair, MacArthur claims to have written this to help Christians come to a genuine assurance of salvation, and in sections of his book (most of part 1 is sound and helpful) he has provided a true service to doubting Christians. The problem is consistency. Solid Reformation teachings in one section of the book are rendered useless by their misapplication in another. MacArthur's eleven tests to determine the genuineness of salvation (part 2 of his book) would drive anyone to despair.

The problem is not so much that MacArthur's descriptions do not describe genuine Christians as that it is nearly impossible to test for them. One of MacArthur's eleven tests of genuine salvation is asking oneself if there is a decreasing pattern of sin in one's life. The pattern of sin in a Christian's life should decrease with time, but at the same time sanctification will cause the Christian to develop a more tender conscience. While the Christian's state improves, in his or her own eyes it will grow progressively worse with the increasing awareness of the horror of sin. While a decreasing pattern of sin may describe the normative Christian life, it is a bad test for it. The same goes for many of MacArthur's other tests.

I do not believe that MacArthur intends to drive these people to despair, but this is the inevitable result when a pastor fails to distinguish between law and gospel in his preaching and teaching.

Chapter 3 *What Is Faith?*

1. Unless stated otherwise, all Hodges quotations are taken from Zane C. Hodges, *Absolutely Free!: A Biblical Reply to Lordship Salvation* (Grand Rapids: Zondervan, 1989).

2. Unless stated otherwise, all MacArthur quotations are taken from John F. MacArthur, Jr., *The Gospel According to Jesus: What Does Jesus Mean When He says, "Follow Me"?* (Grand Rapids: Zondervan, 1988).

3. It should come as no surprise that other noted evangelical leaders support Hodges's diagnosis. Earl Radmacher, president of the Western Conservative Baptist Seminary in Portland, echoes Hodges's remarks. Radmacher laments that false teachers, like savage wolves, are ripping the church apart and that the remedies that these teachers offer for the moral and ethical apathy in the modern church are "cures [which] seem more dangerous than the disease. One such suggested cure is popularly known as 'lordship salvation.'" See Hodges, *Absolutely Free!* ix.

4. That confusion is often caused by attaching adjectives to the word *faith* is illustrated by Earl Radmacher's response to a journal article by John MacArthur on the idea of faith in James's epistle. Radmacher points out that a "problem relates to MacArthur's handling of the word 'faith,' a word that is used sixteen times in James without ever needing a modifier." Yet, as Radmacher goes on to point out, MacArthur uses over twenty different adjectives with the term *faith* in his article ("dead faith," "saving faith," "intellectual faith," and so on). This is very confusing indeed. See Earl D. Radmacher, "First Response to 'Faith According to the Apostle James' by John F. MacArthur, Jr.," in *Journal of the Evangelical Theological Society* 33/1 (March 1990): 35–41.

5. Protestant orthodoxy has traditionally made several precise qualifications regarding the use of the term *cause*. The first distinction is the "efficient cause, or productive, effective cause, which is the agent productive of the motion or mutation in any sequence of causes and effects." A second distinction is the instrumental cause, which is "the means or medium, used to bring about a desired effect." See Richard A. Muller, *Dictionary of Latin and Greek Theological Terms* (Grand Rapids: Baker, 1985), s.v. "*causa,*" "*causa instrumentalis.*" For Hodges, faith is clearly the efficient cause, since the human agent is responsible for all motion, in this case the "appropriation" of eternal life. Protestant orthodoxy has argued that faith is a response to the grace of God, and thereby faith is an instrument, a means of the reception of salvation, not an efficient cause of salvation.

6. Louis Berkhof, *Systematic Theology* (Grand Rapids: Eerdmans, 1986), 505.

7. It is important to point out that a complete treatment of repentance is beyond the scope of this article, except as repentance relates to faith. As with the terminology for faith, both Hodges and MacArthur arrive at different definitions and roles for repentance in the *ordo salutis.*

8. See for example, Rudolf Bultmann and Artur Weiser, in Gerhard Kittel and Gerhard Friedrich, eds., *Theological Dictionary of the New Testament,* trans. Geoffrey Bromiley (Grand Rapids: Eerdmans, 1985), 6:174ff. Also valuable is B. B. Warfield's magisterial article, "The Biblical Doctrine of Faith," in *Biblical Doctrines* (Grand Rapids: Baker, 1981), 467–508. A fine introduction is found in J. I. Packer, "Faith," in Walter A. Elwell ed., *Evangelical Dictionary of Theology* (Grand Rapids: Baker, 1984), s.v. "faith," 399–402.

9. Which is the hiphil form of *'aman.*

10. Packer, "Faith," 399.

11. Warfield, "The Biblical Doctrine of Faith," 470–71.

12. Ibid., 470.

13. Ibid., 471.

14. Ibid., 474.

15. Ibid., 475.

16. Ibid.

17. Ibid., 476.

18. Packer, "Faith," 399–402.

19. Warfield, "The Biblical Doctrine of Faith," 478, emphasis mine.

20. Ibid., 479.

21. Ibid., 481–83.

22. Ibid., 495.

23. Ibid.

24. Ibid., 496.

25. Ibid., 482, 502.

26. Ibid., 504–5.

27. Packer, "Faith," 401.

28. MacArthur argued in his first editions of *The Gospel According to Jesus* that "the Bible does not recognize faith that lacks this element of active repentance" (p. 32); that "repentance is a critical element of saving faith" (p. 162); and that "repentance is a critical element of genuine faith" (p. 172). However, when we discussed the confusion this might cause between faith and repentance, MacArthur changed the text to read "conversion" instead of "faith." This is a substantial change that brings MacArthur into harmony with the Reformation interpretation of these key texts on this point. While faith and repentance are inseparable, and repentance is much more than a synonym for believing in Christ (contra Hodges), they are also distinct; repentance is not faith and faith is not repentance, even though both are certain fruits of conversion or effectual calling (John 1:12–13; Rom. 9:12–18; Eph. 2:1–5).

29. A. A. Hodge, *Outlines of Theology* (Grand Rapids: Zondervan, 1979), 487–89, emphasis mine.

30. Berkhof, *Systematic Theology*, 487.

Chapter 4 *Union with Christ*

1. John Lawson, *Introduction to Christian Doctrine* (Grand Rapids: Zondervan, 1986), 226–27.

2. John Calvin, *Institutes of the Christian Religion*, 2 vols., ed. John T. McNeill, trans. Ford Lewis Battles (Philadelphia: Westminster, 1967), 3.1.1.

3. Bill Bright, *Handbook for Christian Maturity* (San Bernardino, Calif.: Here's Life Pubs., 1981), 133–45.

4. Donald L. Alexander, Gerharde Forde, and Sinclair Ferguson, eds., *Christian Spirituality: Five Views of Sanctification* (Downers Grove, Ill.: InterVarsity, 1988), 57.

Chapter 5 *Calvin and the Council of Trent*

1. For the complete text of Trent's decisions, see "The Canons and Dogmatic Decrees of the Council of Trent," in Philip Schaff, *The Creeds of Christendom* (Grand Rapids: Baker, 1977), vol. 2, 77–206.

2. Ibid., Session Six, chaps. 1 and 5.

3. Ibid., Session Six, chaps. 8 and 11.

4. Ibid., Session Six, chaps. 7 and 16.

5. Ibid., Session Six, chap. 7.

6. Ibid., Session Six, chap. 11.

7. Ibid., Session Six, chaps. 9, 12, and 13.

8. Printed in *Selected Works of John Calvin, Tracts and Letters,* eds. Henry Beveridge and Jules Bonnet, vol. 3 (Grand Rapids: Baker, 1983).

9. Ibid., 113.

10. Ibid., 125.

11. Ibid., 115.

12. Ibid., 116.

13. Ibid., 134.

14. Ibid., 125.

15. Ibid., 135.

16. Ibid., 136.

Chapter 6 *Christ Crucified between Two Thieves*

1. The Puritan/Presbyterian consensus is found in the Westminster Confession of Faith, where the Continental Reformed view is rejected: "This infallible assurance doth not so belong to the essence of faith, but that a true believer may wait long, and conflict with many difficulties, before he be partaker of it." Further, believers who have attained assurance may again lose it "by negligence in preserving of it; by falling into some special sin, which woundeth the conscience, and grieveth the Spirit; by some sudden or vehement temptation; by God's withdrawing the light of his countenance, and suffering even such as fear him to walk in darkness and to have no light: yet are they never utterly destitute of that seed of God, and life of faith . . ." (chap. 18, 3–4). In other words, true faith may exist without assurance. However, Calvin argued that faith implies certainty. Faith "is an *assurance* that renders the conscience calm and peaceful before God's judgment." (3.2.16, based on Col. 2:2; 1 Thess. 1:5; Heb. 6:11, 10:22; Eph. 3:12).

Following Luther, Calvin counseled anxious believers to go back to the means of grace for greater assurance: to the promises of the Word, and the confirmation of that in baptism and Holy Communion. The Puritans offered this counsel, too (cf. Westminster Confession, chap. 14, 1), but emphasized also the role of external evidences of a changed life. I would argue that the Puritans' retention of the importance of the sacraments in this matter saved the best of them from an overindulgence in moral conjecture. Against the Anabaptist rejection of infant baptism, Calvin wrote, "He [Satan] is trying to take away from us the singular fruit of assurance and spiritual joy which is to be gathered from it, and also to diminish somewhat the glory of the divine goodness. For how sweet is it to godly minds to be assured, not only by word, but by sight, that they obtain so much favor with the Heavenly Father that their offspring are within his care?" (*Institutes,* 4.16.32). Holy Communion serves a similar purpose (4.17.1–2). Calvin would have been more eager to send those lacking assurance back to their baptism and the Lord's table for comfort, than to send them to their evidences of conversion. Since both MacArthur and Hodges deny infant baptism, and the tradition from which they both come generally downplays the significance of the sacraments, this essential prop to assurance is removed, rendering the external evidences of changed life the only marks of adoption, in MacArthur's case; and the external evidence of a decision in Hodges'.

2. The belief that faith implies certainty and assurance did not mean, as many of the Puritans seem to have assumed in their rejection of Calvin's position on assurance, that any believer (much less *every* believer) possessed assurance or faith in its fullness. "Surely, while we teach that faith ought to be certain and assured, we cannot imagine any certainty that is not tinged with doubt, or any assurance that is not assailed by some anxiety. On the other hand, we say that believers are in perpetual conflict with their own unbelief" (3.2.17). Nevertheless, for the Puritans, true faith could exist though one were entirely destitute of assurance and certainty. Calvin could not see how someone who truly trusted in Christ would have absolutely no certainty. After all, was not the conviction that

faith is not saving until we can say, "This happened *for me*" at the heart of the Reformation debate? As the Puritan divine Thomas Goodwin put it, "So also faith . . . implies not so much a persuasion that a man's sins are forgiven by God, as having recourse to him to forgive him" (p. 343 below).

3. Zacharias Ursinus, *A Commentary Upon the Heidelberg Catechism,* trans. G. W. Williard (Presbyterian and Reformed, 1852 edition), p. 115.

4. *The Works of George Gillespie,* from the 1846 edition (Edinburgh: Robert Ogle, and Oliver, and Boyd), reprinted by Still Waters Revival in 1991 (Edmonton, Canada), vol. 1, 104–5.

5. MacArthur, *The Gospel According to Jesus,* 21–22.

6. Gillespie, ibid.

7. Ibid.

8. Thomas Goodwin, *The Works of Thomas Goodwin* (Edinburgh: Banner of Truth, 1985), reprinted from vol. 8 of the Nichol edition of 1863, 346.

9. Ibid., 134.

10. Ibid., 128.

11. Ibid., 70.

12. Ibid., 72.

13. Ibid., 498.

14. Ibid., 523.

15. Thomas Hooker, *The Poor Doubting Christian Drawn to Christ* (reprint ed.; Grand Rapids: Baker, 1981), 29–33.

16. Ibid., 75.

17. Ibid., 50.

18. Richard Sibbes, *The Complete Works of Richard Sibbes* (Edinburgh: Nochol, 1862), vol. 1, 57.

19. Joseph Alleine, *A Sure Guide to Heaven* (reprint; Edinburgh: Banner of Truth, 1989), 21.

20. Ibid., 61.

21. Ibid., 75.

22. Ibid., 86.

23. David Hall, ed., *The Antinomian Controversy, 1636–38* (Durham, N.C.: Duke University Press, 1989), 15.

24. Ibid.

25. Alister McGrath, *Iustitia De: II* (Cambridge: Cambridge University Press, 1986), 118.

26. Quoted by Hall, *The Antinomian Controversy,* 19.

27. Ibid., 53.

Chapter 7 *An American Tale*

1. Cf. John F. MacArthur, Jr., *The Gospel According to Jesus* (Grand Rapids: Zondervan, 1988); and Zane C. Hodges, *Absolutely Free!: A Biblical Reply to Lordship Salvation* (Grand Rapids: Zondervan, 1989). MacArthur does allude to this ongoing debate in his first chapter, "A Look at the Issues," 21–33.

2. Cf. MacArthur, *The Gospel According to Jesus,* 25: "Dispensationalism is a fundamentally correct system of understanding God's program through the ages. . . . I consider myself a traditional premillennial dispensationalist."

3. For two interesting overviews of varying evangelical Christian approaches to the doctrine of the Christian life, see: (1) Donald L. Alexander, Gerharde Forde, and Sinclair Ferguson, eds., *Christian Spirituality: Five Views of Sanctification* (Downers Grove, Ill.: InterVarsity, 1988). It contains entries by Gerharde Forde (Lutheran), Sinclair Ferguson (Reformed), Laurence Wood (Wesleyan), Russell Spittler (Pentecostal), and Glenn Hin-

son (Contemplative). And, (2) Melvin E. Dieter, et al., *Five Views on Sanctification* (Grand Rapids: Zondervan, 1989). It contains entries by Melvin Dieter (Wesleyan), Anthony Hoekema (Reformed), Stanley Horton (Pentecostal), J. Robertson McQuilken (Keswick), and John Walvoord (Augustinian–dispensational).

For even more detailed studies on Wesleyan and Pentecostal views, see, respectively, Harold Lindström, *Wesley and Sanctification* (Wilmore, Ky.: Francis Asbury Press, 1980); and Donald W. Dayton, *Theological Roots of Pentecostalism* (Grand Rapids: Zondervan, 1987).

4. For a brief overview of the concerns of "covenant theology," see, for example, John Murray, *The Covenant of Grace* (London: Tyndale, 1954); and, O. Palmer Robertson, *The Christ of the Covenants* (Phillipsburg, N.J.: Presbyterian and Reformed, 1980). For "dispensational theology," see, for example, Charles Caldwell Ryrie, *Dispensationalism Today* (Chicago: Moody, 1965). Also, two graduates of Dallas Theological Seminary and former dispensationalists, Curtis Crenshaw and Grover Gunn, have given a sharp critique of their former beliefs in, Curtis Crenshaw and Grover Gunn, III, *Dispensationalism: Yesterday, Today, and Tomorrow* (Memphis: Footstool, 1985).

5. A scholarly and also popularly written account of Reformation spirituality, particularly as seen in the writings of Luther and Calvin, can be found in, Alister McGrath, *Roots That Refresh* (London: Hodder and Stoughton, 1991). Pp. 170–84, in particular, discuss the relationship of good works to faith.

McGrath has also briefly analyzed Luther's response to Agricola in, Alister McGrath, *Iustitia Dei: A History of the Doctrine of Justification* (Cambridge: Cambridge University Press, 1986), 2:27. Calvin's attack on the Libertines has been translated into English with a historical introduction by Benjamin Farley: John Calvin, *Treatises against the Anabaptists and the Libertines*, trans. and ed. Benjamin Farley (Grand Rapids: Baker, 1982), 159–325.

Three particularly helpful books that deal with the antinomian question among the Puritans are, (1) Dewey Wallace, *Puritans and Predestination* (Chapel Hill, N.C.: University of North Carolina Press, 1982), esp. chaps. 3–5; (2) John von Rohr, *The Covenant of Grace in Puritan Thought* (Atlanta: Scholars Press, 1986), esp. pp. 87–112; and, (3) William K. B. Stoever, *"A Faire and Easie Way to Heaven": Covenant Theology and Antinomianism in Early Massachusetts* (Middletown, Conn.: Wesleyan University Press, 1978), esp. chaps. 3–4 and 7–8.

6. For an account and interpretation of the movement, see, George M. Marsden, *Fundamentalism and American Culture: The Shaping of Twentieth Century Evangelicalism, 1870–1925* (Oxford: Oxford University Press, 1980); hereafter cited as, Marsden, *FAAC*.

7. The classic set of documents on fundamentalism can be found in, Reuban Torrey, A. C. Dixon, et al., eds., *The Fundamentals (Four Volumes)* (Los Angeles: Bible Institute of Los Angeles, 1917). Originally published between 1912 and 1915 in twelve volumes, it contains articles by those from the Princeton camp and the dispensational camp, along with some British spokespersons for evangelicalism like James Orr. Note, Marsden, *FAAC*, 119 (118–123 as a whole):

> *The Fundamentals* . . . had a long-term effect of greater importance than its immediate impact or lack thereof. It became a symbolic point of reference for identifying a "fundamentalist" movement. When in 1920 the term "fundamentalist" was coined, it called to mind the broad united front of the kind of opposition to modernism [of] these widely known, if little studied, volumes. In retrospect, the volumes retain some usefulness in tracing the outlines of the emerging movement. They represent the movement at a moderate and transitional stage before it was reshaped and pushed to extremes by the intense heat of controversy:

8. Space does not permit a detailed examination of all the tensions. The interested reader, however, will find much food for thought in, Marsden, *FAAC*, esp. 43–138.

9. On the history of Keswick and its place in American religious history, see, Marsden, *FAAC*, 77–101.

Not all adherents of Keswick teachings are dispensationalists. Indeed, in Dieter, et al., *Five Views on Sanctification* (n. 3 above), the two views are contrasted. Nevertheless, the sensitive reader of Walvoord (dispensational) and McQuilken (Keswick) in that volume will note that they are extremely close. Cf. pp. 149–83, 194–95, 199–226, and 236–37.

For a sympathetic treatment of Keswick teaching by a former professor of theology at Wheaton College, see, Steven Barabas, *So Great Salvation: The History and Message of the Keswick Convention* (London: Marshall, Morgan, and Scott, 1952).

For two critiques, see, (1) John Murray, "Review of S. Barabas: *So Great Salvation, The History and Message of the Keswick Convention,*" in *The Collected Writings of John Murray* (Edinburgh: Banner of Truth, 1982), 4:281–86; hereafter cited as: Murray, "Review of Barabas" [originally published in *Westminster Theological Journal* 16:1 (1953), 78ff.]; and, (2) J. I. Packer, *Keep in Step with the Spirit* (Old Tappan, N.J.: Revell, 1984), 145–63.

10. For a sympathetic treatment of the Princetonians on the Christian life, see, W. Andrew Hoffecker, *Piety and the Princeton Theologians* (Phillipsburg, N.J.: Presbyterian and Reformed, 1980).

Among the Princetonians, B. B. Warfield, especially, criticized those whom he felt succumbed to "higher life" and "perfectionist" theologies. His most notable work in this regard was a posthumous two-volume collection of previously published essays, B. B. Warfield, *Perfectionism*, 2 vols. (Oxford: Oxford University Press, 1931). An abridged version is available in one volume from Presbyterian and Reformed.

11. Lewis Sperry Chafer, *He That Is Spiritual* (New York: Our Hope, 1918); rev. and enlarged (Philadelphia: Sunday School Times, 1919). The rev. ed. is used here. For a brief biographical account of Chafer, see, Charles C. Ryrie, "Chafer, Lewis Sperry" in *Evangelical Dictionary of Theology*, ed. Walter A. Elwell (Grand Rapids: Baker, 1984), 203.

12. B. B. Warfield, "Review of Lewis Sperry Chafer, *He That Is Spiritual,*" *Princeton Theological Review* 17 (April 1919), 322–27. Hereafter cited as, Warfield, "Review of Chafer." The review is reprinted in appendix 2 of this volume, 000–000.

For a brief biographical sketch of Warfield, see, Mark A. Noll, "Warfield, Benjamin Breckinridge," in *Evangelical Dictionary of Theology*, ed. Walter A. Elwell (Grand Rapids: Baker, 1984), 1156. Also, on Warfield's view of piety, see, Hoffecker, *Piety and the Princeton Theologians*, 95–155.

13. C. I. Scofield, ed., *The Scofield Reference Bible* (KJV with annotations and system of topical references) (New York: Oxford University Press, 1909, 1917), 1213–14 (notes under 1 Cor. 2:14–3:4).

14. Chafer, *He That Is Spiritual*, rev. ed., 10–12.

15. Ibid., 13.

16. Ibid., 40–41.

17. Ibid., 27–38.

18. Ibid., 39.

19. Ibid., 70–73.

20. See, for instance, Calvin's treatment of the *tertius usus leges* (third use of the law, in particular the moral law as codified in the Ten Commandments) in the *Institutes* 2.7.12–13.

The third and principal use [of the law—P.S.], which pertains more closely to the proper purpose of the law, finds its place among believers in whose hearts the Spirit of God already lives and reigns. . . .

Here [in the law—P.S.] is the best instrument for them to learn more thoroughly each day the nature of the Lord's will to which they aspire, and to confirm them in the understanding of it. . . .

Again, because we need not only teaching but also exhortation, the servant of God will also avail himself of this benefit of the law: by frequent meditation upon it to be aroused to obedience, be strengthened in it, and be drawn back from the slippery path of transgression. In this way the saints must press on; for, however eagerly they may in accordance with the Spirit strive toward God's righteousness, the listless flesh always so burdens them that they do not proceed with due readiness. The law is to the flesh like a whip to an idle and balky ass, to arouse it to work. . . .

Certain ignorant persons [probably referring to the Libertine sect and possibly Johann Agricola—P.S.], not understanding this distinction, rashly cast out the whole of Moses, and bid farewell to the two Tables of the Law. *For they think it obviously alien to Christians to hold to a doctrine that contains the "dispensation of death"* [cf. II Cor. 3:7] [somewhat prophetic?—P.S.]. Banish this wicked thought from our minds! For Moses has admirably taught that the law, which among sinners can engender nothing but death, ought among the saints to have a better and more excellent use. . . . *There are not many rules, but one everlasting and unchangeable rule to live by. For this reason we are not to refer solely to one age David's statement that the life of a righteous man is a continual meditation upon the law* [Ps. 1:2], *for it is just as applicable to every age, even to the end of the world.*

[John Calvin, *Institutes of the Christian Religion*, 2 vols., ed. John T. McNeill, trans. Ford Lewis Battles (Philadelphia: Westminster, 1960), emphasis mine.]

21. Chafer, *He That Is Spiritual*, rev. ed., 73–75.

22. Ibid., 77–81.

23. Ibid., 84.

24. Ibid., 104.

25. Ibid., 107.

26. Ibid., 108.

27. Ibid., 110.

28. Ibid., 110–13.

29. Ibid., 120.

30. Ibid., 121.

31. For Chafer on the battle with the world, the flesh, and the devil, see, ibid., 127–34; for Chafer on sanctification, see, ibid., 134–85.

32. Ibid., 177–78; cf., also, 155–63.

33. Ibid., 154–55.

34. Ibid., 160. For more on Chafer's opposition to eradication ideas, see, ibid., 161–62, 165–71.

35. Ibid., 160–62.

36. Ibid., 145–46.

37. Ibid., 148–52. He states on p. 152, "The effect of this deliverance [recorded in Rom. 8:2] is indicated by the blessedness recorded in the eighth chapter as in contrast to the wretchedness of the seventh chapter. It is all the helpless and defeated 'I' in the one case, and of the sufficient and victorious 'I,' by the Spirit, in the other."

38. Ibid., 165.

39. Ibid., 172.

40. Warfield, "Review of Chafer," 322. As stated in n. 10 above, Warfield wrote extensively on and against "Higher Life" teachings. For more on Warfield's understanding of the Higher Life movement, especially in its American manifestations, consult the one-volume abridged version of his *Perfectionism* (Presbyterian and Reformed, 1980), 216–311, 349–99.

41. Warfield, "Review of Chafer," 322.

42. Cf., Chafer, *He That Is Spiritual*, rev. ed., 40–41. Warfield, of course, was reviewing the 1918 edition, not the slightly revised 1919 version. In the edition at hand for Warfield the page numbers are 31–32. Warfield also commended Chafer for repudiating "Pente-

costal manifestations" as necessary for Spirit filling and for rejecting terms like "entire sanctification" and "sinless perfection"; cf. Warfield, "Review of Chafer," 323.

43. Warfield, "Review of Chafer," 323.

44. Ibid., 322–23.

45. Ibid., 324.

46. Ibid., 325.

47. Ibid.

48. Ibid., 326. Interestingly, Warfield said this was "near the beginning of [Chafer's] book." Actually the statement occurred near the middle, on p. 62 of the first edition of *He That Is Spiritual* and p. 84 of the revised 1919 edition.

49. Chafer, *He That Is Spiritual*, rev. ed., 84–85.

50. Warfield, "Review of Chafer," 326–27.

51. Ibid., 327.

52. Chafer, *He That Is Spiritual*, rev. ed., 78–79 n. 1.

53. Ibid., 79 n. 1.

54. Ibid., 80 n. 1.

55. Cf. ibid., 79, where he gives a list of Scripture texts as proofs for his point about "human choice" and then says these are "sufficient evidence"!

56. George Marsden speaks of these problems in, *Reforming Fundamentalism; Fuller Seminary and the New Evangelicalism* (Grand Rapids: Eerdmans, 1987); and, *Understanding Fundamentalism and Evangelicalism* (Grand Rapids: Eerdmans, 1990).

57. In Wheaton's history, not all professors and administrators have been exponents of Keswick teaching. Gordon Clark and Oliver Buswell, both holding a view more in line with the Reformed confessionalists, served Wheaton for a number of years as a professor and as president of the school respectively. For a sympathetic history of Wheaton, see, Paul M. Bechtel, *Wheaton College: A History Remembered, 1860–1984* (Wheaton: Harold Shaw, 1984).

58. For a biography of Murray, see, Iain Murray, "Life of John Murray," in *The Collected Writings of John Murray* (Edinburgh: Banner of Truth, 1982), 3:3–160.

59. Barabas, *So Great Salvation*, vii.

60. Ibid., 188, emphasis mine.

61. Ibid., 107, emphasis mine. Evangelicals must be careful not to think in such an unhistorical manner. Even if one subscribes to Keswick teaching, one should not think that it simply "emerged fully clothed out of Zeus's head" so to speak. Barabas himself noted the background in the conferences of the Pearsall-Smiths' but failed to delve deeper into the roots of their teaching. Also as to sanctification, many Protestant teachers of *varying persuasions* long before Keswick taught to the people in the pews a vigorous doctrine of the Christian life as one lived through faith and by the Spirit's power. Consult the works of John Calvin, Richard Sibbes, John Owen, John Bunyan, Jacob Spener, John Wesley, Jonathan Edwards, Nicholas von Zinzendorf, and George Whitefield to name a few.

A friend of mine once made a similar claim about the teachings on the "Spirit-filled life" by the teacher of a group in which we were both involved. He said: "Luther rediscovered the truth of justification by faith in 1517, but it wasn't until our leader spoke of Spirit filling in this century that Christians knew the power for service."

62. See n. 9 above.

63. Barabas, *So Great Salvation*, 41. Hodge wrote: "The Protestant Churches at the time of the Reformation did not attempt to determine the nature of sin philosophically. . . . Founding their doctrine . . . upon the Word of God, they declared sin to be the transgression of, or want of conformity to, the divine law." (Charles Hodge, *Systematic Theology* [New York: Scribners, 1888], 2:180–81.) As with Barabas's commendation of the Reformed confessionalist Hodge on the doctrine of sin, so too does Keswick advocate J. Robertson

McQuilken commend Hodge's definition of faith. He writes that it "is superb, useful to those of any theological persuasion." Cf. Dieter, et al., *Five Views on Sanctification*, 245.

64. Chafer, *He That Is Spiritual*, rev. ed., 139, emphasis mine.

65. Barabas, *So Great Salvation*, 54–69.

66. Ibid., 99.

67. Ibid., 94.

68. Ibid., 85.

69. Ibid., 124–25. Of course, the question could be posed that if the crisis decision can come piecemeal at times, have we found a third type of Christian: the "carnal Christian," the "spiritual Christian," and "the somewhat-on-the-way-to-being-the-spiritual Christian"?

70. Murray, "Review of Barabas," 4:281–82.

71. Ibid., 4:286.

72. For more on Murray's perspective on the Christian life, see, John Murray, *The Epistle to the Romans* (Grand Rapids: Eerdmans, 1968); *Redemption: Accomplished and Applied* (Grand Rapids: Eerdmans, 1955); and *The Collected Writings of John Murray*, Parts III–V (Edinburgh: Banner of Truth, 1977), 2:123–320.

73. Murray, "Review of Barabas," 4:283–86.

74. I had hoped to discuss some of the materials of InterVarsity Christian Fellowship as well, but space will just not permit. Like Crusade and Navigators, InterVarsity has been influential in the lives of thousands of students. It has served the general Christian populace as well through InterVarsity Press and the triennial Urbana conferences. For one example of how an InterVarsity staff worker deals with the issues of justification and sanctification—and in this he seems fairly representative of the whole—see, Will Metzger, *Tell the Truth: The Whole Gospel to the Whole Person by Whole People* (Downers Grove, Ill.: InterVarsity Press, 1981), esp. 77–84. Also pertinent to our discussion are InterVarsity's *Bible and Life* training sessions for students. The first major talk at Level I is on the lordship of Christ in salvation. This should give the reader some idea of IV's position.

75. For a biography of Bright, see, Richard Quebedeaux, *I Found It! The Story of Bill Bright and Campus Crusade* (San Francisco: Harper and Row, 1979).

76. All references to *Have You Made the Wonderful Discovery of the Spirit-Filled Life?* in this chapter are from, Campus Crusade for Christ Staff, *Basic Training Manual* (San Bernardino: Here's Life, 1975), 154–55.

77. Evan Hopkins in Barabas, *So Great Salvation*, 91.

78. Cf. John Bunyan, *The Pilgrim's Progress* (Edinburgh: Banner of Truth, 1977), 6–38.

79. Bill Bright, "Ye Shall Receive Power," in Campus Crusade for Christ Staff, *Basic Training Manual* (San Bernardino: Here's Life, 1975), 159.

80. Ibid., 163–67.

81. Ibid., 167–73.

82. Ibid.

83. R. C. Sproul, *Pleasing to God* (Wheaton: Tyndale House, 1988), 150.

84. The text of the "Four Laws" that I have before me is from, Campus Crusade for Christ Staff, *Basic Training Manual* (San Bernardino: Here's Life, 1975), 47ff. Since the publication of that manual, the text has been modified somewhat. Instead of saying in law 1, "God Loves You and Has a Wonderful Plan for Your Life," it reads, "God Loves You and Offers a Wonderful Plan for Your Life." Other than that, it is essentially the same.

85. Charles C. Ryrie, *Balancing the Christian Life* (Chicago: Moody, 1969), 170.

86. Keswick proponent J. Robertson McQuilken also stresses this in Dieter, et al., *Five Views on Sanctification*, 160–62.

87. Bill Bright, ed., *Ten Basic Steps to Christian Maturity, Teacher's Manual* (San Bernardino: Here's Life, 1965), *passim*. One example: Bright tells leaders of groups using the *Ten Basic Steps* booklet: "Ask the class, 'What is a carnal Christian?' [Give them] Ruth Paxon's def-

inition: 'The carnal man has accepted Christ as his Saviour but he has little or no appreciation of a life of complete surrender to, and full appropriation of, Jesus Christ as Lord of his life. Christ has a place in the heart but not *the* place of supremacy and pre-eminence. . . . He attempts to live in two spheres, the heavenly and the earthly—and he fails in both.' The carnal man is undoubtedly a Christian, for Paul calls the carnal church members at Corinth 'brethren' in verse 1, a term he never applies to unbelievers. But the life of the carnal Christian is inconsistent and unhappy."

88. Francis M. Cosgrove, Jr., *Essentials of New Life* (Colorado Springs: NavPress, 1978).

89. Jerry Bridges, *The Pursuit of Holiness* (Colorado Springs: NavPress, 1978).

90. Cosgrove, *Essentials of New Life*, 33.

91. Ibid., 117, 131–32.

92. Ibid., 135–36.

93. Ibid., 162.

94. Walter Henrichsen, *Disciples Are Made—Not Born* (Wheaton: Scripture Press, 1974).

95. Bridges, *The Pursuit of Holiness*, 39.

96. Ibid., 52–69.

97. Ibid., 81.

98. Ibid., 84–85.

Chapter 8 *A Battle Royal*

1. Indeed, the British edition of MacArthur's book, in keeping with the typical British distaste for exotic titles, has been renamed *You Call Me Lord?*

2. MacArthur does make reference to it on p. 215, but this is in an appendix. I could not find any references to it in Hodges.

3. Unless stated otherwise, all Hodges references are to Zane C. Hodges, *Absolutely Free!: A Biblical Reply to Lordship Salvation* (Grand Rapids: Zondervan, 1989).

4. Sinclair B. Ferguson, *Taking the Christian Life Seriously* (Grand Rapids: Zondervan, 1981), 30–32, 41.

5. B. B. Warfield, "Review of Lewis Sperry Chafer, *He That Is Spiritual*," *Princeton Theological Review* 17 (April 1919), 326.

6. Ernest Reisinger, *What Should We Think of "The Carnal Christian"?* (Edinburgh: Banner of Truth, n.d.), 21–22.

7. Cf. MacArthur, *The Gospel According to Jesus*, 87–88, where he professes: "Salvation is by grace through faith (Eph. 2:8). That is the consistent and unambiguous teaching of Scripture. . . . I do not believe, and have never taught, that a person coming to Christ must understand fully all the implications of sin, repentance, or the lordship of Christ. Even after growing in his understanding for years as a Christian, he will not know all of these in their full depth. [Will any believer, no matter how mature, this side of eternity know these implications 'in their full depth'?—P.S.] But there must be a *willingness* to obey. Furthermore, repentance and submission are no more human works than faith itself."

8. John Calvin, *Institutes of the Christian Religion*, 2 vols., ed. John T. McNeill, trans. Ford Lewis Battles (Philadelphia: Westminster, 1960), 3.18.9, emphasis mine.

9. MacArthur, *The Gospel According to Jesus*, 187–89. MacArthur states:

[The man] missed the point. While justification and sanctification are distinct theological concepts, both are essential elements of salvation. God will not declare a person righteous without also making him righteous. Salvation includes *all* God's work on our behalf, from His foreknowledge of us before the foundation of the world to our ultimate glorification in eternity future (Rom. 8:29–30). One cannot pick and choose, accepting eternal life while rejecting holiness and obedience. When God justifies an individual He also sanctifies him. As D. Martyn Lloyd-Jones wrote, "Do we realize that if we truly understand the doctrine of justification by faith we have already grasped the essence and the nerve of the New Testament teaching about holiness and sanctification? Have we realized that to be justified by faith guarantees our sanctification, and that therefore *we must never think of sanctification as a separate and subsequent experience?*". . .

Hebrews 12:14 does not make holiness a prerequisite for salvation, but it recognizes it as the sure result. In other words, sanctification is a *characteristic* of all those who are redeemed, not a *condition* for their receiving salvation. Those who really believe are certain to become holy, and those who do not believe can never be holy. They have no hope of seeing God, except to stand before Him in judgment.

[Emphasis his. The Lloyd-Jones quotation is from, D. Martyn Lloyd-Jones, *Romans: The New Man* (Grand Rapids: Zondervan, 1974), 190.]

10. There has been in this century a rise in interest in the Puritans among pastors and the laity, which some have termed a neo-Puritan revival. MacArthur has moved far into these circles. But as with Puritanism itself, and any revival, different adherents will have different emphases. (I use the term *revival* here both as a sociological phenomenon and theologically, since a revival of interest in anything, an old TV show, for example, will spark off heated debates among adherents over who is the most loyal to the original!)

Dr. Martyn Lloyd-Jones, who for years served as pastor of Westminster Chapel in London and is known to most conservative evangelicals, was one of the patriarchs of this neo-Puritan revival. To get a glimpse at how he understood the Puritans, see, D. M. Lloyd-Jones, *The Puritans: Their Origins and Successors (Addresses Delivered at the Puritan and Westminster Conferences, 1959–1978)* (Edinburgh: Banner of Truth, 1987), especially his 1967 address entitled "Sandemanianism" on pp. 170–90 for an interesting look at another lordship controversy. For a quite sympathetic biography of Lloyd-Jones, see, Iain Murray, *D. Martin Lloyd-Jones*, 2 vols. (Edinburgh: Banner of Truth, 1982 [vol. 1] and 1990 [vol. 2]). Some of Lloyd-Jones's views, however, have been criticized by other Reformed confessionalists. See, for example, Donald Macleod, *The Spirit of Promise* (Tain, Scotland: Christian Focus, 1986), esp. iv–x, 49–56.

11. Cf. esp. MacArthur's "Appendix 2: The Gospel According to Historic Christianity," 226–37. MacArthur quotes Thomas Vincent's exposition of the Westminster Shorter Catechism, William Guthrie, Thomas Manton, Joseph Alleine, Thomas Watson, and Thomas Goodwin, among others.

12. The reader is here directed to chap. 8 n. 5 above for a selection of books that talk about what I am calling "the Puritan spectrum." See also, Brooks Holifield, *The Covenant Sealed: The Development of Puritan Sacramental Theology in Old and New England, 1570–1720* (New Haven, Conn.: Yale University Press, 1974).

Dr. J. I. Packer of Regent College introduced me to the concept of Puritanism as a movement of revival. For a selection of essays giving his interpretation of Puritanism, see, J. I. Packer, *A Quest for Godliness: The Puritan Vision of the Christian Life* (Wheaton: Crossway, 1990). For his definition of "Puritanism as a movement of revival," see 35–48.

Another quite sympathetic study of the Puritans, but one that also recognizes their shortcomings, should be noted as well since it was written to introduce laypersons to Puritanism: Leland Ryken, *Worldly Saints: The Puritans as They Really Were* (Grand Rapids: Zondervan, 1986).

13. The Banner of Truth Trust has reprinted 23 of the 24 volumes of the 1850–1855 Goold edition of Owen's works. I would start with *Volume Six: Sin and Temptation,* for this describes a Puritan view of the Christian life at its best. Banner of Truth also publishes an exposition of Owen's teaching that could serve as a "reader's guide" (for Owen is quite prolix!); see, Sinclair B. Ferguson, *John Owen on the Christian Life* (Edinburgh: Banner of Truth, 1986).

14. Thomas Vincent, *The Shorter Catechism of the Westminster Assembly Explained and Proved from Scripture,* original edition published 1674 (Edinburgh: Banner of Truth, 1980), 226–27.

15. Is it not interesting that Hodges's opening proposition in this quotation bears a striking similarity to the answer to the Shorter Catechism question noted above and to Vincent's exposition of it? As seen, both the catechism and Vincent would agree that "saving faith is taking God at His Word in the gospel." Maybe the problem is that Hodges does not like how they exposit what that "gospel" is in which one "takes God at His Word." This is a very different issue from saying, as he apparently does, that Puritanism denies faith in the gospel as God's way of salvation by adding something to faith. What is really being dealt with here is the biblical interpretation of "saving faith [alone]," "gospel," and "taking God at His Word." Theological and historical reflection is required, not verbal abuse of an entire tradition.

16. R. T. Kendall, *Calvin and English Calvinism to 1649* (Oxford: Oxford University Press, 1979); and M. Charles Bell, *Calvin and Scottish Theology: The Doctrine of Assurance* (Edinburgh: Handsel, 1985).

17. For critiques of Kendall, see, (1) Richard Muller, *Christ and the Decree: Christology and Predestination in Reformed Theology from Calvin to Perkins* (Grand Rapids: Baker, 1986), esp. 25–26, 131–32, 194 nn. 31 and 38; (2) Paul Helm, *Calvin and the Calvinists* (Edinburgh: Banner of Truth, 1982); (3) John von Rohr, *The Covenant of Grace in Puritan Thought* (Atlanta: Scholars, 1986), esp. 26–31; (4) Patrick Collinson "England and International Calvinism," in *International Calvinism, 1541–1715,* ed. Menna Prestwich (Oxford: Oxford University Press, 1985), 197–223; (5) W. Stanford Reid, "Review of R. T. Kendall: *Calvin and English Calvinism to 1649,* " *Westminster Theological Journal* 43 (1980), 155–64; (6) Mark Shaw, "Drama in the Meeting House: The Concept of Conversion in the Theology of William Perkins," *Westminster Theological Journal* 45 (1983), 41–72; (7) Mark Shaw, "The Marrow of Practical Divinity: A Study in the Theology of William Perkins," Ph.D. dissertation, Westminster Theological Seminary, 1981; (8) Peter Lillback, "The Binding of God: Calvin's Role in the Development of Covenant Theology," Ph.D. dissertation, Westminster Theological Seminary, 1985; (9) Joel Beeke, *Personal Assurance of Faith: English Puritanism and the Dutch "Nadere Reformatie"* (New York: Peter Lang, 1991); and, (10) Andrew Woolsey, "Unity and Continuity in Covenantal Thought: A Study in the Reformed Tradition to the Westminster Assembly," Ph.D. dissertation, Glasgow University, 1988 (forthcoming from Oxford University Press).

The reader should also consult works that agree with the Kendall and Bell thesis of discontinuity between Calvin and later Calvinists. Two such works are, Basil Hall, "Calvin against the Calvinists," *John Calvin: A Collection of Distinguished Essays,* ed. G. E. Duffield (Appleford, England: Sutton Courtenay, 1968), 19–37; and Alan Clifford, *Atonement and Justification: English Evangelical Theology, 1640–1790* (Oxford: Oxford University Press, 1990).

Also of interest is to note William Stoever's book mentioned in chap. 8 n. 5. He and Kendall wrote at the same time and did not interact with one another. What is of interest is to see their very different interpretations of John Cotton, the great New England teacher at First Church, Boston. Kendall views him as the only true Calvinist of the Puritans he examines, albeit he argues that Cotton is too subjectivistic. Stoever, however, interprets Cotton as one in the antinomian struggle in New England who became almost a "crypto-sectary" in his strong nature/grace split. This shows that good scholars can easily differ when discussing the same historical figure! Cf. Kendall, *Calvin and English Calvinism to 1649,* 167–83; and Stoever, *A Faire and Easie Way to Heaven,* 34–57, 161–83.

Consider also this statement by Patrick Collinson, a noted Puritan scholar and professor of history at Cambridge University. It is found on pages 216–17 of his article listed above:

"Calvin against the Calvinists" has been an attractive slogan, drawing attention to the significant changes in theological method which are detectable in the work of Beza, Zanchius, and Perkins, and thereafter in much English and New English divinity. And it makes a useful point which has some general validity, as indicating the difference which necessarily exists between a religious founder and the movement which acquires his name.... Nevertheless, to mean by "Calvinist" something other than a follower of Calvin will always seem a trifle perverse, while the extent to which Calvin's legacy was falsified by his immediate successors has been exaggerated.... As for English Calvinism, it may be simple ignorance of concurrent developments in continental theology which has sometimes led to undue stress on the particular deviance of the English school. These writers were such attentive students to the whole body of Reformed divinity that their treatment of the life of the individual Christian, ... sometimes regarded as an English peculiarity, may represent a practical application of what they had learned rather than any conspicuous departure from it.

18. Two books that will alert the reader to the issues involved in this controversy are, R. T. Kendall, *Once Saved, Always Saved* (London: Hodder and Stoughton, 1983); and, the rebuttal, Richard Alderson, *No Holiness, No Heaven!* (Edinburgh: Banner of Truth, 1986).

19. For example, twice (207–8 n. 7 and 215 n. 4), Hodges quotes at length from Kendall and Bell on Calvin's view of faith and assurance. The first reference is to a Kendall statement in which Hodges says Kendall "nicely summarized" Calvin, and the second reference is to a Bell statement in which Hodges says Bell "aptly summarized" Calvin. The problem is that Hodges neither proves that he personally has grappled with Calvin's *Institutes* nor gives the reader many extensive Calvin quotes. To do responsible research in historical theology, one should go to the original text first, with sensitivity to its historical context, and grapple with what it says before going to secondary sources. In this, it is somewhat like using sound Bible study methods. It must be said, however, that Hodges does a little better with Luther, giving some longer citations. But even those tend to come from only one major Luther work, "The Babylonian Captivity of the Church" (cf. 222–23 n. 5).

20. For more on this issue as discussed by Luther and Calvin (especially Calvin), see Michael Horton's introduction to this collection and also Bob Godfrey's chapter, "Calvin and the Council of Trent."

21. For example, see, Anthony Hoekema, *The Christian Looks at Himself* (Grand Rapids: Eerdmans, 1975), 61–67; and D. Martin Lloyd-Jones, *Romans: The Law: Its Functions and Limits: Exposition of Chapters 7:1–8:4* (Grand Rapids: Zondervan, 1974), 176–317.

22. Warfield, "Review of Chafer," 327.

23. My thanks to D. Bruce Hindmarsh of Christ's Church College, Oxford University, for drawing my attention to this quotation.

Conclusion: *Christ Died for the Sins of Christians, Too*

1. Robin Leaver, *Luther on Justification* (St. Louis: Concordia, 1975), 16–41.

2. See Warfield's review of Lewis Sperry Chafer's *He That Is Spiritual* in the *Princeton Theological Review* (April 1919) in the appendix.

3. Roland Bainton, *Here I Stand* (New York: Abingdon, 1950), chaps. 1–3.

4. *Summa Theologiae* 1–2, q. 113. Cf. Leaver, *Luther on Justification*, 17–22.

5. Philip S. Watson, *Let God Be God* (Philadelphia: Fortress, 1959), 52–59.

6. Ibid., 48–52.

7. Ibid.

8. William Hordern, *Living by Grace* (Philadelphia: Westminster, 1975), 25.

9. M. Strommen et al., eds., *A Study of Generations* (Minneapolis: Augsburg, 1972).

Contributors

W. Robert Godfrey is professor of church history at Westminster Theological Seminary in California. The author of numerous articles, he is also the editor of *Through Christ's Word* (Presbyterian and Reformed) and co-editor of *Theonomy: A Reformed Critique* (Zondervan). Educated at Stanford (B.A., M.A., Ph.D.) and the Gordon School of Theology (M.Div.), he has chaired the Consultation on Conversion for the Laussane Committee for World Evangelization and is ordained in the Christian Reformed Church (CRC).

Michael S. Horton is president of Christians United for Reformation (CURE) and the author of *Putting Amazing Back into Grace* (Thomas Nelson), *Made in America* (Baker), and *The Law of Perfect Freedom* (Moody), as well as the editor of *The Agony of Deceit* (Moody) and *Power Religion* (Moody). Educated at Biola University (B.A.) and Westminster Theological Seminary (M.A.R.), and currently engaged in doctoral studies at Wycliffe Hall, Oxford, Horton is ordained in the Presbyterian Church in America (PCA).

Kim Riddlebarger is vice president of Christians United for Reformation (CURE) and has contributed to *Power Religion* (Moody), in addition to his regular contributions to *Modern Reformation* magazine. Riddlebarger is also dean of CURE's Academy, a center for lay adult education, and is ordained in the Christian Reformed Church (CRC). He was educated at California Sate University Fullerton (B.A.), the Simon

Greenleaf School of Law (M.A.), and is currently engaged in doctoral studies at Fuller Theological Seminary.

Rick Ritchie is a staff writer for CURE's bi-monthly magazine, *Modern Reformation*. A Missouri Synod Lutheran, Ritchie was educated at Christ College Irvine and Gordon–Conwell Theological Seminary.

Rod Rosenbladt is director of CURE's Center for Reformation Studies and professor of theology at Christ College Irvine. In addition, he has contributed to *Christianity for the Tough-Minded* (Bethany) and *The Agony of Deceit* (Moody). Rosenbladt was educated at Pacific Lutheran College (B.S.), Capitol Theological Seminary (M.Div.), Trinity Evangelical Divinity School (M.A.), and the University of Strasbourg (Ph.D.) He is ordained in the Lutheran Church-Missouri Synod.

Paul Schaefer is a freelance writer living in Philadelphia, Pennsylvania. He was educated at the University of Pennsylvania (B.A.), Harvard University, Westminster Theological Seminary, Emory University (M.A.), and is a candidate for the D.Phil. at Oxford University.

Robert Strimple is professor of systematic theology at Westminster Theological Seminary in California. His Ph.D. is from the University of Toronto, and he is ordained in the Orthodox Presbyterian Church.